History of the Vikings and Norse Culture

by Njord Kane

History of the Vikings and Norse Culture

By Njord Kane

Published on: August 30, 2019 by Spangenhelm Publishing

Interior Design and Cover by: Njord Kane

Library of Congress Control Number: 2019911282

ISBN-13: 978-1943066292

ISBN-10: 1943066299

1. Vikings 2. Norse 3. History 4. Europe 5. Scandinavia

First Edition.

10 9 8 7 6 5 4 3 2 1

 **Spangenhelm
Publishing**
United States

Table of Contents

Preface

This book is divided into two parts. The first part tells the Norse story chronologically from an anthropologist / historian's point of view. The saga of the Norse people begins early during the Stone Age when they migrated as hunter-gathers following herds of megafauna, such as Mammoths. They progressed out of the Nordic Stone Age and began to gradually settle and form into a complex societies.

Along the way, we shall detail the steps of Norse society and the people who evolved into the far reaching "viking" explorers that changed and modified the world we know today.

The second part of this book highlights specifics about ancient Norse culture, technology, beliefs, and practices.

The Norse were a major indigenous people of Scandinavia and Northern Europe. When we refer to them, we often see the words 'Viking' and 'Norse' used interchangeably without discrimination. So which term is correct when referring to these people?

Do we call them Vikings or Norse?

At first thought, we usually call them vikings. This is because when we mention the vikings, immediately everyone knows we're talking about the Norse. Plus, it is used to refer to the Norse so commonly.

However, the term "viking" is not actually what the Norse people called themselves.

It was something they did.

The word viking comes from the Old Norse word "víkingr," a term which meant to go raiding and it wasn't always by boat. The word viking was only later used to refer to the Norse people who were conducting these raids.

There are a variety of other stereotypes commonly associated with "vikings." Most are simply false stereotypes such as the horned or winged helmet, for example.

Calling them "vikings" is technically incorrect. However it's of such common use today that when we call them vikings, everyone knows that we're referring to the Norse. Even though viking was something they did (raid) and not what they were called.. or how they referred to themselves. They were actually called the Norse or Northmen.

A statement of fact is: all vikings were Norse, but not all Norse were vikings.

In fact, most Norse were farmers – just like everyone else on the planet during the time.

I'll repeat myself on this topic.

The purpose of this book is not only to provide a concise and up to date historical chronicle about the Norse people, but also of their culture and beliefs.

With so many recent discoveries by archaeologists studying the Norse, there are many things that we had previously thought we knew about this ancient culture that have changed. This makes the Nordic story as previously taught out of date and in need of being retold.

This book tells the Norse story current to today's discoveries, presented in short chapters through each epoch of Nordic history.

We start our story about the Norse from the first proof of existence as an identifiable and distinct people. A people who migrated into Scandinavia and the Northern European area many thousands of years ago. We then take you through their progression from hunter-gathers into the agricultural settlements that eventually grew into societies.

A journey through the rise and expansion of Nordic culture that forever help form Europe and Western Culture as a whole. Highlighting new discoveries in Norse knowledge and technologies that were previously a mystery to scientists.

This book is not the single work of the author, but the combined works of hundreds of years by thousands of researchers who've spent lifetimes trying to unravel the story and mystery of the Norse people. There has been so many recent discoveries by modern researchers that the Nordic story has been rewritten from what we thought we knew about their obscure history.

A history that was almost lost in time with obscure myths and legends.

The Beginnings of a People

Chapter 1 - Who were the Norse?

The Norse were an ancient Germanic people who inhabit Northern Europe and Scandinavia. The Norse are also known as Northmen or Norsemen or as they are referred to in popular media, the Vikings.

The Norse people were spread across Northern Europe, particularly in the regions known today as: Scandinavia (Norway, Sweden, and Finland), Germany, Denmark, Poland, Netherlands, the United Kingdom (England, Scotland, Ireland, and the surrounding islands), Iceland, Russia, Latvia, Lithuania, and Estonia.

These northern people as a whole spoke as their native language, one the various dialects of Norse. The Norse language was a Northern Germanic / Scandinavian language that was in wide use before the christianization of Northern Europe, Russia, and Scandinavia.

The Norse are today most commonly known to people as the "Vikings." However, the term "viking" was not actually what the Norse people called themselves. It was something that they did. The word "viking" comes from the Old Norse word "víkingr," a term which meant to go raiding for loot and it was something that wasn't always done by boat. A Viking was a Norse Raider.

The word viking was only later misused when referring to the Norse people as a whole, instead of just those specific Norsemen who conducted the Viking raids. Simply put, a "Viking" is a raider, or more correctly; a Norseman who went raiding. In more precise terms, a Viking is a Norse Raider.

With this in mind, we know that calling the Norse people "Vikings" as a whole is incorrect. However it is of such common use today that when someone calls them Vikings, everyone knows that they are talking about the Norse. Although, in most cases, they are referring to Norse Raiders, in which case, "Vikings" would be correct. But to reiterate, viking was something they did (raid) and the people were actually called the Norse.

A statement of fact is: **all Vikings were Norse, but not all Norse were Vikings**.

In fact, most Norse were farmers and tradesman – just like everyone else on the planet. I had said all of this in the preface of this book, but found it necessary to repeat myself because I simply can't stress this fact enough.

There are also many other misunderstandings and stereotypes that are commonly associated with the term

"Viking." One of the most common false stereotypes about the Norse and especially of viking raiders is that of the horned or winged helmet for example.

The Norse never wore winged or horned helmets - that is fiction. The types of helmets the Norse wore is discussed further ahead in this book's chapter about *Norse Arms and Armor.*

The winged and horned helmet were mistakenly used to depict Vikings in an opera. The opera singer's costumes of winged and horned helmets stuck as a common belief as to what the Norse used to look like and what they wore.

Statue of a Viking in Gimli, Manitoba (Canada).[42]

As glorious as many of these false depictions may be; such as horned helmets being a sort of universal icon as to identify Vikings.

We'll clear up these misconceptions as we go further along in the book and look closely at what the Norse really did and what they were really like. We'll look at the facts of what was real about the Norse people and their culture. We'll also look specifically at the Norse that infamously raided during the Viking Era, giving them the label as Vikings.

The history of the Norse people goes all the way back to the Stone Age, but they are best known for a period of time when they raided several parts of Europe known as the Viking Age.

The Viking Age is typically recorded in history as occurring approximately around 793 AD to 1066 AD. This period of time is not the time span of the Norse people themselves, nor was it the peak of their civilization. This is merely the height of the time when the Norse people were mostly written about. The time when they reached out and went out on viking adventures. A time when the World noticed them and were fearful.

The Viking Age began somewhere just before the date of 800 AD. The actual beginning of the Viking Age is a bit foggy and different locations argue different time periods of when viking raids actually began to occur.

To abolish this argument, it is generally accepted in the academic community that the official beginning of the Viking Age is to have begun on the 8th of June 793 AD. This date is when there is a formal recording made of when Norse Raiders (Vikings) made an attack on the monastery at Lindisfarne, an island off the northeast coast of England.

The attack came unexpected, as it was an unguarded religious community of Christian monks. An easy target for Vikings sailing around the coast in search of a place they can easily raid and loot.

The Viking raiders were seeking an easy target that was close to the water, so they didn't have to go far from their boats. The Norse preferred to raid near their boats to allow them a hasty escape before reinforcements could come.

Allowing the Vikings to surprise attack, loot, and vacate before anyone really knew what happened.

Lindisfarne Priory Viking stone, a 9th Century grave marker. [41]

Lindisfarne was a defenseless place known as the "Holy Island." The viking raid on it caused much consternation throughout the Christian World and is most often marked as being the "official" beginning of the Viking Age.

This map shows the location of the Holy Island, Lindisfarne on the northeastern coast of Northumbria of the modern day UK Island. The raiding Norse had probably landed near the location from the sea and sailed up or down the coast until they spotted a location to attack.

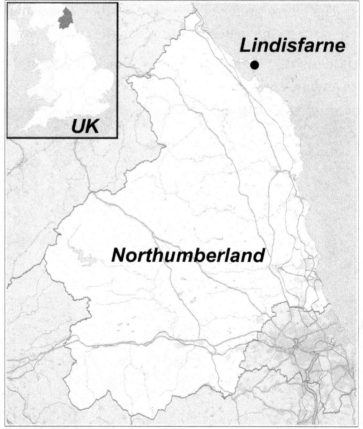

Holy Island of Lindisfarne shown within Northumberland, UK.[43]

The Viking Age is the period of time when the Norse are most often talked about. The Age when the Norse invaded much of Europe during a time when they became known as the Vikings.

The Viking Age is not the beginning of the Norse people or the start of their culture. The roots of the Norse go back even further. All the way back to the Megalithic and Neolithic Eras of the Stone Age.

The Stone age for the Norse was very different than what we were taught about the Stone Age in regards to other cultures. Other cultures such as the Mediterranean Cultures are where we gathered most of our information about the stone ages, the bronze age, and the iron ages of humankind in general. But the Norse people experienced the change of the Ages much differently than other cultures.

The Stone Ages, the Bronze (Copper) Age, and the Iron ages for the Norse progressed very different that that of the rest of the World. So different were the early stages of Nordic cultural evolution that they have their own separate categories and classifications for their cultural evolutionary eras. The culturally specific Norse classifications are labeled as: *The Nordic Stone Age, The Nordic Bronze Age,* and *the Nordic Iron Age.* The Nordic Iron Age is broken down into its own separate stages as well.

The Norse made the best of what they had available to them and with their unique regional situation, adapted with an uncanny sense of innovativeness. Their ability to trade and reach areas of trading to better improve their way of life was unmatched by any other culture in their day.

Nordic innovative technology that is still unmatched today. Their willingness to reach out far to other populations and cultures made them one of the most influential cultures out there.

Chapter 2 – The Nordic Stone Age

From around the time during the Lower Paleolithic Era, which was about 1.8 million years ago, into the Upper Paleolithic Era, or 20,000 years ago; Europe was sparsely populated by Homo Erectus and Homo Neanderthalensis. These were the ancient ancestors of modern humans. They were a hunter-gather type of people who were eventually replaced by Homo Sapiens, modern humans.

Survival was hard and basic survival techniques were limited in an ever changing and unpredictable climate. The general practice of survival was to hunt and find whatever it was that they could scavenge to eat in order to survive. Hunting megafauna (large animals) was one of the most practiced means by groups that were able to survive in this environment.

To hunt these large animals, they had to develop ways to take them down. This included designing specialized tools such as spears and javelins to hunt. Archeologists have found 380,000 year old wooden javelins belonging to these hunters in the Nordic Stone Age area. These javelins are the oldest complete hunting weapons ever found anywhere in the world and they were discovered in Schoningen, Germany.[1]

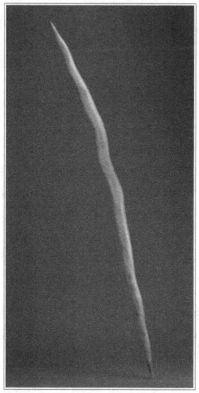

One of three wooden spears found at Schöningen, Germany.[44]

During the Upper Paleolithic to the Mesolithic Era, ranging from about 43,000 to 6,000 years ago, Europe's homo sapiens (human) hunter-gatherer populations gradually began to increase in number. During the last glacial maximum (Ice Age), much of Europe was depopulated because of the changed climate. After the thaw, Europe was then re-settled again approximately 15,000 years ago.

During this period of repopulation, groups of Europeans migrated long distances following the edge of the glacial ice in search of food. They were mostly hunting seals and following them along the edge of the ice and the sea. Some groups that were following seals and other marine food stuffs had made it all the way to North America traveling along the ice's edge that bridged across from Europe to North America.

We know that Stone Age Europeans had crossed over into North America during this time because several dozen European-style stone tools, dating back between 19,000 and 26,000 years, have been discovered at six different locations along the U. S. East Coast. What's more, chemical analysis carried out on a 19,000 year old stone knife found in Virginia, USA revealed that it was made of a French-originating flint.

That's a long distance for Stone Age people to travel, but it was necessary for their survival. They followed the food they were hunting in order to survive the exceptionally harsh climate.

What became of the Stone Aged Paleo-Europeans that had migrated to North America is still a puzzle for researchers to unravel. It is unclear as to whether or not they completely died out or if they attempted any form of settling. The most probable conclusion is that they continued to wander, hunting and searching for food until they eventually died out.

We do know Paleo-Europeans began entering the previously uninhabited North America at about the same time as the Paleo-Indians began crossing over via the Bering Sea land-bridge, known as Beringia. Similarly, Paleo-Indians followed game across the land-ice bridge much the same way as the Paleo-Europeans did on the opposite side of the continent.

As the glacial ice receded and the climate warmed up, the fauna that these stone aged hunter-gatherers hunted changed as some of the large herd animals began to become more scarce. There were fewer mammoth herds as the number of these animals began to dwindle.

Fortunately, the warmer climate brought new sources of meat, such as growing herds of reindeer, that had become more readily available over time. Eventually, reindeer became a main source of hide, bone, antler, and of course a primary source of meat.

It was during this time of the Nordic Stone Age that the Norse people existed as nomadic reindeer hunters. From 13,500 BC to 11,000 BC is a period of time during the Nordic Stone Age that is called the **Hamburg Culture.** This time period is classified by the shouldered spear and arrow points discovered that date to the period and zinken tools found that the Hamburg Culture people used as chisels when working with horns.

Also specific to the Hamburg Culture are the tanged Havelte-type arrow head points found which are described as being unique to the Hamburg Culture exclusively.

14

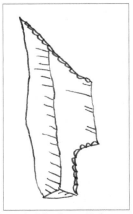

An illustration of a Hamburg Culture Arrow Head.[2]

Rock circles were also found in small settlements that are attributed to being used as weights to hold down the coverings of teepees. A teepee (also tepee and tipi) is a conical tent usually made of animal skins and supported by wooden poles. Teepees were used by primitive Nordic people just like the Great Plains Indians of North America and Saami people North of them in Scandinavia.

Within these sites were a great amount of reindeer horn and bone remnants which shows that the reindeer were a very important prey. It appears that they lived in small groups that ranged from East of Poland to Northern France and Southern Scandinavia. It has also been discovered that they migrated along the Norwegian coast during the summer months because the sea level at the time was about 50 meters lower than it is today.

After this period in the late upper paleolithic age at around 11000 BC to 10000 BC came the **Ahrensburg Culture** with the complete extinction of megafauna, such as the mammoth. The ice began to recede in lower Sweden and Denmark from the Younger Dryas event (The Big Freeze) which caused much deforestation and there were land stretches exposed which are now under the North and Baltic Seas. This allowed these migrating hunter groups to reach areas by foot that later could only be reached by boats.

These Nordic nomads continued to hunt grazing wild reindeer and now had more incentive to exploit marine resources that became more accessible.

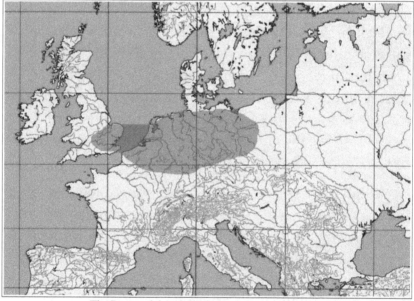

The Range of the Ahrensburg Culture. (Albin L. 2009)

The arrowheads of this time period changed to a shouldered, tanged point. This was a marked improvement in hunting methods as better tools were being made. With improved weapons and tools, hunters were able to hunt more proficiently and expand the variety of prey they hunted.

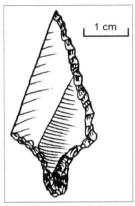

Drawing of an Ahrensburg Culture arrow head.[3]

Fish hooks have also been discovered, showing an improvement from relying on spear fishing by having the ability and knowledge to angle for fish. This may have contributed to a slowing in culture development, because the Neolithic Age (New Stone Age) is estimated to have begun around 5,000 BC in Northern Europe. This is about 4000 years after the Neolithic Age had already began in Southern Europe.

The **Linear Pottery culture** (Linearbandkeramik) was the next major archaeological horizon of the Northern European Neolithic Age happening at around 5500 BC to 4500 BC. This culture migrated less and began the gradual process of more permanently settling in areas. It was during the Linear Pottery culture that a trait started to co-evolve with the culture of dairy farming.

A significant change in lifestyle when agriculture began to develop with the keeping of livestock in lieu of complete dependency of hunting and gathering for survival. This was also a time where the transition from living a nomadic lifestyle in teepees to remaining in one place and living in more permanent structures such as communal long houses.

Excavations have revealed a large fortified settlement at Oslonki, Poland which dates to around 4300 BC that had nearly thirty trapezoidal longhouses located within in. The rectangular longhouses were between seven and forty-five meters long and were between five and seven meters wide. They were built with massive timber posts chinked with wattle and daub mortar.

Within them, and the nearly eighty grave sites on location, simple pottery items were found consisting of simple cups, bowls, vases, and jugs without handles. These pottery items were obviously designed as kitchen dishes and for transport and trade of food and liquids.

Linear Band Pottery.[4]

The use and life style associated with the Linear Band Pottery Culture began somewhat inland nearer other cultures and was most probably a learned concept from neighboring peoples to the South and East. The culture did not spread North or near the coastlines until later.

The culture that developed simultaneously to the North of the Linear Band Culture was the **Ertebølle culture.** This culture existed predominately in the Southern Areas of Scandinavia from about 5300 BC to 3950 BC.

These people were hunter-gatherers that also relied on fishing and had some pottery making within their culture as well. This was about the time that this culture had some sparse transition to animal husbandry, such as cows and pigs. They didn't practice cultivation yet, but they did trade for barley and emmer wheat (also known as farro or hulled wheat) from tribes south of them and engaged in seasonal cultivation of wild crops.

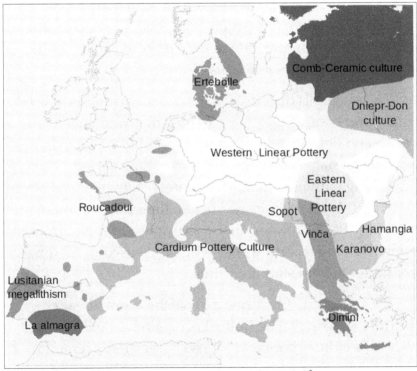

Map of European Middle Neolithic Period.[5]

By looking at the map above, you can see the proximity of the Western Linear Pottery cultures and the Ertebølle Cultures which encompass the majority of the Early Norse inhabited areas. This explains the trade exchanges and similarities between the cultures at that time. Their proximity and regular interaction with each other allowed exchanges in technology and ideas.

The climate became warmer than it is today in those regions and the water level soon became significantly higher. It was about five to six meters higher on the Baltic coastline than it is Today. Jutland (Denmark) was an archipelago during this time of small island chains and groups. The inland waters were rich with fish and the people living there flourished from this. They fished for these abundant marine life in their dugout canoes while also hunting whales and seals.

The materials they used were mostly made from wood, antler and bone as they lived in huts that were made of brush and light wood that was in abundance due to the warmer climate occurring during this time period. This was along with having milder winters. Fire pits made from mud and clay were formed outside their huts. In these fire pits, they used firewood that was usually collected from the shorelines (dried drift wood) while they used dried fungus for tinder to help start their fires.

Evolving out of this culture was the **Funnelbeaker Culture** (Trichterbecherkultur) of around 4300 BC to 2800 BC. This culture is named for its characteristic ceramics with funnel-shaped tops which were probably used for drinking.

The people of this culture lived more inland in settlements that were located near those of the previous Ertebølle culture on the coast. They lived in single-family waffle and daub houses that were made from weaved lattice strips of wood or sticks and then 'daubed' with sticky material generally made from mud, clay, and straw mixtures.

The livelihood of these people relied on farming and animal husbandry which became their major sources of food. They raised sheep, cattle, pigs, and goats but also continued to rely on some hunting and fishing for food stuffs. They grew primitive wheat and barley on small patches, but these resources were fast depleted and still had not developed into a major dietary staple yet.

There was some small scale mining and collection of flint stone, which was traded into areas that lacked flint stone, such as the Scandinavian hinterlands. This culture also traded and imported copper items from Central Europe, especially tools, daggers, and axes.

During this time period a communal pile dwellings, also called stilt houses, were built and improved over several years by some communities that were only inhabited during the summer months. These buildings were used as social centers where clans gathered for festivities after the summer's hunting and harvesting season.

This may also have been an early concept of the Norse "Thing," where free men from different clans met to trade and negotiate disputes and make agreements. There were usually about 100 hearths made of limestone that were evenly distributed across the pile dwelling in huts that were supported by the many hazel stilts.

Around these limestone hearths, researchers found an abundance of residue from meals of charred wheat and barley, split and charred crab apples, hazel nut shells, and bone from cattle, sheep and pigs. There were also remains from game such as red deer, moose, wolf, and bear. Additionally, researchers found remains from fowl such as mallard and black grouse and the remains of fish such as northern pike and perch. This shows how expanded their diets were becoming and the variety of meat consumed that they fished and hunted for.

The ceramics of these people were the same as those of the hunter-gatherer Pitted Ware culture, but the tools and weapons were the same as those of the Funnelbeaker culture. This shows a mixture of culture and technology shared between them.

The remains of craftsmanship were relatively few, suggesting that their tools were transported to the communal pile dwellings from the workshops where they lived the majority of the time. Meaning, they only came to the communal sites for short periods of time to trade and exchange ideas. Additionally meeting for religious rites and probably to make sacrifices to their gods.

Among the most remarkable finds in these communal sites were double edged battle axes, which appear to have played an important role in their culture as far as being symbols of status.

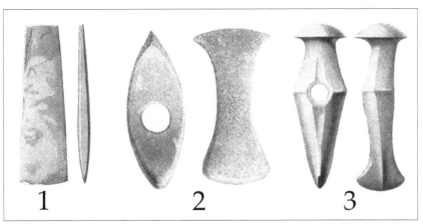

Axes from the Funnelbeaker culture. 1. thin-neck ax, 2. double-edged battle ax, 3. polygonal battle ax.[6]

During the time of these Nordic Stone Age cultures, a prevalence of a gene that allowed adults of Northern European descent to digest lactose originated and spread to other cultures to become virtually universal. This was a genetic variant that was either rare or completely absent in early farmers from Central Europe.

Lactase is an enzyme produced in the digestive system of infants and some (mostly European) adult humans to break down lactose. The lactase enzyme is essential in the digestion of whole milk. The absence of the lactase enzyme is what causes a person consuming dairy products to experience the symptoms of lactose intolerance. Ancient DNA extracted from three individuals belonging to the Funnelbeaker Culture in Gökhem, Sweden were found to possess these traits.

This genetic trait made cattle an even more important resource to the Norse than just that of meat and hide. The milk could now be regularly harvested for consumption, which later evolved into cheese, butter and other dairy products which became a very important part of their culture.

Evolving from this culture followed the **Battleaxe Culture**, also known as the **Boat-Ax Culture** or more accurately, the **Corded Ware Culture** of approximately 2800 BC that continued well into the Nordic Bronze Age that began around 1700 BC. The name 'boat-ax' comes from the fact that the over 3000 battle axes found scattered throughout the Nordic areas of Scandinavia made from ground stone were shaped similar to that of boats.

Boat-shaped battle axes typical of the Battle Ax Culture.[7]

This time period has also been nicknamed the Age of Crushed Skulls by Swedish writer Herman Lindqvist. due to evidence of skull damage in grave sites caused by axes. This is also highly suggestive as to why the style of spangenhelm helmets worn by the Norse may have evolved to the distinctive conical shape as a means to protect the head from such blows.

The culture of this age gets its more accurate label as the Corded-Ware Culture, because of the change in pottery during this time period. Pottery that was highly influenced from pastoral societies on the Central European steppes.

Corded-Ware pottery from around 2500 BC.[8]

The span of Corded-Ware Culture coincides with the Funnel-Beaker Culture as improvements were learned from neighboring groups and a greater reliance on farming began to evolve. Much of the early distribution of this culture was more inland in its beginnings than from the coastal regions. The people of this culture shared many features of the Funnel-Beaker Culture such as use of horses and wheeled carts (which were possibly drawn by oxen) that originated from the European steppes.

The improvements from this culture spread quickly to other settlements due to the aforementioned higher sea levels which instead of being a hindrance and dividing the cultures, allowed them to use the dividing waterways and the seas as highways. This developed into a maritime culture that enhanced their geographical spread and economies with expanded trade.

Chapter 3 – The Metallic Ages

The Norse "Metallic Ages," so called because they date in the time periods of when the Norse people are recorded to have been working with metals such as: copper, bronze, and iron. This time period also includes the **Migration Period,** also the period called the **Age of Heroes**.

These events happened during the time of the Germanic Iron Age when there were great southerly migrations of the Nordic people.

The period of the Norse Metallic Ages were:

- The Nordic Bronze Age 1700 BC –500 BC.

- The Pre-Roman Iron Age 500 BC – 1 AD.

- The Roman Iron Age 1 AD - 400 AD.

- The Germanic Iron Age 400 AD – 800 AD.

- The Migration Period ("The Heroic Age") 400 - 800 AD.

The **Nordic Bronze Age**, also called the Northern Bronze Age, occurred approximately 1700 BC through 500 BC.

The Norse people, particularly those in Scandinavia, joined the European Bronze Age relatively late. Their entrance into the age began from importing various goods from other cultures.

Through means of trade was usually how they obtained items from Europe and the Mediterranean that were made from bronze and gold.

The other way was from plunder.

It was also during this time that many rock carvings depicting ships began showing up. This tells us how much ships became tied to their culture. There wasn't a written language developed during this Age yet and most stone carvings depicted either ships or elk. The stones are dated in comparison with bronze axes and swords, along with other items found from the same era.

It was during this era of the Nordic Bronze Age that the early burial custom of making monument "Stone Ship" burial mounds began showing up.

These Stone Ships varied in size from being relatively small to being huge and they were generally around other burial grounds and religious ceremonial locations.

To the heathen Norse, these were the hallowed grounds of their ancestors and loved ones.

It's believed that the building of these ships, along with equipping the bereaved with other items, would help them along in their journey to the underworld of Hel.

Two Stone Ships (Burial Grounds).[9]

Also marking the Nordic Bronze Age was the fact that there was a warmer climate in the region similar to that of Northern France today due to climate change that happened around 2700 BC.

This allowed Norse communities to live closer together in denser populations as they experienced better farming conditions. Grapes were even grown in parts of Scandinavia during this time.

This did change because during the end of the Norse Bronze Age, from around 850 BC through 650 BC, the climate changed again becoming colder and wetter which dramatically altered living conditions and southerly migrations began.

The Norse then developed into what's called the **Pre-Roman Iron Age** that ranged from around 500 BC through until the 1st century BC when they came into contact with the Romans. This time line is the earliest part of the Nordic Iron Age that occurred in Norse inhabited areas where a wealth of archaeological artifacts have surfaced leading scholars to believe that Pre-Roman Iron Age Norse evolved without completely making a transition out of the Nordic Bronze age.

Although the use of iron began to increase, bronze was still mostly used during this time. The Norse use of iron gradually increased with strong Celtic influences until greater contact with the Romans in the 1st century BC, when Nordic use of Iron became even more influenced by Roman culture.

It was during this period of the Nordic Pre-Iron age before 71 BC, that many Norse came down to unite with a Germanic leader by the name of Ariovistus. Ariovistus had promised the Norse lands for resettlement in Gallic areas as reward for joining his army and fighting for him.

Ariovistus is described by Julius Caesar's firsthand account of the Gallic Wars, as rex Germanorum (King of Germania), even though Germania wasn't united under a single King. The Celtic/Gallic Sequani People asked Ariovistus for assistance in their war against their hereditary rivals, the Gallic Aedui. The Aedui people were aligned with the Romans and the Sequani were in need of assistance in their war against them. Ariovistus seen this as an opportunity for expansion.

Ariovistus, with an army built up from various Germanic and Norse tribes, came to the assistance of the Sequani and defeated the Aedui. However, the Sequani people ended up worse off then before and had lost a third of their lands that were seized by Ariovistus, who threatened to take a third more because he had to make room and provide the promised settlements for the approximate 24,000 Norse Harudes that had come to assist him from the North.

He had also subjugated the Sequani people he had come to help into semi slavery.

The Harudes (or Charudes) were the Norse/Germanic group first mentioned by Julius Caesar as one of the tribes who'd joined Ariovistus crossing the Rhine River to battle the Gallic Aedui.

The Norse Harudes had gathered in Jutland (Denmark Today) from the North in Scandinavia and then came South to join with the Germanic tribes that were forming. Their name suggests that they may have come from Hardanger region in the county of Hordaland, Norway and sailed to Jutland.

The Sequani, who had asked Ariovistus for help but became subjugated and lost their lands in doing so, appealed to their previous enemies the Romans for help now. Julius Caesar came to their aid and drove back the Germanic and Norse tribesmen across the Rhine in 58 BC. However afterward, various tribesmen continued opportunistic raids on Gaul.

They would cross the Rhine to raid and then afterwards sought refuge from retaliation by crossing back to the eastern side of the Rhine. This pushed Caesar to build a bridge to cross the Rhine and confront the opportunistic raiders and to show support for the Germanic tribe, the Ubians that were also allied with the Romans.

The first bridge Caesar had built in 58 BC, was built with a Legion of 40,000 troops in ten days. He crossed his army into Germania and burnt down some villages, but the tribes had moved eastward and converged together to meet Caesar's army in force. Caesar had heard of this plan and crossed back over the Rhine into Gaul and took the bridge down with him. He had only been in the area for 18 days.

In 55 BC, Caesar came again with his army and built a new bridge within a few days and again crossed the Rhine. However, the tribes retreated so Caesar returned back into

Gaul and took his second bridge down as he did so. Caesar had displayed to the Norse and Germanic tribes that the Rhine wasn't a natural obstacle that would provide them with security from the Romans, as Rome could cross the river at any time they wished. This act secured the eastern front of Gaul, which later had built permanent bridges for trade with allied Germanic tribes that sought out the stability that Rome offered.

This was during the time period known in the Nordic Iron Ages as the **Roman Iron Age**, which ran from around 1 BC to 400 AD, when the Roman Empire had the greatest hold and influence over the Germanic tribes to the north of their empire. A Roman influence that reached all the way into Scandinavia, as climate change continued to push many Norse south to seek places for resettlement.

This was also a time when a great amount of imported goods spread throughout Scandinavia that originated from the Roman Empire such as coins, glass beakers, bronze and iron items such as weapons and other objects. More gold and silver came into Nordic regions towards the end of the Roman Iron Age when Rome began to falter and were ransacked more often by neighboring Germanic tribes.

At the end of the Roman Iron Age, cultural change began happening in Norse areas that was again also influenced by climatic changes that had caused dramatic changes in the flora and fauna.

This period in Scandinavia is called the "**Findless Age**" due to the lack of archaeological finds resulting from the scarcity of populations in the area that left behind few traces of their presence. The deteriorating climate pushed Norse populations south as they sought better more arable lands.

This "findless" time period is called the **Migration Age** which happened at the same time as the **Germanic Iron Age** that occurred from 400 AD to 800 AD. It is a time period that is also called the "Heroic Age" and the period of "Barbarian Invasions," because of the consequence of Norse southerly migrations that encroached into the lands of other tribes that were already present.

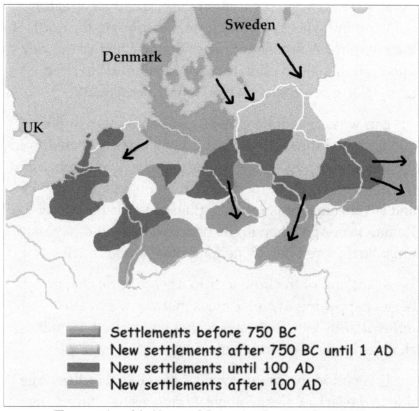

The expansion of the Norse and Germanic tribes 750 BC– 100 AD.

This Nordic incursion caused much friction between pre-existing populations and resulted in many battles and wars. The result of some of these many battles became Sagas about warrior heroes – making it the Heroic Age.

The waning of the once powerful Roman Empire and the growing Celtic and Germanic Kingdoms led to an increase in gold flowing in the north resulting in many works of gold as the Norse used it to make decorative ornaments. After Rome fell, gold then became scarce in the northern regions and the Norse began to use gilded bronze once again. Falling of Rome in the West also led to a mass migration of Nordic and Germanic tribes into the south and Britannia.

This was the Nordic Migration Period and it happened in two phases.

The first phase happening between 300 AD to 500 AD, which put control of the then Western Roman Empire into the hands of the Germanic people.

The second phase of migrations took place 500 AD through 700 AD with settlements expanding into Central and Eastern Europe. This expansion spread all the way into the Lombardy region of Northern Italy.

There is some dispute among some scholars as to whether this period of time in Norse history should be called *the Migration Period* or *the Invasion Period*. This is because there are several explanations as to why the sudden and heavy appearance of 'barbarians' on the Roman frontiers.

Some argue that climate change may have pushed populations south into more fertile croplands and the effect of tribes coming in from every direction pushing one people into another, causing a 'domino-effect.'

It's also seen that the increased 'barbarian', or rather Nordic-Germanic migrations into formerly controlled Roman lands are the result of a falling Rome, not the cause as has previously been claimed by some historians.

Nevertheless, this mass migration is often viewed as being a time of Nordic-Germanic invasion. Mostly by those in the former provinces of Roman Britannia, Gaul, and the rest of Europe which was previously governed under the protection of the Western Roman Empire.

Chapter 4 – The Nordic Migration Period

The Nordic Migration Period was a time of massive migrations, of not only the Norse and Germanic people, but of almost all cultures across Europe. It was a time of great change that took place in two phases over a span of four centuries from around 284 AD to 700 AD.

This period of time began just before the Early Middle Ages, often referred to as 'the Dark Ages' *(from 5th to 10th centuries)*. This is a time when Rome was losing its hold on Western Europe and along its western frontiers.

A period when all of Europe began its migrations as power dramatically shifted across the land when the Roman Empire split in half.

In 284 AD, the Roman Emperor Diocletian split the Roman Empire in half, separating East from West. He kept the eastern portion of the Roman Empire to rule for himself, which later became known as the Byzantine Empire. The western portion of the Roman Empire came under the rule of Emperor Maximian.

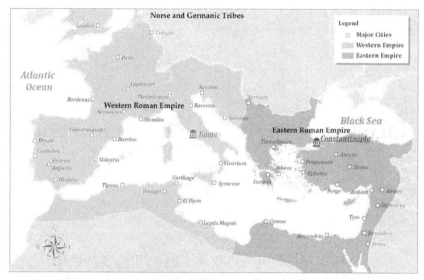

Map of the Western half of the Roman Empire split from the Eastern half of the Roman Empire (Byzantine Empire).

With Rome no longer pushing in 300 AD, the first phase of these Norse-Germanic migrations took place through to 500 AD, when the Roman Empire's control began to loosen and fall into the hands of tribes in Germania and Britannia.

The second phase of these migrations took place from 500 AD through to 700 AD with settlements expanding deep into Central and Eastern Europe.

This expansion of 'barbarian' tribes into former Roman controlled areas spread all the way into the Lombardy region of Northern Italy.

At the beginning of the migrations, in most cases, prosperity continued in some places after the Roman Empire split in half, such as Britannia until the Roman government withdrew its military protection in 410 AD.

Soon after, instability swept the area of Britannia with a combination of renewed Pictish, Irish, and now Jute, Anglo, and Saxon invasions causing great destruction, from which the Romano-British civilization never recovered.

The Goths rose to prominence out of the North during this time as well.

In "The Origin and Deeds of the Goths" written by Jordanes in 551 AD, the origin and history of the Gothic people begins with an ethnological descrition of the North, especially that of a land they called Scandza (Scandinavia).

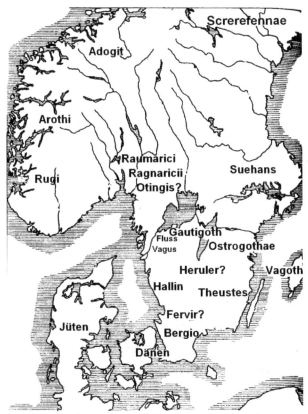

Map of Scandza, with a selection of tribes

Jordanes begins the history of the Goths with their emigration of three ships from Scandza (Sweden) to Gothiscandza (Poland) in a distant past.

He tells of how these ancient Goths sacked "Troy and Ilium" just after the Greeks recovered somewhat from the war with Agamemnon at the time of the Trojan War.

Written in Late Latin, Jordanes also claimed the Goths as having encountered the Egyptian pharaoh Vesosis.

Jordanes' gives an account of when the Goths encountered Roman military forces in the 3rd century AD. His writing concludes with the defeat of the Goths by the Byzantine general Belisarius, in which he writes a passage to honor those who were victorious over the Goths after a history of 2030 years.

Although Rome did not begin until 753 BC, this would mean that possibly the Greeks had been fighting Norsemen since 1479 BC, based on Jordanes having written it 'around' 551 AD and being in the Eastern part *(Greek speaking)* of the Roman Empire.

If there's any accuracy to his record, this would have been just after the Egyptian Pharoah Hatshepsut, the second historically-confirmed female pharaoh, came to the throne of Egypt in 1478 BC.

This was during the Mycenaean Greek civilization at the end of the Greek Bronze Age from 1600 to 1100 BC, just before the Greek Dark Ages which lasted from around 1200 to 800 BC.

The possible Goth conflict with Egyptians would have

been in a time when the New Kingdom of Egypt was pushing it's way up into the gates of what would be later known as Europe.

The War of Vesosis and Tanausis is described in Jordanes' account of the Goths as happening in remote antiquity when Vesosis, king of the Egyptians, made war against them.

Map of New Kingdom of Egypt, 15th Century BC.

He writes that in a battle at the river Phasis in Colchis (modern Georgia), Tanausis, king of the Goths, met Vesosis, king of the Egyptians, and there inflicted a severe defeat upon him, pursuing him even to Egypt.

This would explain why so many items discovered of ancient Norsemen of the time period have a Scythian influence in the design of many items such as spangenhelms. The Goths have been around for a while.

The Goths expanding and pushing against the now faltering Roman Empire, pushed also on the Germanic tribes west of them, which in turn pushed further migrations into the West and into Britannia.

The Goths were later followed by the Huns coming from the east and they pushed Europe ever more to the south and west as they pressed against Rome and the Goths.

The destruction of the Gothic kingdoms by the Huns in the early 370's AD triggered more Germanic migrations well into the following century. When the city of Rome, the heart of the ancient Roman Empire, fell to the Visigoths in 410 AD, the face of Europe changed. To make sure Roman Empire never rose again, the Vandals followed suit in 455 AD and 'vandalized' the Rome again.

The former Western Roman frontier was now open.

No longer protected by the Roman military against the constant threat from the Picts and Scots of the North, the Celts felt themselves increasingly vulnerable to attack. Around 430 AD, the ambitious Celtic warlord Vortigern invited the Jutish brothers Hengest and Horsa (from

46

Jutland in modern-day Denmark), to settle on the east coast of Britain to form a bulwark against sea raids by the Picts, in return for which they were "allowed" to settle in the southern areas of Kent, Hampshire, and the Isle of Wight *(later known as Southern England).*

But the Jutes were not the only newcomers to Britain during this period. Other Germanic tribes soon began to make the short journey across the North Sea. The Angles (from a region called Angeln, the spur of land which connects modern Denmark with Germany) gradually began to settle in increasing numbers on the east coast of Britain, particularly in the north and East Anglia.

The Frisian people coming from the marshes and islands of northern Holland and western Germany, also were being pushed onto the mainland of Britannia beginning in 450 AD.

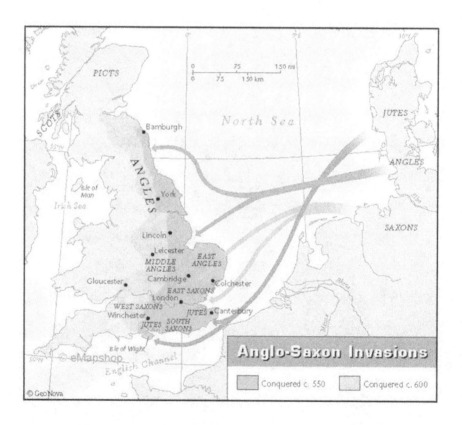

From the 470's AD, the Saxons coming from the Lower Saxony area of modern-day northwestern Germany began increasingly pushing their way into the southern part of the British mainland.

Overtime, these Germanic tribes began to establish permanent bases and to gradually displace the native Celts.

By the middle of the 5th century large numbers of Anglo and Saxon tribes began to migrate into southern and eastern England. The hallmarks of Roman life, the towns, villas, use and literacy of Latin along with Christianity, declined steeply.

These Anglo-Saxons tribes established a number of small kingdoms in eastern Britain. By around 600 AD, these merged into larger kingdoms. These larger formed the kingdoms of Northumbria, Mercia, and Wessex gradually extending their territory westward as they conquered more and more lands of the Britons.

After being profoundly changed from Roman occupation so many years ago, Britannia was dramatically changing again.

From the end of the sixth century, the Anglo-Saxons began converting to Christianity. However, to what extent this religion had survived in the localities from Roman times is a matter for debate.

Records tell us that the Irish were being converted to Christianity in the 5th century. Additionally, it's recorded that the Christian church began sending missionaries to Scotland and northern England in the 6th century.

There is also record of a mission led by Augustine in the south of England in 597 AD.

Map of Britian, 600 AD.

By the end of the 7th century and the 'official' beginning of the Viking Age, it's recorded that all of England and Scotland had converted to Christianity, with Ireland following.

However, the Christianization of England, Scotland, and Ireland was by no means done peacefully.

When the Norsemen (Vikings) attacked England, most of them were returning Norse and Germanic clans who'd previously been pushed out by emerging Kingdoms under Christianity.

The Viking Age was really no different that the American Indian Wars with the same results. The conqueror claimed *'Manifest Destiny'* under the name of Christ against the heathen occupants, slaughtering them and seizing their lands.

Take the Jutes of Kent and the Isle of Wight for example. It was just decades before the "official" date of the "Viking Age" in 686 AD when the Jutes were slaughtered under the command of a bishop by the neighboring Christian kingdom (ironically using Norse mercenaries).

It is believed that some of the surviving Jutes may have fled to Norway and Denmark (Jutland) to later return as so called 'viking invaders'.

In a sense, the Viking Age is really just when the Norse began fighting back against expansion of Christian kings united by the Roman Church.

The records of clergy, especially that of Bede, the kingdoms and monasteries that were attacked, you see the presence of well established Germanic or Nordic tribes being condemned as heathens or idol-worshippers and pushed out by force. Their families slaughtered and lands taken in the name of the church to allow 'Christian Settlers'.

When you trace the Vikings that attacked them, you find these expeditions were led by descendants of those very tribes that were pushed out of their lands. They came with some kindred help of opportunistic Norsemen with the promise of lands and the right to gather and claim anything they could capture.

In comparison, imagine Americans taking Texas back if some foreign power took it from them. Most of the Texans would have been killed fighting to defend their lands. Once they were defeated, the survivors would flee to neighboring "friendlies" for refuge and seek help to reclaim their lands in Texas.

Hey, guess what - that happened!

Remember the Alamo!

The Viking attacks were no different.

Fighting back was the birth of the Viking Age.

The Viking Age was actually a war against Christian expansionism, as the Viking Age ended upon Norse conversion to the Church, at least by the land rulers.

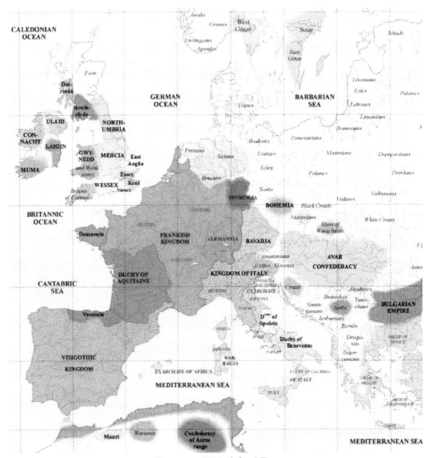

Europe, 700-ish AD.

53

Chapter 5 – The Viking Age

In most cases, the Norse "Viking Age" is recorded to have officially began in 793 AD with the first recorded raid on an undefended monastery through to 1066 AD, ending with the Battle of Hastings. However, these dates vary upon scholars. The Battle of Hastings wasn't exactly the end of the Viking Age, because the Norse were spread out across Europe and Viking raids continued to take place in other locations.

With that said, dating the conclusion of the Viking Age is fairly generic because Viking raids were sporadic in many locations and when one area was under control, another area was being raided. Additionally, this was because Viking raiders weren't unified efforts and most Norsemen tended to 'vikingr' (raid) at their own whim.

This places the conclusion of the Viking Age at approximately the beginning of the 12th Century-ish. This is also about the time when Norse and other Kingdoms were becoming increasingly solidified and more able to repel Viking incursions. This was also around the time when the

Christianization of Northern Europe and Norse dominated lands began to take a firmer hold. So dating the exact end of the Viking Age is vague at best.

The same can be said about the approximate beginning of the Viking Age as well. Although it's officially marked by most scholars as beginning in 793 AD with the raid on the Lindisfarne Monastery, it wasn't a new concept for the Norse to go "vikingr' (raid). Viking raids were already occurring in a vast range of other areas, including France.

Nevertheless the most accepted official start of the Viking Age is recorded to have begun on June 8th, 793 AD when Norse raiders landed on the island of Lindisfarne and attacked the Christian Monastery located there, killing the monks and seizing the valuables.

Viking raids by opportunistic Norsemen also began occurring in frequency at other locations, such as the island of Iona in Scotland in 794 AD. By 795 AD, Christian Monasteries along Ireland's coast were being raided regularly by small Viking groups for the first 40 years. After that, large Viking fleets began showing up.

Viking Raids had begun with regularity on the western coast of Francia (France) in 790 to 800 AD. Normandy, where they had been raiding, actually takes its name from the Viking raiders who they called Normanii (Norsemen or Men of the North). The Norse raiders seized upon internal turmoil within the leadership of France, so they invaded and seized the region, which later became known as Normandy.

So Viking raids were already occurring in many

locations at the time. What made the Lindisfarne significant to mark it as the official beginning of the Viking Age was because it was the earliest official recording of a Viking raid.

The raid had caused much stir in the Christian world because the Norsemen attacked an unarmed religious compound and killed all the monks that inhabited it. At the time, it was naturally assumed that a religious compound such as a Christian monastery was safe from any kind of attack. The Norse dissolved this illusion.

Although the Viking raids were sporadic, they were very violent when they occurred. The speed and violence of these raids happened without warning and spread much fear to everyone that heard about them. These speedy violent attacks from coastlines and rivers marked the beginning of the **Viking Age of Invasion** by means of the Longship.

Viking Ship, Pre-800 AD.[46]

What helped the Viking raiders during this time period was the fact that England was relaxed with its isolated communities along the edges of coasts, islands, peninsulas, and other waterway inlets. These communities were completely unguarded without a second thought to any dangers from the sea.

This complacency opened the door to Norse raiders as being easy pickings. There was simply an abundance of unguarded and unarmed settlements located near the water that were ripe for Viking raids that were easily reachable by longboat. This allowed the Norse raiders to arrive conveniently by longboat, quickly raid the settlement, and then leave with their plunder uncontested.

Sporadic small scale Viking raids continued across the northern and eastern coastal shores of England, Scotland, and Ireland. The extensive raids in Ireland eventually led to settlements and the founding of Limerick in 812 AD.

At this time, a Norwegian Viking by the name of "Naddodd" became one of the first settlers of the Faroe Islands. He's also credited for discovering Iceland when he was sailing from Norway to the Faroe Islands and got lost. After briefly exploring the Island looking for inhabitants, he returned to his boat and it started snowing, so he named the place Snæland (Snowland), which later became called Ísland (Iceland).

As time passed and word got around about the easy picking of the Islands, the number of raiders grew in size. In 832 AD, a large Viking fleet of about 120 ships had invaded kingdoms in Ireland's eastern and northern coasts. More Norse settlements began to form and the Norse presence started growing even larger in the region.

The Danes came upon the Isle of Sheppey in 835 AD, which is just off the northern coast of Kent, England. After successfully raiding the Isle, they began moving northward looking for more places to raid. Raids by various Norsemen started becoming a regular occurrence to the inhabitants of England, Scotland, and Ireland.

Three years later, in 838 AD, a small Viking party entered the River Liffey and established a base called a "Longphort." This base eventually became the city of Dublin. The Vikings also established other longphorts in locations now called Cork, Limerick, Waterford, and Wexford. The Vikings could sail through on the main rivers and branch off into different areas of the country.

In Scotland, the highly navigable Rivers Tay and Earn were entered by a large Viking fleet in 839 AD. The Norse invaders were able to reach into the very heart of the Pictish kingdom of Fortriu. The Norse defeated the King of the Picts, Eogán mac Óengusa, his brother Bran and the King of the Scots of Dál Riata, Áed mac Boanta, along with many other members of the Pictish aristocracy which were all killed in battle against the invaders.

Depiction of a Pict Warrior.[45]

The Norse, rather than their usual summer raids sailing from Scandinavia or the mainland, waited in Ireland where they had established several strategic bases and then raided parts of England during the winter between 840 AD and 841 AD. Whereas when inhabitants were already worried about the Vikings attacking in the Summer months, now had to now worry about the Winters too.

It was during this time, which was during the reign of Louis the Pious, the King of the Franks, the Vikings were also carrying out raids on Frankish areas primarily in the summer and then wintering in Scandinavia. It wasn't long until several coastal areas had become lost to the Norse invaders as Vikings took advantage of the quarrels within the Frankish royal family caused after the death of Louis the Pious.

The royal family's quarrels caused so much instability in the Frankish region that the Norse seized the opportunity to settle their first colony in the southwest (Gascony) of the Kingdom of Francia. This area had been more or less abandoned by the Frankish kings after their two defeats at Roncevaux Pass on the Spanish border.

The incursions on the River Seine in Francia in 841 AD had caused severe damage to Rouen and Jumièges. The Vikings attacking these Francia regions sought to capture the treasures stored at monasteries, which were easy prey given that the monks lacked any defensive capability.

The Vikings had set up a permanent base in the mouth of the Loire River in 842 AD where they could now strike at places as far as Northern Spain, such as Cadiz which was attacked in 844 AD. In some of their raids on Spain, the Vikings were crushed either by the Kingdom of Asturias or the Emirate armies. The Vikings that did settled in these areas in Spain, such as in Al-Andalus, had eventually become "Hispanized," but kept their ethnic identity and culture.

In 844 AD, many dozens of Dragon Ships (Drakkars) appeared in the mouth of the Tagus river, along the border of Portugal and Spain. After a siege, the Vikings successfully conquered Lisbon (Al-Ushbuna). The Norse invaders left after 13 days, following a resistance led by Alah Ibn Hazm and the city's inhabitants. Another raid on Lisbon was attempted by the Norse in 966 AD, but was without any success.

Viking raids ruthlessly continued on the divided kingdoms of Francia (the Kingdoms of the Franks, Modern France). The infamous **Ragnar Lothbrok** with 120 ships and 5000 warriors landed in Francia near the mouth of the Seine River and began ravaging Western Francia. During these attacks, the city of Rouen had fallen to the Norse invaders.

Then Carolivenna fell victim and was attacked next in the Viking's search for silver and other valuables. Even the city of Paris fell and King Charles "the Bald" was forced to pay Ragnar a large bribery of silver not to sack it in 845 AD.

However, opportunistic Vikings still regularly patrolled the rivers and waterways of West Francia after discovering the easy pickings of the rich churches and monasteries.

Legend has it that many of the raids conducted on England, Francia and Frisia during this time were led by Ragnar Lothbrok. **Ragnar Lothbrok** (also Ragnar Lodbrok or Ragnarr Loðbrók which means "Ragnar Hairy Breeches" in Old Norse) was a legendary Norse ruler and hero who became known as the scourge of England and France. He was said to be the son of Sigurd Hring, a King of Sweden and succeeded the throne upon his father's death.

Ragnar Lothbrok had been married three times. His first wife was **Lagertha**, who he had met in a battle while avenging his grandfather's death, King Siward. King Frø of Sweden invaded Norway and killed the Norwegian King Siward.

To add insult to injury for public humiliation, King Frø ordered that the surviving women of King Siward's family into a brothel. When Ragnar Lothbrok heard about King Frø's invasion of Norway, he came with an army to avenge the death of his grandfather.

When Ragnar arrived, some of the women King Frø had ordered into the brothel dressed in men's clothing and helped fight on Ragnar's side. Among these women dressed as men and fighting in front among the bravest was the skilled shield-maiden Lagertha.

Lagertha fought as ferociously as a man and only the loose locks of her hair flowing over her shoulders revealed her as being a women. This impressed Ragnar greatly and lead him to court her. Lagertha pretended to be interested in his proposals and Ragnar came to seek her hand in marriage.

However when he arrived, Lagertha had a bear and a great hound which were guarding her home, attack Ragnar when he arrived. He killed the bear with his spear and choked the hound to death. By doing this, he won Lagertha's hand in marriage. Ragnar had three children with her, a son named Fridleif and two daughters (whose names are lost to history).

Unfortunately, Ragnar continued to hold a grudge against Lagertha for having her two beasts attack him when he originally sought out her hand in marriage and divorced her and returned to Denmark.

When he returned to Denmark, Ragnar was faced with a civil war and sent word to Norway for support. Lagertha, who still loved him, heeded his call and came to his aid in Denmark with 120 ships full of warriors. Lagertha arrived with her ships of warriors and saved the day for Ragnar with a counterattack by circling around and attacking the enemy from the rear. She took Ragnar's enemies by surprise and turned the tide of the battle, causing their opponents to panic.

Upon returning to Norway, she quarreled with her new husband (*name unknown*) and slew him with a spearhead that she had concealed in her gown. She then usurped the whole of his name and sovereignty, as she found it better to rule without her husband than to share the throne with him.

Ragnar Lothbrok's second wife was the daughter of King Herrauðr of Sweden, Thora Town-Hart (Þóra borgarhjörtr). King Herrauðr had acquired an egg from Bjarmland (Arkhangelsk Oblast, Russia, next to Finland). The egg had hatched into a lindworm (wyrm or dragon) and grew into a great serpent that encircled her bower (apartment). Her father promised Thora's hand in marriage to whoever could slay this great serpent. This is when Ragnar famously wore the hairy breeches that gained his nickname, "Lothbrok" (Loðbrók) which means "Hairy-

Breeches."

Ragnar went to Västergötland (West Gothland, in Southwest Sweden) where her bower was located and dressed himself in shaggy clothes and the hairy beeches that he treated with tar and sand to protect him from the serpent's poison. He took a spear and approached the serpent which spewed poison at him, but Ragnar protected himself with his shield and was also protected by his tar and sand treated clothes. He speared the serpent through its heart and cut off its head. married Thora.

Thora gave Ragnar two sons Eiríkr (Erik) and Agnar, who later died of an illness.

The name of Ragnar's third wife was Aslaug (Aslög). Aslaug was said to be the daughter of the legendary Norse hero Sigurd (Old Norse: Sigurðr) and the shield-maiden Brunhild (also spelled Brynhildr or Brünnhilde). Upon the deaths of her parents, Sigurd and Brunhild, she was then raised by Brunhild's foster father Heimer. However, Heimer was concerned about Aslaug's safety and kept her identity hidden. Legend states that he built a large harp to hide her in and traveled as a poor harp player, keeping the girl concealed within it.

They arrived at Spangereid at Lindesnes in Norway, where they stayed for the night in the house of the peasants Åke and Grima. Åke believed that the mysterious large harp contained valuables and told his wife Grima about it. Grima then convinced him to murder Heimer while he was sleeping. However, after they murdered Heimer and broke the harp open, they discovered the hidden little girl, who they named Kråka ("Crow") and raised as their own child. In order to hide her beauty, the accepted sign of her noble origins, they rubbed her in tar and dressed her in a long hood.

However, one day when as she was bathing, she was discovered by some of Ragnar Lothbrok's men, who were confused by Kråka's beauty and allowed the bread they were baking to burn as they watched her. When Ragnar inquired about the mishap with the bread, they informed him about the beautiful girl they'd seen.

Ragnar then sent for her and to test her wits,
he commanded her to arrive
neither dressed nor undressed,
neither hungry nor full,
and neither alone nor in company.

To this challenge, Kråka arrived dressed in a
net, biting an onion, and with only a dog as
her companion.

Ragnar's challenge to test Kråka's wits.

Ragnar was genuinely impressed by her ingenuity and felt that she would be a wise companion. Ragnar proposed marriage to her, but she refused until he'd accomplished his mission in Norway.

When Ragnar visited Östen Beli, the viceroy of Sweden, he had told him of the maiden Kråka (Aslaug), but Östen persuaded him to reject Kråka and instead to marry Ingeborg, a Swedish princess. On Ragnar's return home, "three birds" had already informed Kråka of his plans to marry the princess Ingeborg and so she expressed her disapproval of this to him and revealed to him her true noble origins. In order to prove she that she was indeed the daughter of the hero Sigurd who had slain the dragon Fafnir, she told him that she'd bear him a child whose eye would bear the image of a serpent.

Fulfilling this, she bore him a son who had the image of a snake encircling the pupil and he was named Sigurd "Snake-in-the-Eye." When Östen learned of Ragnar's change of plans to marry the princess Ingeborg, he rebelled against him but was slain by Ragnar's sons at Kråka's (Aslaug) bidding.

Aslaug (Kråka) bore Ragnar four more sons: Ivar the Boneless, Björn Ironside, Hvitserk, and Ragnvald.

Although these marriages were recorded consecutively in history/lore, Ragnar Lothbrok was a bit of a ladies' man and shared the beds of all three, Lagertha, Thora and Aslaug. Each bearing children to him before being married, because there is mention of the deeds of Ragnar's sons before he was betrothed to their mothers.

Ragnar's sons grew up and set out to prove themselves as equals to their father. They made wars far and wide and conquered such places as Zealand, Reidgotaland (Jutland), Gotland, Öland and all the surrounding small islands. Ivar, who was the cleverest, was their leader and installed himself at Lejre on the island of Zealand, East Denmark.

Ragnar's sons grew to be strong warriors of their own accord and became even more ambitious. Ragnar didn't want his sons to overshadow him and seek his kingdom from him. So he appointed Eysteinn Beli to be the king of Sweden in his stay and instructed him to protect it from his son's ambitions.

One summer when Ragnar was out Viking (pillaging) in the Baltic region, his two sons from Thora, Erik (Eiríkr) and Agnar, came to Lake Mälaren in Sweden seeking the kingdom. They send a messenger to Gamla Uppsala, which is the seat of Swedish Kings and a place in Sweden that hosted regular sacrificial rites and royal burials, and asked King Eystein to meet them.

Upon his arrival, they demanded that the King be their vassal and to give his daughter Borghild to Erik to be his wife. When King Eystein heard their demands, he consulted the Swedish chieftains and they made the decision to attack Erik and Agnar. After a long battle against overwhelming numbers, the brothers lost against the Swedish forces. Agnar was slain in the battle, but Erik survived the battle and was captured alive.

King Eystein desiring peace and wanting to seal a peace treaty went ahead and offered his daughter to Erik and as much from the *Uppsala öd* as he wanted. The *Uppsala öd* was the ancient collection of royal estates that financed the Swedish Kings.

But Erik declined the King's offer and stated that he didn't wish to live after such a humiliating defeat. The defeated Erik asked the King to be raised him up on the points of spears above the slain in the battlefield, so he'd be pierced by the spears and slain on the field of battle.

He wished to be put to death in this manner so he could

enter Valhalla with the rest of the battlefield's slain. A demand which, the Swedish rulers granted. This was the end of Ragnar Lothbrok's sons by Thora.

In 850 AD, Dane Vikings overwintered for the first time on the Isle of Thanet near Kent, England. Usually they went home to winter and returned to England in the warmer summer months to raid. They were securing areas now where they felt safe to winter over.

After the year 851 AD, Norsemen began to also stay in the lower Seine Valley of Francia for the winter as they began to secure a better hold of the area. This was occurring also in Kent, Scotland, and in Ireland as Norsemen began to stay throughout the year. In Ireland near Waterford for example, the Norse had established a more permanent settlement in 853 AD. Viking raids were intensifying everywhere the Norse could reach and their reach was fast expanding.

By 854 AD a raiding party overwintered a second time, at the Isle of Sheppey in the Thames estuary, where the River Thames runs into the North Sea and by the following year in 855 AD, the Isle of Sheppey became a regular wintering camp for the occupying Danes. The unguarded River Thames provided a convenient gateway for Viking raiders seeking island targets and also as a entrance port from the mainland reaching into Francia.

The raids following the rivers and hitting inland Francia became more regular. By 858 AD, Vikings had captured and burned Chartres, Francia. They did it twice more in the 860's AD. Vikings simply rowed to Paris and left only when they acquired sufficient loot or were bribed by the Carolingian rulers. These Viking raiders are believed to have been led by none other than Ragnar Lothbrok himself.

The Viking raids by these invading Norsemen were getting so frequent and bad that by 862 AD, the King of West Francia, Charles the Bald (later known as Charles II) had to put a stop to it.

Portrait of Charles the Bald (823-877).[56]

King Charles II put a stop to much of the raiding by defending his rivers and fortifying his towns. By doing so, he effectively made it more difficult for the Vikings to easily raid or attack. Many religious communities and monasteries were moved inland and out of reach from Viking opportunists, this eliminated the easy pickings by raiders.

By this time, many Norsemen had already settled in

Shetland, Orkney, the Hebrides and Man, and parts of mainland Scotland. These Norse settlers were to some extent integrating with the local Gaelic population in the Hebrides Islands and the Isle of Man. These areas were ruled over by local Norse Jarls that were originally captains of ships.

Hersirs were Norse leaders that were followed by large bands Viking raiders that also claimed the land where they settled and occupied. The Jarl of Orkney and Shetland however, claimed supremacy over all of the Isles with the other Jarls or Hersirs under him.

"King Rorik"[47]

With Francia becoming increasing more difficult to raid, Viking bands diverted their attention more on England. In 864 AD they reverted to the Isle of Thanet for their winter encampment before conducting summer raids.

Desiring to show himself as a better warrior than his sons, Ragnar Lothbrok decided to conquer England with only two knarr ships. Knarrs were a type of merchant ship used by the Norse traders at the time. The ships Ragnar had were built in Vestfold, Norway and were indeed enormous ships.

Ragnar's wife, Aslaug didn't approve of this idea because such large ships weren't fit for attacking the English coast, only the more maneuverable longships were more capable for that task. However, Ragnar refused to heed her advice and arrived safely with his army in England and began a campaign to ravage and burn his way across the country.

Sometime late in 864 or early 865 AD, Ragnar had made his way to Northumbia and became shipwrecked off the coast. Hearing the news of Ragnar being shipwrecked, King Ælla of Northumbria mustered an overwhelming force and defeated Ragnar's army while they were vulnerable. They were able to take Ragnar alive and held him prisoner. King Ælla, mocking the tales he'd heard of Ragnar's immunity to snakes during the time when he courted Thora and slew the serpent, had Ragnar Lothbrok thrown into the snake pit.

King Ælla having Ragnar Lothbrok put to death in a pit of snakes.[48]

However, it is said that Ragnar was protected by an enchanted silken shirt that Aslaug had made for him. It was only when this shirt had been removed from him that the snakes were able to bite Ragnar and kill him with their venom.

Before 865 AD, most Viking raids were predominately hit and run operations, but by that year in 865 AD they changed into invasions with the intent to conquer. It is believed that pressure from tyrannous kings in Nordic regions forced them to seek new lands and start new lives. Norsemen were now looking for farm land to settle their families.

The legend in the Sagas of Ragnar's Sons (Ragnarssona þáttr) claims that some of the attention of England by Ragnar Lothbrok's sons was because of the death of their father, Ragnar Lothbrok who was killed by the king of Northumbria, Ælla, during a raid in which Ragnar was taken prisoner and thrown into a snake pit. The following year, Ragnar's sons build a substantial force and sought vengeance for their father against King Ælla.

In 865 AD, the **Great Heathen Army**, otherwise known as the **Great Viking Army** was formed by uncoordinated bands of Norse Vikings that came from Denmark, Norway, and Sweden. They were led by Ragnar Lothbrok's sons, Ivar Ragnarsson (Ivar the Boneless), Halfdan Ragnarsson (Halfdene), and Ubbe Ragnarsson (Hubba), along with the Dane Viking chieftain Guthrum.

The Norsemen were well aware of the civil war that had weakened the great northern kingdom in England and as warriors these Norse were extremely opportunistic.

The Norse consolidated their forces as they came in and wintered in East Anglia. To protect their realm and as an opportunity to see their rivals in Northumbria attacked, East Anglia made a peace agreement with the Norse army. They allowed the Norse to use their lands to gather their army and provided them with horses. The Norse used it as a staging point for their invasion into Northumbria.

By late 866 AD, the Great Heathen Army marched into Northumbria and on November 21st they seized York, which they called Jórvik. York (Jórvik) had a great defensive and was a strategic stronghold that was well protected by the walls the Roman Army had built for it previously.

Kings Ælla and Osberht united their forces and made an attempt to retake York months later on March 21st 867 AD. But two days later on March 23, 867 AD, as they continued their attempt to retake York from the Great Heathen Army, the battle ended when King Osberht was killed and King Ælla was captured. King Ælla was horrifically subjected to traditional Norse warrior practice of the Blood Eagle ordeal by having his ribs torn out and folded back to form the shape of an eagle's wings.

Routes taken by the Great Heathen Army from 865 to 878 AD.[57]

Reputedly, it was punishment for King Ælla's alleged murder of Ragnar Lothbrok by throwing him into a pit of snakes after his failed raid on Northumbria the prior year.

After that battle and the Norse seizing control of the region, the Northumbrians paid the Vikings off and the Great Heathen Army's collected leaders established as King in their place, Egbert (Ecgberht I). King Egbert was put in place to be a puppet leader and tax collector in Northumbria. The Great Heathen Army then set off for the Kingdom of Mercia, where in 867 AD they captured Nottingham.

King Burgred, the king of Mercia and Kent, requested help from his brother-in-law King Æthelred I, the king of Wessex, to help in defense against the Viking invaders.

King of Mercia Athelred seen on the exterior of Lichfield Cathedral.[51]

King Æthelred and his brother Alfred, the future Alfred the Great, led a West Saxon army from Wessex and Mercia and besieged the Norse occupied city of Nottingham with no clear result. The Mercians settled on paying the Vikings off to leave instead.

The Vikings of the Great Heathen Army returned to Northumbria in the Autumn of 868 AD and stayed the winter in York,. They remained in York for most part of the year 869 AD. Some remained in hopes of starting a new life in York, but most sought land of their own. It was the main reason they'd come in the first place and their leaders reassured them there was more areas available.

The Great Heathen Army returned to East Anglia and spent the winter of 869/870 AD at Isle of Thetford. This time when the Norse arrived there wasn't a peace agreement between the East Anglians and the occupying Viking army. The East Anglians weren't caught by surprise this time and the Great Heathen Army wasn't as numerous as before either. They seen this as an opportunity to repel the Norse invaders from their land, so the local King Edmund fought against the Norsemen to no avail. He was captured and killed. Subduing the East Anglians, the Great Heathen Army wintered there and prepared to attack further Anglo lands as soon as weather permitted,

The Battle of Englefield was a battle that took place on New Years Eve, December 31st, 870 AD at Englefield near Reading, which is now the English county of Berkshire. It was one of a series of battles that took place following an invasion of the then Kingdom of Wessex by an army of

Danes. During these battles in which the Danes had established a camp at Reading. Both the battle and campaign are described in the Anglo-Saxon Chronicle.

Three days after their arrival in Reading, a party of Danes, led by two of their jarls, rode out towards Englefield. It was here that Æthelwulf, the Ealdorman of the shire, had mustered a force and was waiting for them. In the ensuing Battle of Englefield, many of the Danes, including one of the jarls named Sidrac, were killed while the rest of the Danes were driven back to Reading.

A battle between 'Anglo-Saxons' and 'Vikings' staged by re-enactors.[50]

However, the Saxon victory at Englefield did not last long. Four days later the main West Saxon army, led by King Ethelred and his brother, Alfred the Great attacked the main Danish encampment at Reading and were bloodily repulsed. This battle became known as the First Battle of Reading. Among many of the dead on both sides was Æthelwulf, who had repelled the invading Norse in the first place.

In 871 AD, King Bagsecg came to England from Scandinavia and brought with him the **Great Summer Army.** He arrived and added his forces to the Great Heathen Army which had already had much success in overruning much of England.

King Bagsecg and Halfdan Ragnarsson dispatched a few raiding parties to attack the Kingdom of Wessex which remained vulnerable to Viking style raids and they captured Reading and Berkshire where they set up camp within the towns. On January 4th, 871 AD, Alfred attempted to attack the camp, however Bagsecg won a great victory at what's called *The Battle of Reading* where he inflicted terrible losses on Prince Alfred's army.

Reenactors depicting King Alfred with the West Saxon (Wessox) forces battling the Danish Norsemen of the Great Summer Army.[52]

The Battle of Ashdown, in Berkshire (possibly the part now in Oxfordshire), took place on January 8th, 871 AD. Both forces met for battle on the North Wessex Downs in Berkshire. The Vikings horde were commanded by Bagsecg and Halfdan and five other Danish Jarls. The Viking army itself was outnumbered in comparison to the West Saxons led by Alfred. This battle would determine the fate of Wessex and its king.

Alfred's elder brother King Æthelred of Wessex was busy praying in a church and refused to fight until his other army arrived. This left Alfred in command and the West Saxon and Viking armies met and the battle itself lasted all day. King Bagsecg was killed along with his five Danish Jarls.

According to the Anglo-Saxon Chronicle, King Bagsecg was slain by a sword while Halfdan fled from the field of battle with the rest of the army back to Reading.

The Battle of Ashdown itself was a limited West Saxon Victory, because two weeks later they would meet the Norsemen on the battlefield again.

The Battle of Basing was a battle that took place on January 22nd in the year of 871 AD at Old Basing in what is now known as the English county of Hampshire. It was one of a series of battles that took place following an invasion of the then kingdom of Wessex by an army of Danes. These Dane Norse were remnants of the merged Great Heathen Army and Great Summer Army.

The Danes had established a camp at Reading and the previous battles of Englefield, the Battle of Reading and the Battle of Ashdown, had proved indecisive with victories to both sides.

Two weeks after following the costly Saxon victory at Ashdown, King Æthelred and his brother Alfred were forced to retreat their army to Basing, where the two armies met again. The Saxon army led by King Æthelred was beaten by the Dane forces led by Ivar the Boneless (Ingvar). However, just like the preceding battles, this battle was also indecisive and two months later was followed by the Battle of Marton that happened on March 22nd, 871 AD where the Saxons prevailed.

These were the last known battles to be fought by King Æthelred against the Danes that year and the King is reported to have later died shortly later on April 15th, 871 AD.

Whether he died in battle or died shortly afterward on April 23rd as a result of wounds he suffered in battle is unclear.

Ether way, King Æthelred died and was succeeded by his younger brother Alfred, who later became known as Alfred the Great. King Alfred inherited both the throne of Wessex and its immediate need of defense against the Norse invaders.

The English continued to suffer defeats and after the defeat at Wilton, King Alfred's optimism that he'd be able to defend his kingdom from the Norsemen was deteriorating and he was forced to make peace with them. The terms of this peace agreement are unknown, but the Norse withdrew from Reading in the Autumn of 871 AD and wintered in London before returning to Northumbria in 872 AD.

The Northumbrians had rebelled against the puppet leader previously installed by the Norse, so the Great Heathen Army returned to restore power and then wintered in Lindsey for the winter of 872-873 AD. The Mercians continued to pay off the Viking invaders in exchange for peace and the Norse took up quarters in Repton for the following winter of 873-874 AD.

The following year in 874 AD, the Great Heathen Army conquered Mercia and drove the Mercian King Burgred into exile, placing the Mercian, Ceolwulf II, in power as a puppet leader and demanded oaths of loyalty.

After the Vikings had conquered the Kingdom of Mercia, the Great Heathen Army had split in two with half of the Viking army following Halfdan Ragnarsson who led his band north into Northumbria and then wintered by the River Tyre. Following the winter of 875 AD, he led his Viking band North to battle the Picts and Britons in the Kingdom of Strathclyde.

The year following in 876 AD, Halfdan then returned South and shared out the land with the other Norsemen in a region that became known as **The Danelaw.**

The Danelaw was the land conquered in England by the Great Heathen Army and then was occupied by the remaining Norsemen that settled there. This region fell under the Norse laws followed by the occupying Viking

Danes.

The second band of Vikings in the Great Heathen Army which were led by Guthrum, Oscetel, and Anwend, had left Repton in 874 AD and established a base camp at Cambridge for the winter of 874–875 AD. In the late of 875 AD, this band of Vikings moved on to Wareham, where they raided the surrounding areas and then occupied a fortified position to secure it. However, King Alfred of Wessex made a treaty with this group of Norsemen and they agreed to leave the Realm of Wessex. Nevertheless, it wasn't long until they started raiding other parts of Wessex and forced King Alfred to take up arms and fight back again.

Statue of King Alfred at Wantage holding an ax.[53]

By 876 AD, the Viking King Guthrum (Guðrum) had acquired various parts of the Kingdoms of Mercia and Northumbria and was now turning his attention to acquiring the Kingdom of Wessex, where his first confrontation with Alfred had taken place on the southern coast. The Viking King Guthrum sailed his army around Poole Harbour and linked up with another Viking army that was invading the area between the Frome and Trent rivers which were also ruled by King Alfred.

King Guthrum had won his initial battle against King Alfred and he'd successfully captured the Castellum as well as the ancient square where a convent of nuns was located that is known as the Wareham.

King Alfred then negotiated a peace settlement with the Viking invaders, but by 877 AD this peace agreement was broken when King Guthrum led his Viking army to raid further into the Wessex realm.

This action forced King Alfred to confront the Vikings in a series of skirmishes that King Guthrum continued winning. After King Guthrum had successfully captured Exeter, King Alfred was forced to seek a peace treaty that resulted in King Guthrum leaving the Kingdom of Wessex to winter in Gloucester.

The peace treaty lasted until on the night of 6th January 878 AD, King Guthrum made a surprise attack in the darkness on King Alfred and his court at Chippenham, Wiltshire. It was the Christian feast day of Epiphany and the Anglo Saxons were taken by surprise by the Vikings. However, it's also possible that Wulfhere, the Ealdorman of

Wiltshire, had allowed the attack because when King Alfred returned to power later that year, he stripped Wulfhere of his role as Ealdorman.

King Alfred was forced to flee from the attack with a few retainers and took shelter in the marshes of Somerset where they stayed in the small village of Athelney.

King Alfred spent the next few months building up his force while waging a guerrilla war against King Guthrum's secured refuges located in the fens. After a few months King Alfred was able to call forth men loyal to him to Egbert's Stone, where they then traveled to Ethandun and fought the Viking invaders that were led by King Guthrum.

This fighting went on until King Alfred was eventually able to defeat the half of the Viking Great Heathen Army led by King Guthrum in the Battle of Edington in May of 878 AD.

At the battle, King Alfred had routed the remains of King Guthrum's band from the Great Heathen Army. The Viking remains fled to their encampment and King Alfred sieged them for two weeks until eventually defeating them and making the Peace Treaty of Wedmore.

The peace treaty was made and the Viking King Guthrum was baptized as a Christian and assumed the new christening name of Æthelstan. Guthrum, now known as Æthelstan converted his faith while also accepting King Alfred as his godfather.

This treaty had established peace between the two rulers and also clearly defined the borders between the realms of

King Alfred and King Æthelstan (Guthrum).

The Kingdoms of Wales was not colonized by the Vikings as heavily as eastern England, Scotland, Ireland, and the surrounding Isles were. The Vikings did, however, settle in the South around St. David's, Haverfordwest, and Gower, among other places.

These were fairly easily accessible locations that could be reached by boat. The Vikings did not subdue the Welsh mountain kingdoms because they were not as easily accessible by waterways that the Vikings were so accustomed to and a dwindling army the Norse were now from previous engagements. The remains of the Great Heathen Army that swiftly conquered much of England, Scotland, Ireland, and the surrounding isles was now broken up and scattered into separate areas.

The Viking son of Halfdan the Black, Harald Fairhair (also known as Harald Halfdansson or Harald Hårfagre) was born in the Petty Kingdom of Rygjafylke in 850 AD. This located in what is called Rogaland, Norway today.

He was the son of Halfdan the Black, who was King of Vestfold (a petty kingdom) and a member and heir of the House of Yngling (a legendary Swedish royal clan with kings, which includes Ragnar Lodbrok, that is also mentioned in the Sage of Beowulf).

When King Halfdan the Black died, Harald Fairhair became the sovereign of several small and scattered petty kingdoms in Vestfold, Norway that his father had acquired through conquest and inheritance.

Statue of the first King of Norway, Harald Hårfagre (Fairhair).[54]

King Harald Fairhair went on to unify Norway and became the first King of Norway as a result. The unification of Norway began from a rejection of King Harold's marriage proposal from Gyda, the daughter of King Eirik, King of Hordaland (a petty kingdom in southern Norway).

When he proposed marriage to her, she is said to have refused to marry King Harald unless he was King of all of Norway. Upon this, Harald took a vow to never comb or cut his hair until he was the sole king over all of Norway.

In 866 AD, King Harald began a series of conquests against the several petty kingdoms of Norway until in 872 AD, after a great victory at the Battle of Hafrsfjord, when King Harald (now known as King Harald I of Norway) became the sole ruler of a now unified Norway.

However, not everyone shared King Harald's enthusiasm for a unified Norway nor of King Harald being the sole ruler of it. As a result his realm of the now unified Norway became under constant threat from many opponents that were forced to flee Norway and seek refuge in either Iceland, the Orkney Islands, Shetland Islands, Hebrides Islands, Faroe Islands, Scotland, Ireland, Northumbria, Mercia, or in the northern European mainland in what became Normandy.

This explains the sudden surge of the numbers that were so easily added to the Great Heathen Army and the increase in the number of Viking expeditions appearing along, just about every coastline in Northern Europe and the Isles in general. This was because of King Harald I of Norway and leaving wasn't entirely voluntary because many Norwegian chieftains who were wealthy and respected were perceived as a threat by King Harald Fairhair. They were therefore subjected to much harassment from King Harald and by those loyal to him. This prompted them to vacate their lands and seek refuge in Iceland, the isles and mainlands of Ireland, Scotland, and England.

Most of the Viking invasions of the 9th Century were not acts of piracy, but acts of necessity and desperation as many

Norse had suddenly become homeless and were forced to seek out new places to settle. This was when the Viking raids changed into Viking invasions and permanent occupation.

In 875 AD, King Harald Fairhair sent a fleet from Norway to Scotland in an attempt to unite it with the Kingdom of Norway. He had discovered that many of the Norse that were opposed to his rising power and unification of Norway had fled there. Many of them had taking refuge in the Isles by Scotland.

From these locations in the Isles, his opposition were launching raids and attacking Norway itself. To deal with this problem he organized a fleet that was led by Ketill Bjornsson (Ketill Flatnose) to subdue the Norse rebels and bring the rebellious independent Jarls under the control of his Kingdom of Norway. Many of the Norse rebels that had fled to Iceland were attacking Norway as well.

King Harald's commissioned fleet had successfully subdued the Norse rebels on the Isles and King Harold then found himself ruling not only Norway, but now the Isles of Man and parts of Scotland of which he annexed into the Kingdom of Norway.

However, Ketill Bjornsson, who been sent to subdue the rebels and seize the lands on the King of Norway's behalf, had decided to claim the captured Isles for himself and thus sent no tribute to King Herald of Norway.

Because of this betrayal, King Harald seized the possessions of Ketill Bjornsson that were in Norway and also banished Ketill's sons from Norway as well. The

Viking Ketill and his family was now outlawed and fearing the bounty put on his head Ketill decided to flee to Iceland, where most of his family eventually migrated with him as a result of King Harald of Norway actions against him.

It was Ketill's grandson, who was the son of Olaf the White King of Dublin, that sought loyalty to the King of Norway and invaded Scotland to extract tribute from nearly half the kingdom until his eventual death in battle.

Map of England 878 AD.[10]

By 879 AD, Guthrum's remaining army left Wessex, with some following him to his new Kingdom and some leaving to live a more settled life in York, Northumbria. Some assembled on the Thames to form a new army to return to the European continent to begin new campaigns and take advantage of the political turmoil in Francia with the death of King Charles the Bald (Charles II) in 877 AD.

Although with the treaty in place between King Alfred of Wessex and King Guthrum of the Danelaw, Alfred was saved any major conflicts but still had to deal with the occasional Viking raid here and there upon his kingdom. Alfred had reorganized his army, rebuilt and built new defenses around the countryside and formed a navy.

Peace between lands of the Danelaw and Wessex continued until in 884 AD when King Guthrum of the Danelaw attacked Wessex. Alfred defeated him and made a peace agreement that was outlined in the Treaty of Alfred and Guthrum. This peace treaty formally drew the boundaries of the Danelaw and allowed for Danish self-rule in that region.

In November 885 AD, a Viking named Rollo (Hrólfr, possibly Ganger Hrolf (Hrolf the Walker)) was one of the lesser leaders of the Viking fleet which besieged Paris under the leadership of Sigfred. The Vikings initially demanded a ransom, but the Count of Paris, Odo denied it to them, even though he could only muster a few hundred soldiers to defend the city. However, even though the Vikings used a variety siege engines, they failed to breach the Parisian Walls. Some of the Vikings left with Sigfred to pillage further up the River Seine. Yet some stayed with Rollo to continue with the siege on Paris and by the following year in October of 886 AD, King Charles the Fat of Francia arrived with his army.

Viking Ships besieging Paris.[55]

To the disappointment to the Parisians, who had defended the city so tenaciously, King Charles the Fat did not attack the Vikings but instead sent an emissary to find the Viking's chieftain in order to negotiate, but the Vikings replied that they were all chieftains of their own accord.

Eventually he was able to pay them a sum of 700 pounds of silver to leave Paris and allowed them to sail further up the River Seine to pillage Burgundy, which was in revolt at the time.

In 911 AD, the Viking leader Rollo, who fell foul to the Norwegian King Harald Fairhair, returned to the River Seine with his followers and invaded the area of northern France again. He launched an attack on Paris before laying siege to Chartres. On July 20th 911 AD, Frankish forces were to repel the Viking attack led by Rollo at the Battle of Chartres.

Then on August 26th, 911 AD, after another Frankish victory near Chartres against Rollo's forces, Charles the Simple (King Charles III), who was now King of Western Francia and of Lotharingia felt Rollo and his army of Norsemen would be worthy allies instead of adversaries and negotiated the Treaty of Saint-Clair-sur-Epte.

In this Treaty, King Charles the Simple in exchange for the Viking's loyalty and pledge of feudal allegiance, gave the city of Rouen and the area of what is present-day Upper Normandy to Rollo and his men in what established the **Duchy of Normandy**, named from the Frankish word for the Viking Men of the North, or Northmen (Normanii).

This was the land between the River Epte and the sea, as well as Brittany, which was an independent country that the Franks had failed to conquer. Additionally, Rollo and his Northmen were to defend the shores of the River Seine.

As a token of goodwill, Rollo also agreed to be baptized Christian as Robert I and to marry King Charles' daughter, Gisela. Legend states that when Rollo was required to kiss the foot of King Charles, as was custom to the condition of the treaty. Rollo refused to perform such a humiliation, in such that when Charles extended his foot to him, he ordered one of his warriors to do so in his place. When his warrior lifted King Charles' foot up to his mouth, it caused the king to lose his balance and fall to the ground.

In accordance to the Treaty of Saint-Clair-sur-Epte, Rollo honored his word and defended the shores of the River Seine. However, Rollo continued to make attacks on Flanders (Modern day Northern Belgium).

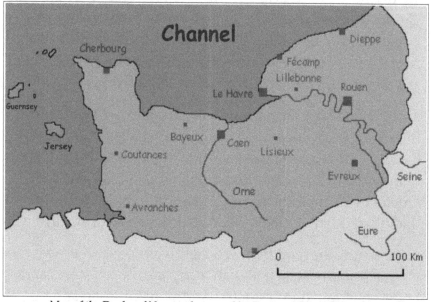

Map of the Duchy of Normandy created by Treaty of Saint-Clair-sur-Epte.[58]

Alfred the Great had died in 899 AD and was succeeded by his son, Edward the Elder. He, along with his sister, Æthelflæd, who was known as the Lady of the Mercians, conquered several Danish territories in the Midlands and East Anglia in a series of campaigns during the 917 AD. The Danish Jarls who submitted were allowed to keep their lands. Upon the death of his sister in 918 AD, Edward the

Elder also became King of Mercia. At this time, the balance of power in England was shifting out of the hands of the Viking conquerors controlling the Danelaw and into the hands of the Anglo-Saxon King. The Kingdom of Northumbria continued to be ruled by Norsemen.

Robert I of Western Francia, King of the Franks.[59]

In France, King Charles the Simple was deposed of by Robert I in 922 AD. Robert I instilled himself upon the throne as King of Western France, King of the Franks.

Rollo considered his oath to King Charles of France to now be null and voided. The Normans led by Rollo began a period of expansion westwards. In an attempt to stop

Rollo's attacks, Frankish Barons made negotiations which ended with Rollo being given Le Mans and Bayeux. Even with the newly gained land, Rollo continued with the seizure of Bessin in 924 AD and the following year Rollo's Normans attacked Picardy.

Rollo statue in Normandy in the town square of Falaise.[61]

In the same year Rollo was attacking Frankish areas, King Edward the Elder died on July 17th, 924 AD while leading an army against a Welsh-Mercian rebellion at Farndon-Upon-Dee. Edward the Elder was then succeeded by his son **Athelstan** (Æthelstan) who became King of the Anglo-Saxons from the time of his father's death until the year 927 AD when he conquered the remaining Viking hold in York. This victory effectively made King Athelstan the first King of all of England.

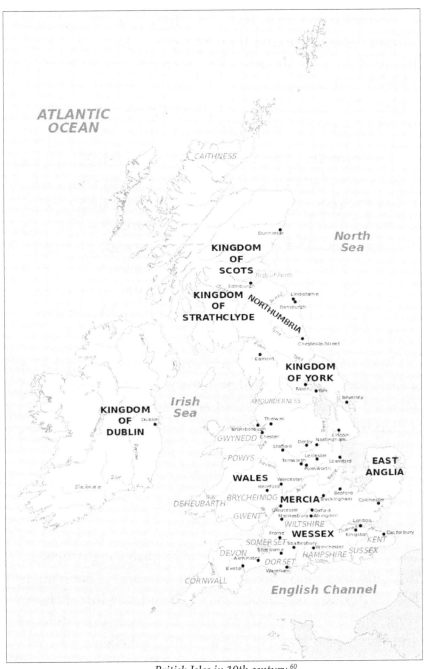

British Isles in 10th century.[60]

While England was becoming unified, in Normandy the Viking Rollo began dividing the lands he had conquered between the Epte and Risle Rivers among his chieftains and himself. Rollo then settled in Rouen, making it the capital city of Normandy. In 927 AD, Rollo passed the fief of Normandy to his son William Longsword.

It's uncertain when Rollo died, but he probably lived for a few years after that, but historians are certain that died before the year 933 AD. It is recorded by the historian Adhemar, that Rollo had gone mad towards the end and at one point had 100 Christian prisoners beheaded in front of him to honor the pagan gods who he worshiped and then later distributed 100 pounds of gold around to the churches in honor of the Christian God he'd been baptized in the Treaty of Saint-Clair-sur-Epte.

Even though Rollo had converted and been baptized as a Christian, as was typical of many converted Norse, he retained the religious roots of Norse beliefs and simply added the Christian god with the rest of his gods, as many polytheists do when converted.

Normandy began to form from a Frankish land once conquered and settled by Norsemen into a land of Norman identified themselves as Normans.

In England during 939 AD, the English King Athelstan died and was succeeded by his son Edmund I. Soon after King Edmund's coronation, he faced military threats from King Olaf Guthfrithson (Olaf III of the Norse-Gael dynasty and also the King of Dublin) who still laid claim to York which had been conquered by King Athelstan of England.

King Olaf III attacked Northumbria and forced King Edmund I into a treaty which granted King Olaf Northumbria and part of Mercia.

When King Olaf died a couple years later in 942 AD, King Edmund reconquered the Mercian midlands and by 944 AD, took back Northumbria. Two years later in 946 AD, King Edmund himself had died and was succeeded by his brother, King Eadred. Northumbria had once again become unstable until a new wave of Norwegian Vikings appeared in England in 947 AD led by Erik Bloodaxe (Eric Haraldsson). He was the son of King Harald Fairhair of Norway and as soon as he arrived, he'd captured York and claimed Northumbria for himself.

Silver penny of Eric Bloodaxe hailing him as King Eric (Eric Rex). A coin of the last Viking King of York. It circulated during the Viking Age at 947 to 954 AD.[63]

However, King Erik's rule in Northumbria was just as unstable as was when it was in English hands. The Northumbrian's (Scot-Welsh-Norse) loyalty bounced from that of King Edmund (English), to Dublin King Olaf (Norse-Gael), to the Norwegian King Erik (Norse).

Norwegian Viking rule effectively ended in Northumbria when King Erik Bloodaxe was driven out by the Northumbrians in 954 AD.

Note: This is also the year Erik Bloodaxe died, but whether he was slain or killed in battle is not clear. It is possible that he was killed when he was dethroned and expelled from Northumbria, but records point more to him being ambushed and murdered while traveling on an old Roman road.

Erik Bloodaxe was also the last last King of Northumbria. The lands of the former Kingdom of Northumbria were reduced to a Earldom that were disputed between England and Scotland.

By the end of 10th Century, Viking presence in Ireland, Scotland, and England changed from raiders to that of settlers that began to blur into the native population as Norse settlers became permanent inhabitants and effectively became English, Scottish, or Irish.

In 990 AD, Sigurd Hlodvisson (Sigurd the Stout) became the Earl of Orkney and took control of the Hebrides, which he placed a Jarl named Gilli in charge of. It wasn't long before Sigurd faced trouble from his southern neighbors. Earl Finnleik of Moray led an army against him and Sigurd found his men outnumbered seven to one.

Upon the advice of his mother, Sigurd's men carried the Raven Banner (a symbol of Odin) as their battle standard into battle and were victorious. However, as Sigurd's mother had predicted the standard-bearer was killed.

Raven's Banner (hrafnsmerki) as used by Jarl Sigurd.[63]

After a previous period of peace, a series of raids and attacks had been taking place along the coast of England by Danish Vikings which were porting in Normandy. Tensions between England and the Normans became grave enough that Pope John XV attempted to resolve the conflict and engineer peace between them. However, this failed when a sizable Danish fleet began a campaign on England. It was then after the Battle of Maldon that in 991 AD King Æthelred II (Æthelred the Unready) was forced into paying Danegeld (tribute) to the Danish King Sweyn I Forkbeard.

Unfortunately, the tribute paid in Danegold did not stop the Danish Viking attacks on England. Viking raids continued along the English coast until in 994 AD, when the Danish fleet swelled bigger than it was before in 991 AD. This was when Danish fleet had began attacking while they headed up the Thames towards London. The battle was inconclusive and King Æthelred II met with the leaders of the Danish fleet, of which King Olaf Tryggvason, King of Norway was foremost amongst them.

As a result of the negotiations, 22,000 pounds of gold and silver were paid to the Viking raiders and a peace treaty was signed between King Æthelred II and King Olaf.

In 994 AD King Olaf Tryggvason, who was already a baptized Christian, was confirmed as a Christian in a ceremony and then after receiving gifts, Olaf made an oath to never come back to England in hostility. After which, King Olaf returned to Norway and never came back to England again. After the peace agreement, some of the Vikings decided to stay in England and entered into King Æthelred II's service as mercenaries, based on the Isle of Wight.

On his way to Norway, King Olav stopped on the Northern Isles to Christianize them by summoning Jarl Sigurd and ordered him, along with all his subjects to be baptized as Christians. Stating that if he refused, he'd have him killed on the spot and would ravage every island with fire and steel. Not surprisingly, Jarl Sigurd agreed to King Olaf's demand of being baptized and the islands converted to the Christian religion in 995 AD.

This was not the end of Viking expansionism. Earlier, **Eric the Red** was expelled from Norway for manslaughter and resettled in Iceland with his family as many Norse refugees from Norway had before him. In 982 AD, the Icelanders had also expelled him at a "thing"(assembly) from Iceland for three years for some killings over a dispute he had committed there.

Erik the Red statue at Qagssiarssuk, Greenland.[64]

This is when Eric the Red made his way to Greenland. Greenland had been discovered previously by Gunnbjörn Ulfsson who had discovered it by accident when strong winds had driven him to the 'land mass' which he called Gunnbjarnarsker. Later, a Viking named Snaebjörn Galti attempted to settle Greenland, but it had ended in disaster. Eric the Red made the first successful settlement in Greenland. Eric had spent his three years in exile exploring the land. When his time in exile had ended, he returned to Iceland with tales of how great "Greenland" was, giving it the appealing name "Greenland" to lure potential settlers.

After spending the Winter of 985 AD in Iceland, Eric the Red returned to 'Greenland' with a large number of settlers. They established two successful colonies in the only areas suitable for summer farming. Eric the Red's son, Leif

Ericson, explored further West.

In about 985 or 986 AD, Bjarni Herjólfsson, while sailing to Greenland to visit his parents had been blown off course and discovered a land with low lying hills with forests some distance to the West. He did not stop to explore the newly discovered lands, but continued searching for Greenland, eager to see his parents. He eventually found Greenland and then eventually returned to Norway, where he told of this land he had found, but no one showed any interest. It is believed the land he had seen was North America.

Leif Erikson statue in front of Hallgrimskirkja.Iceland.[86]

Fifteen years later in 999 or 1000 AD, Leif Erikson had acquired the ship that Bjarni had sailed with when he spotted the land West of Greenland in hopes of finding the land himself and exploring it. Lief hired a crew of 35 men and set out to find it, following the route in reverse that Bjarni had sailed.

Leif and his crew first landed in a rocky, desolate place that he named "Helluland." meaning "Flat-Rock Land"possibly Baffin Island. They ventured further by sea and landed in a forested place he named "Markland," meaning "Forest Land" possibly Labrador. After sailing at sea for two more days, they landed in a place he named "Vinland." It was at this place where he and his crew built a small winter camp he called Leifsbúðir. After having wintered in the newly discovered settlement in Vinland, Leif returned to the settlement "Brattahlíð" in Greenland during the Springtime with a cargo of grapes and timber. It has believed that the site of Leifsbúðir (Leif's settlement) that is located in L'Anse aux Meadows, Newfoundland (a Canadian province).

In 1004 AD, Leif's brother Thorvald Eiriksson sailed to explore Newfoundland with a crew of 30 men and spent the winter at Leifsbúðir (Leif's camp). In the Springtime, Thorvald attacked nine of the local indigenous people, who the Norsemen called **"Skrælingar"(Skræling)**, that were sleeping under three skin-covered canoes. One of the victims survived the attack, escaping and came back to the Norse camp with a force. The indigenous people retaliated by attacking the Norse explorers and Thorvald was killed by an arrow that had passed through their defensive barricade. Brief hostilities continued as the remaining Norse explorers stayed through the winter until they left the following Spring.

A depiction of the death of Thorvald Eriksson in North America in 1004 AD.[66]

Thorvald and Leif's brother, Thorstein Ericson along with his wife Guthrith (Gudrida), sailed to the New World to retrieve his dead brother's body. Unfortunately, his expedition got lost and never reached Vinland. Turning back, they returned to Greenland and by the end of the first week of winter they landed at Lysufiord, Norway where Thorstein fell ill and died. The following Spring, his wife Gudrida returned to settlement Greenland of Brattahlíð, called Ericsfiord at the time.

In 1009 AD Thorfinn Karlsefni (Thorfinn the Valiant),

with three ships that contained livestock and 160 (some sources say 250) men and women, sailed south and landed at Straumfjord in Newfoundland. However, they later relocated to Straumsöy, Newfoundland. The Norse settlers began with peaceful relations between the indigenous people (Skræling) as they bartered with furs and gray squirrel skins for milk and red cloth. The Norsemen claimed the natives tied the red cloth around their heads, wearing them as a sort of headdress.

A bull that belonged to Thorfinn Karlsefni came storming out of the wood and frightened the natives so bad that they ran to their skin-covered canoes and fled away. The natives returned in force three days later and attacked the Norsemen. It is said that the natives used a form of catapults where they hoisted a large dark blue sphere on a pole and fired it. When fired, the sphere projectile flew over the heads of the men and made an ugly assortment of noises.

The Norsemen retreated from the native's attack, however Leif Ericson's half-sister Freydís Eiríksdóttir who was pregnant and unable to keep up with the retreating Norsemen. She called out to her kinsmen to stop fleeing from "such pitiful wretches," claiming that if she had weapons she would do better. At one point, Freydís picked up a sword that belonged to a man who had been killed by the natives. She pulled one of her breasts from out of her bodice and struck it with the sword she had picked up. This frightened the natives and made them flee.

Meanwhile on the Island of Ireland, disputes over the

lands of Ireland rose as King Brian Boru, the King of Munster, began making moves to be High King of all of Ireland. Political maneuvers and manipulations were taking place and even lands were attacked as he sought to become the High King. Tensions rose to a point that by 1014 AD, King Brian's army was mustered and marching to Dublin to unseat the Irish-Norse King Sigtrygg II Silkbeard Olafsson of Dublin.

King Sigtrygg convinced Brodir of the Isle of Man and Sigurd of Orkney to side with him in the Battle of Clontarf. King Sigtrygg stayed with reinforcements at Dublin while Brodir and Sigurd led the battle that lasted all day. King Brian was killed in the battle, yet the Irishmen prevailed and ultimately drove back their enemies into the sea. Sigurd himself was also killed in the battle, apparently while still holding a Raven banner.

As Britain, the Isles, and the Northern mainland became more settled and prepared to defend themselves against Vikings, other Norsemen sought opportunity in more southerly reaches of mainland Europe, such as Spain. In 1015 AD, a Viking fleet is recorded to have entered the River Minho and sacked the city of Tui Spain. The attack was so devastating that it left the city of Tui abandoned to be later re-established at its current location.

The Norse did not totally give up their designs on England. In 1016 AD, King Cnut the Great became the ruler of the English kingdom, which itself was the product of a resurgent Wessex. With England, Denmark, Norway, and part of Sweden, King Cnut the Great controlled a North Sea

Empire until his death in 1035 AD, when his empire was split up by his successors.

Upon King Cnut's death, the throne of England was succeeded by his son Harold Harefoot until he died in 1040 AD. Upon his death, Harthacnut (another of Cnut's sons) who was already on the Danish throne, took the English throne, which reunited the previous North Sea Empire of his father, Cnut the Great. However, King Harthacnut only lived another two years after his brother and died in 1042 AD.

At this point in 1042 AD, the monarchy in England reverted back to the English line after being held by the Norse in Danish hands for such a long time. The restored English line's king was Edward the Confessor, who is known as being the last King of Wessex.

The Norse had still not given up their hopes on ruling over England however. There was a continuing close alliance on the Isles that were tied with the Kingdom of Norway. In the year of 1058 AD, a Viking fleet that was led by the king of Norway's son came united with men and ships from Orkney, the Hebrides, and Dublin to seize the throne of England, but had failed in their attempt.

King Edward the Confessor died in January of 1066 AD without an obvious successor and this caused much controversy as both King Harald of Norway and Duke William of Normandy believed they were the rightful heirs to the throne of England. However, Harald Hardrada (Harald Sigurdsson) also had a claim to be the rightful heir to the throne of England. He landed and attacked with a

Viking army in hopes of taking control of York and thus seize the English crown, but he was defeated and killed at the Battle of Stamford Bridge.

King Harald Hardrada hit in the neck by an arrow at Battle of Stamford Bridge.[49]

This event is often cited as the end of the Viking era as being the last Viking invasion.

However the Viking Era is better marked as coming to a conclusion when the Duke of Normandy, William the Conqueror (also a descendant of Vikings), successfully took the English throne and became the first Norman King of England in the same year of 1066 AD at the Battle of Hastings.

This event of 1066 AD marks the end of the Viking Age.

The Norse petty kingdoms became absorbed into countries and the Christian religion spread throughout Europe.

Chapter 6 – The Jómsvíkings

The Jómsvíkings were a legendary group of much feared Nordic and Slavic pagan mercenaries during the height of the Viking Age in the 10th and 11th centuries.

Being mercenaries, they'd reputedly fight for any lord able to pay their substantial fees. Even though most of them were adamantly Norse or Slavic Pagans, they were known to fight alongside Christian rulers on occasion.

"Christian silver spends the same as Pagan silver."

The legend of the Jómsvíkings appears in the Jómsvíkinga saga, which was written in Old Icelandic. Legend states that their stronghold, called 'Jómsborg', was located on the southern shore of the Baltic Sea. This was a region known as Wendland in medieval times, which is now known as Pomerania. Unfortunately, the exact location of the Jómsvíking stronghold is long lost and disputed by modern historians and archaeologists.

Most scholars locate it on the hill Silberberg, north of the town of Wolin on Wolin island in modern day Poland near the border of Germany.

Google map location in Wolin, Poland - bordering Germany.

The Jómsvíking saga says that the settlement was founded by Pálnatóki who'd received the location from the Wendish ruler, Burislav. Pálnatóki showed up on his shores with forty ships and the Wendish King fearing being attacked by this renowned viking Pálnatóki, offered him the land called Jóm. In exchange for the land, Pálnatóki and his men were to help defend the Wend territory.

Pálnatóki agreed and the Jómsborg stronghold was built. The stronghold is described in the Jómsvíking Saga as being a great and strong fortification which 'jutted' out to sea, making it a huge fortified harbor.

The attached Jómsborg harbor is said to have been large enough to hold 300 ships, and that's with them all locked safely in the harbor's fortification.

The Jómsborg fortification was also said to have great walls, locking gates, and catapults for its defense.

The Saga of the Jómsvíkings relates that Pálnatóki then made the following laws:

- First of their laws was that no man may join their company over the age of fifty or under the age of eighteen.

- Kinship was not to weigh in when considering membership. Meaning, you couldn't use your relation or family status to become a member.

- No member was to flee from any man who was his equal in bravery and as well armed as himself.

- Each member must avenge any other member as if he were his brother.

- No one was to utter words of fear or be afraid of anything, however hopeless matters looked.

- All the loot brought in from expeditions was to be carried to the standard, of whatever value, big or small, and anyone not abiding by this rule must leave the company.

- No one within the fort was to start a quarrel.

- If news of importance came to any man's knowledge he was not to have the temerity to make it known to all, because Pálnatóki was to announce all news.

- No one was to have a woman in the fort.

- No one was to leave for more than three days.

- If any member was discovered to have killed their father or brother or other close kin, Pálnatóki was to be the judge, as with all other matters.

There are, however, different accounts for the origins of the Jómsvíking order besides that of the Jómsvíking saga.

The Gesta Danorum, a Danish history written in the 13th century by Saxo Grammaticus, tells that a settlement named 'Julinum' which was conquered by the King of Denmark, Harald Bluetooth. King Harald then gave it to the Swedish prince 'Styrbjörn the Strong', also providing him with a strong force of which Styrbjörn used to terrorize the cold North and Baltic Seas.

A golden disc (called the Curmsun Disc) bearing the name of Harald Bluetooth and Jómsborg appeared in Sweden in autumn 2014.

The Gesta Danorum *(Danish History)*, Styrbjarnar þáttr Svíakappa *(Tale of Styrbjörn the Swedish Champion)*, and Eyrbyggja saga *(The Saga of the People of Eyri)* all tell of the exiled Swedish prince 'Styrbjörn the Strong' in the early 980's AD.

These records and sagas tell of Styrbjörn as having brought the Jómsvíkings to a devastating defeat against his uncle 'King Eric the Victorious' at the 'Battle of the Fýrisvellir' at Uppsala in an attempt to take the crown of Sweden by force.

Styrbjörn, now ruler of the Jómsvíkings, wanted to gather an even greater force in order to take the Swedish crown. The very crown which had denied of him by the Swedish Thing (assembly) on his father's death. A death by poisoning which he suspected was done by his uncle Eric who now wore the crown for himself.

In order to accomplish this, Styrbjörn pillaged far and wide the newly created kingdom of Denmark until its king Harald Bluetooth asked for a settlement by giving Styrbjörn his daughter Tyra as his wife.

Styrbjörn went away, but later returned to Denmark with 1000 longships and forced the Danish king Harald Bluetooth to give him 200 ships and whoever among them he saw fit to take with him.

This included the king himself.

The armada of 1000 Jómsvíking longships led by Styrbjörn the Strong and 200 Danish longships led by Harald Bluetooth set sail for Sweden.

When Eric the Victorious learned that Styrbjörn's navy had entered Mälaren from the Baltic Sea, he sent the *fiery cross*** in all directions and rallied the conscripted leidang defense fleet at Uppsala.

**The 'fiery cross', also called a 'bidding stick', is a wooden club or baton carried by a messenger to rally people for 'thing assemblies' and defense for war.

A Finnish boy with a "fiery cross" (bidding stick) in 1876.

At the advice of Þorgnýr the Lawspeaker, King Eric put stakes in the waterway which led to Uppsala in order to impede the Danish backed Jómsvíkings.

When Styrbjörn's saw that his longship armada could not sail further, he vowed that he'd never leave Sweden, but to win or die.

Much as was later repeated in 1519 AD by Hernán Cortés when he set sail in conquest of Mexico, he ordered the ships to be set on fire and left his men with no other option but to press on and fight to the death!

King Harald Bluetooth, however, did not want to take part in this and left with the Danish longships and men.

Styrbjörn swallowed his pride at this and marched the Jómsvíkings towards Uppsala to battle for the crown. When the Swedes attempted to halt their progress the Swedish forest, Styrbjörn threatened to start a forest fire. This convinced the Swedes to let Styrbjörn and his men pass through the forest without harm.

Again Þorgnýr the Lawspeaker advised king Eric and told him to tie together cattle and harness them with spears and swords. When the enemy approached on the Fýrisvellir marshy plain south of Uppsala, thralls pushed the weaponized herd of cattle towards the advancing Jómsvíkings.

This move successfully caused chaos among their ranks of the Jómsvíkings, but Styrbjörn was an excellent warchief and was able to restore order.

When the armies met, the fight lasted all day and into the evening which ended in a stalemate. The next day's battle also ended in stalemate, notwithstanding the large number of reinforcements King Eric received that day.

During the night, Styrbjörn sacrificed to Thor, but the red-bearded god showed himself angry and foretold a great defeat.

King Eric, however, went to the Temple at Uppsala and sacrificed to Odin, promising himself to him after ten years.

It is said that a tall man in a blue cloak and a broad-brimmed hat showed himself to Eric.

Eric praying to Odin before the Battle of Fýrisvellir, as envisioned by Twentieth century artist Jenny Nyström (1854-1946).

Odin gave King Eric a cane (*or spear?*) and told him to throw it over the Jómsvíkings and to say: "Óðinn á yðr alla" (I give all of you to Odin).

On the third day of battle, Eric obeyed Odin's command and a hail of arrows fell over the Jómsvíkings.

A hailstorm that the men called "Odin's arrows".

When Styrbjörn understood that the battle was all over, he screamed to his men to stand and fight. He then thrust his banner into the bloodied soil of the battlefield and rushed into the Swedish army with his best champions.

Few men fled that day.

There are three runestones from this time that mark the event. A reference on the Högby Runestone reading:

"The brave valiant man Ásmundr fell at Fýrisvellir"

Side "B" of Ög 81, referred to as the Högby runestone (Högbystenen).

On the Hällestad Runestone labeled 'DR 295' reads:

"he did not flee at Uppsala"

DR 295 of the Hällestad Runestones located in the walls of Hällestad Church in Torna-Hällestad, Sweden.

The Sjörup Runestone located in Scania, Sweden says:

"He did not flee at Uppsala, but slaughtered as long as he had a weapon"

The Sjörup Runestone is generally associated with the Jómsvíking attack on Uppsala, the Battle of the Fýrisvellir. It says: Saxi placed this stone in memory of Ásbjörn Tófi's/Tóki's son, his partner. He did not flee at Uppsala, but slaughtered as long as he had a weapon.

All three of these runestones relate to honorable deaths at Uppsala who were all probably Jómsvíkings.

The battle is also commemorated in poetry by Thórvald Hjaltason, an Icelandic skald who'd taken part in the battle on the Swedish side of the Battle of the Fýrisvellir.

As a result of this battle, the Swedish king Eric became known as "King Eric the Victorious".

This was not the only great historic battle that the Jómsvíkings were known to have suffered such a defeat.

The Jómsvíkinga saga tells of the Jómsvíkings attacking Jarl Haakon Sigurdsson in Norway and being defeated in the Battle of Hjörungavágr in 986 AD.

The Battle of Hjörungavágr was between the fleet of Jómsvíkings led by Sigvaldi Strut-Haraldsson and those of Haakon Sigurdsson and Sweyn Haakonsson.

During this battle, Haakon felt the battle was turning against him in favor of the Jómsvíkings and went to the island Primsigned and prayed to his patron goddess, Thorgerdr Holgabrudr. The saga said that the goddess repeatedly refused his offerings, until she finally accepted the blót (sacrifice) he offered of his 7 year-old son.

Haakon tasked his slave, Skopti, to slaughter his son for the blót offering to the goddess Thorgerdr.

After which, Haakon returned to his fleet and pressed his men to engage in another attack against the Jómsvíkings with the aid of his satiated patron goddess.

An illustration depicting the goddess Thorgerdr Holgabrudr facing the fleet of Jómsvíkings by Jenny Nyström in 1895 AD.

Haakon enters his ship and the fleet rows forward for the attack. As the battle ensues, the weather becomes thick and clouds cover the sky with thunder and lightning ringing out as it begins to rain.

Jómsvíkings fighting in a hail storm at the Battle of Hjörungavágr in an 1897 illustration by Halfdan Egedius.

The Jómsvíking fleet fights facing the storm and cold wind. They struggle to stand due to the heavy wind and attempt to throw weapons, missiles, and stones at Haakon's fleet but the winds turn their projectiles right back at them.

The Jómsvíking saga points to this battle as the beginning of the end for the Jómsvíkings. After these two decisive defeats, the power of the Jómsvíkings began to wane.

Olaf Trygvasson's Saga relates that the Jómsvíkings played a decisive, if treacherous, role in the Battle of Svolder in 1000 AD.

At Battle of Svolder, a Jómsvíking force led by Jarl Sigvaldi Strut-Haraldsson abandoned King Olaf of Norway and joined forces with his Danish enemies to annihilate his fleet.

The Battle of Svolder, at which the Jómsvíkings fought with Denmark against Norway, maybe with a swap of allegiance to side with Forkbeard's advantage, of his 400 ships to Tryggvason's 100. (Otto Sinding painter).

This action may have been intended to fight the christianization of Scandinavia, which had been forcibly promoted by Olaf who'd converted to Christianity after his wife died in Wendland.

The sea battle ended with the King Olaf, the great-grandson of Harald Fairhair, first King of Norway, jumping overboard from the last ship to be taken.

As it happened though, the Danish king Sweyn Forkbeard, who won the Norwegian throne when the sea battle ended, was a Christian. He and his father, King Harald Bluetooth of Denmark, are reported to have been baptized in 965 AD.

Beyond these historic battles, Jómsvíkings are also reported as having raided parts of eastern England and various Scandinavian territories in the early 11th century.

Jómsvíking re-enactors at the annual Wolin festival in Poland.

At around 1013 AD, the Jómsvíkings were campaigning in England on behalf of Sveyn Forkbeard, but switched sides to collect their own Danegeld from the English. This took place while the main Viking invasion force drove Ethelred the Unready to Normandy.

The decline of the Jómsvíkings steadily continued over the next few decades.

According to the Heimskringla *(Old Norse kings' sagas)*, King Magnus I of Norway decided to put an end to the Jómsvíking threat.

Slavic and Viking re-enactors at the annual Wolin festival in Poland.

As part of consolidating his control of Denmark, King Magnus I sacked Jómsborg, destroying the fortress and killing many of the inhabitants in 1043 AD.

This effectively put an end to the problematic Jómsvíking mercenaries.

128

Chapter 7 – The Varangian Rus'

The Varangians were a Nordic people who, during the Viking Age between the 9th and 11th centuries, ruled the medieval state of Kievan Rus'. These people settled and spread out in territories known today as Belarus, Russia and Ukraine.

They also formed the Byzantine Varangian Guard.

The Kievan Primary Chronicle was a history compiled in 1113 AD of the Kievan Rus' from about 850 to 1110 AD. It is also called "The Tale of Bygone Years", which originates from the record's opening sentence, which reads:

"These are the narratives of bygone years regarding the origin of the land of Rus', the first princes of Kiev, and from what source the land of Rus' had its beginning."

This chronicle states that a group of Varangians known as the Rus' had settled in Novgorod in the year 862 AD. The record states that these Varangian Rus' were under the leadership of Rurik.

Rurik was a Varangian chieftain of the Rus' who in the year 862 AD had seized control of Ladoga, a prosperous multi-ethnic trade settlement. This post, located on the Volkhov River near Lake Ladoga in modern-day Russia, was said to be dominated by Scandinavians who were called by the name of Rus'.

Rurik and his brothers arrive in Staraya Ladoga.
Painting by Viktor Vasnetsov, 1913.

These Rus' under Rurik built the Holmgard settlement near Novgorod, which was a major trade route between the Scandinavian Baltics to the Greek Byzantiums. Rurik remained in power until his death in 879. On his deathbed, Rurik bequeathed his realm to his kin, Oleg.

In 882 AD, Oleg conquered Kiev and established the state of Kievan Rus' and became supreme ruler of the Rus' until his death in 912 AD. Legend states that his death was prophesied by the Slavic pagan volkhvs (*priest-seerer equiv. to old Norse völva*).

Oleg the Seer, Grand Prince of Rus', also known as Oleg of Novgorod. Painting by Viktor Vasnetsov.

The Kievan Rus' would later by ruled by Rurik's descendants beginning with Rurik's son Igor who would rule the Rus' after Oleg's death in 912 AD.

From 913 AD, the Rus' plundered the Arabs in the Caspian Sea and in 941 AD, Igor sent fleets to besiege Constantinople itself.

He besieged Constantinople again in the year 944 AD until Greek fire destroyed part of his fleet. A treaty was made putting Rus' viking incursions in check in the region.

Leo the Deacon, a Byzantine historian and chronicler, describes how Igor met his death while collecting tribute from the Drevlians in 945 AD:

"They had bent down two birch trees to the prince's feet and tied them to his legs; then they let the trees straighten again, thus tearing the prince's body apart."

The Rurik dynasty continued to rule the Kievan Rus' and its successor states, including the Grand Duchy of Moscow and the Tsardom of Russia, until 1598 AD; when Tsar Feodor, son of Ivan the Terrible, died without an heir and ended the Rurik Dynasty.

The Varangians engaged in trade, piracy, and various mercenary activities while they roamed the river systems and portages north of the Black Sea.

They controlled the Volga trade route between the Varangians and the Arabs, which connected the Baltic to the Caspian Sea, and the Dnieper and Dniester trade routes leading to the Black Sea into the capital of the Byzantine Empire.

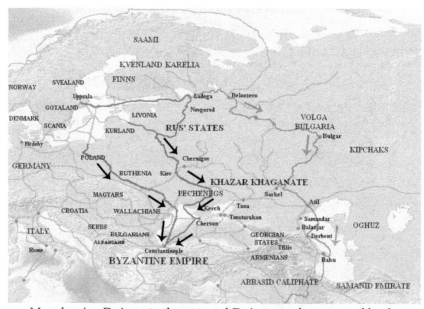

Map showing Dnieper trade route and Dniester trade route used by the Varangians into the Byzantine Empire, with the Volga trade route to the east into the Arabic world.

Those were the critically important trade links which connected Medieval Europe with wealthy and developed Arab Caliphates and the Byzantine Empire. Most of the silver in the West came from the East via those routes.

Many Varangians served as mercenaries in the Byzantine Army from the early 10th century constituting the elite Varangian Guard (the personal bodyguards of Byzantine Emperors).

In 988AD during the reign of Vladimir the Great began the christianization of Kievan Rus'. Eventually most of the Varangian Rus', both within the Byzantine Empire and throughout Eastern Europe, were converted from their ethnic heathen beliefs to that of Orthodox Christianity,

By the 11th century, the influx of Scandinavians to Rus' lands stopped and Varangians became gradually assimilated with East Slavs.

The terms "Varangian" and "Rus" can often be used interchangeably, save for slight variations between the two groups.

Both terms refer to people of Scandinavian and Slavic descent who settled in the Dnieper-Volga region after the 8th century.

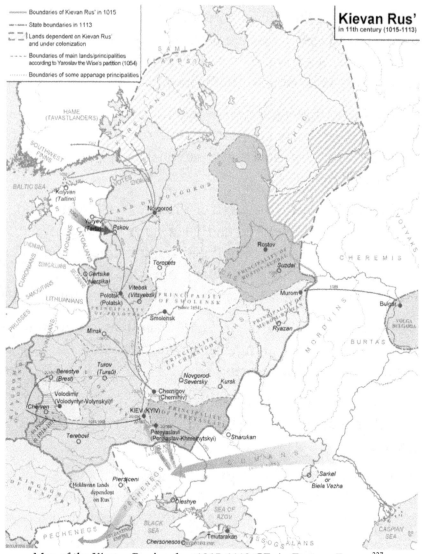

Kievan Rus'
in 11th century (1015-1113)

Map of the Kievan Rus' realm, 1015-1113 CE, in Eastern Europe[227].

The Varangians were predominately Scandinavians and Slavs in Eastern Europe who were often joined the Byzantine emperor's personal Varangian Guard or were a part of Byzantine Army as mercenaries from the 10th century through to the 14th century.

The Rus' were predominately people of Scandinavian origin who assimilated or adopted Slavic cultural and generally settled in towns with their families. The Rus are considered to be a people of mixed Scandinavian/Slavic ethnicity but with a distinctly Slavic culture.

"Rus" eventually developed from the name of a group of people into the name of a political entity and area of land.

Chapter 8 – Northmen in the Muslim World

There are many documented encounters between the Muslim World and the Viking World.

Although recent events has left many Scandinavians with mixed feelings about their relationship with the Islamic world; the relationship between the Nordic world and the Islamic world goes way back further than most would expect. Far enough back that their histories are actually intermingled with one another.

In March of 2015, news regarding the discovery of a ring found on a Viking woman in an ancient burial ground with the inscription 'For/To Allah' erupted in mainstream media everywhere.

The ring itself wasn't a new discovery, it was originally discovered during a late 19th century grave excavation in the town of Birka, on Björkö island, about 19 miles (30 kilometers) from Stockholm.

Birka was a key trading center during the Viking Age.

The ring is part of the Swedish History Museum's collection, originally cataloged as being made of gilded silver and violet amethyst, bearing the inscription "Allah."

Researchers say it is the only ring with an Arabic inscription ever found at a Scandinavian archaeological site.

The non-gilded silver alloy ring was found in a 9th century woman's grave at the Viking trading centre in Birka, Sweden.

The owner of the ring was found wearing traditional Scandinavian clothing, but the researchers said it was impossible to determine her ethnicity due to the decomposed state of the bones in the grave. However, researchers say, "It is not impossible that the woman herself, or someone close to her, might have visited — or even originate from — the Caliphate (which then stretched from Tunisia to the borders of India) or its surrounding regions."

The ring is set with a violet glass stone inscribed with Arabic Kufic writing, interpreted as reading "il-la-lah" (for/to Allah").

Kufic is the oldest calligraphic form of the various Arabic scripts and consists of a modified form of the old Nabataean script. Arabic Kufic writing developed around the end of the 7th century in Kufa, Iraq, and used by the Abbasid Caliphate to the 10th century until the Turko-Persian Seljuk Empire controlled the region.

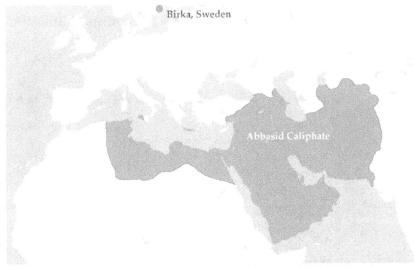

Location of Abbasid Caliphate and ring discovery in Birka, Sweden.

The Arabic Kufic written language developed around the end of the 7th century in Kufa, Iraq, and used by the Abbasid Caliphate to the 10th century until the Turko-Persian Seljuk Empire controlled the region.

Location of Seljuk Empire

When we look at the trade routes used during this time period, we can see how deep Norse trade routes go into the Islamic regions of the world.

Map showing the major Varangian trade routes: the Volga trade route (in red) and the Trade Route from the Varangians to the Greeks (in purple). Other trade routes of the eighth-eleventh centuries shown in orange.

Map showing the major Varangian trade routes: the Volga trade route (in red) and the Trade Route from the Varangians to the Greeks (in purple). Other trade routes of the eighth-eleventh centuries shown in orange.

When you compare the map above showing the Volga Trade Route and compare it with the map below which shows the Sunni Muslim Khazar controlled lands; there is a vast reach that goes deep into Muslim lands. There were many settlements along this route as trade was conducted on a regular and daily basis. This is where the two cultures, that of the Vikings and that of the Muslims, converged and interacted.

The two cultures got to know each other and each other's ways really well.

It is not just possible, but most likely probably that there was also regular cultural conversions between the two peoples. Norse Rus converting to Islam and permanently settling in the region and some converts that returned back to their homelands North. This also goes for many Muslims of a variety of origins, ranging from Turk or Persian or Arab or Khazar, that embraced the Norse culture and returned home or relocated North.

Map showing extent of Khazar lands

These cultural interactions took place during the same time period that we hear from Ahmad ibn Rustah, a 10th-century Persian explorer and geographer. He tried to describe the Northmen that had, not just regular, but career contact with Muslims in and out of Islamic lands:

"They sail their ships to ravage as-Saqaliba [the surrounding Slavs], and bring back captives who they sell at Khazaran and Bolghar... They have no estates, villages, or fields; their only business is to trade in sable, squirrel, and other furs, and the money they take in these transactions they stow in their belts. Their clothes are clean and the men decorate themselves with gold armlets. They treat their slaves well, and they wear exquisite clothes since they pursue trade with great energy."

He also stated:

"They carry clean clothes and the men adorn themselves with bracelets and gold. They treat their slaves well and also they carry exquisite clothes, because they put great effort in trade. They have many towns. They have a most friendly attitude towards foreigners and strangers who seek refuge."

This shows how friendly the Norsemen were towards foreigners and even offered hospitality towards them as they would their own kindred. This friendliness went to the point that the Islamic observer even noticed how well the Northmen treated their slaves (thralls). He was so marvelled at it, that he mentioned it twice – along with their cleanliness.

Slaves that are treated well often gain favor and sometimes get their freedom.

According to Norse Law, it was possible for a thrall (slave) to purchase their freedom and become a "freedman." This made it very possible for Muslim thralls to become freed and able to live their lives amongst the Norse. Their descendants would eventually became freemen (Karls) and considered native Norse by the Norse around them. Muslims that were once slaves (thralls) that became fully assimilated into Norse culture.

This is very possible and very probable, as Norse law allowed for this.

These interactions made it possible by distant foreigners to merge into Norse society, even imported Muslims that were once slaves.

This map of Europe and the Near East, 800 AD, shows the proximities of Viking, Christian, and Muslim territories.

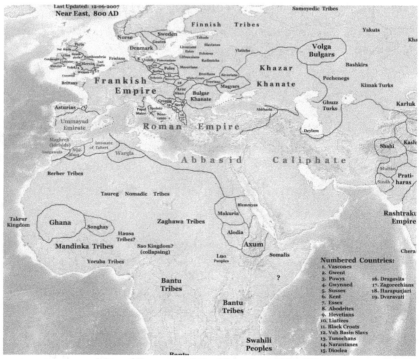

Map of Europe and the Near East, 800 AD.

The most well known interaction between Muslims and Northmen comes from ibn Fadlan.

In 921-922, ibn Fadlan was a member of a diplomatic delegation sent from Baghdad to Volga Bulgars, and he left an account of his personal observations about the Rus of the Volga region, who dealt in furs and slaves. This is the same "Arab" referred to in the film, "The 13th Warrior" based on the novel, "Eaters of the Dead by Michael Crichton."

Johannes Brøndsted interpreted ibn Fadlan's commentary as indicating that these Rus (Northmen) were in Islamic lands, they retained their Scandinavian customs regarding weapons, punishments, ship-burials, and religious sacrifices. Ibn Fadlan's account includes a detailed description of the Rus praying and making sacrifices for success in trade:

"On anchoring their vessels, each man goes ashore carrying bread, meat, onions, milk, and nabid [possibly, beer], and these he takes to a large wooden stake with a face like that of a human being, surrounded by smaller figures, and behind them tall poles in the ground. Each man prostrates himself before the large post and recites: 'O Lord, I have come from distant parts with so many girls, so many sable furs (and whatever other commodities he is carrying). I now bring you this offering.' He then presents his gift and continues 'Please send me a merchant who has many dinars and dirhems (silver coins issued in Islamic countries), and who will trade favourably with me without too much bartering.' Then he retires.

If, after this, business does not pick up quickly and go well, he returns to the statue to present further gifts. If results continue slow, he then presents gifts to the minor figures and begs their intercession, saying, 'These are our Lord's wives, daughters, and sons.' Then he pleads before each figure in turn, begging them to intercede for him and humbling himself before them. Often trade picks up, and he says 'My Lord has required my needs, and now it is my duty to repay him.' Whereupon he sacrifices goats or cattle, some of which he distributes as alms. The rest he lays before the statues, large and small, and the heads of the beasts he plants upon the poles. After dark, of course, the dogs come and devour the lot -and the successful trader says, 'My Lord is pleased with me, and has eaten my offerings."

This shows a tolerance of different religions at these trading areas and made integration into each other's society much easier. When there is tolerance for each other's beliefs, customs, and religious practices, then each culture learns from each other and there is an exchange ideas. Whenever one culture mingles with another culture, that culture cannot help but to absorb some of the other's culture, beliefs, and practices.

The Norse have long 'mingled' with the Muslim world and have had very long trade relationship.

There are many other accounts of Norse and Muslim interactions.

There are many other scholars that have recorded interactions between the Norse world and the Muslim world, such as:

Muhammad al-Idrisi (1100-1165),

Ibn Khurradadhbih / Ibn Khordadbeh (820-910),

al-Tartushi (1059-1127),

al-Mas'udi (896-956),

al-Muqaddasi (940-991),

Ibn Rustah (10th Century) ,

Miskawayh (932-1030),

Ibn Hawqal (10th Century),

Ahmad al-Ya'qubi (897-898),

Ibn Qutiya (10th Century),

Yaqut al-Rumi (1179-1229),

Yahya Ibn Hakam al-Bakri (772 – 866),

al-Maqqari (1578-1632), and

Ibn al-Athir (1160-1233).

They also share their observations of these "saqalibah", a term first employed in the 10th century translated as "fair-haired, ruddy-complexioned population of Central, Eastern and North-Eastern Europe"

Regular contact between Muslim and Norse cultures has occurred for centuries, mostly by means of trade, but also by invasions, conquests, and wars between the various cultures as they clashed into each other from every direction. Many times, the conquered people of one culture retained much of their original culture and practices as they become part of the new culture that now dominated. The previous culture mixed with the new one and often creating a new culture from the blend. Usually this new culture had a new sense of national identity, like suddenly becoming Franks, Danes, Caliphates, or Magyars with their religion chosen for them.

Muslim (Saracen), Magyar, and Viking Invasions of Europe during the 10ᵗʰ century

During this time period, captured slaves from all parts of the known world were a common sight everywhere. Muslims slaves brought into the North lands would have been as common as any other slave or item traded.

Besides the raids to the Muslim world to the South, southeast, and east of the Rus and other Northmen, Norse from the West sailed south and attacked the Muslim world.

The Vikings had set up a permanent base in the mouth of the Loire River in 842 AD where they could now strike at places as far as Spain. Muslim areas in Spain under

Moorish control, such as Cádiz (Qādis) was attacked in 844 AD.

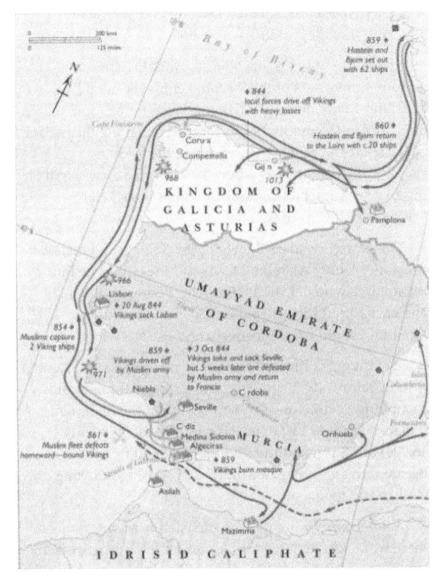

A viking fleet of 100 ships plundered up the Garonne

river and attacked Toulouse and then sailed to Spain and attacked the Asturians and Gijón, on the coast of Asturias, was the first place they made landfall and they later attacked Muslim provinces in Spain.

In 844 AD, Vikings attacked Al-Andalus, the administrative area of the Iberian Peninsula ruled by Muslims. Many dozens of Dragon Ships (Drakkars) appeared in the mouth of the Tagus river, along the border of Portugal and Spain. After a siege, the Vikings successfully conquered Lisbon (Al-Ushbuna), sacking it on the 20th of August. After that, Seville was sacked by Vikings on the 3rd of October.

The Norse invaders then left after 13 days, following a resistance led by Alah Ibn Hazm and the city's Muslim inhabitants who defeated them. The Viking survivors fled and carried out further raids on Al-Andalus but the Muslims fought back effectively and thwarted their efforts.

The Vikings retreated and in the next weeks they looted Lisbon before advancing on the river Guadalquivir and occupying Sevilla for forty-two days. But the Blammen ("Black Men", Arabs) defeated a large host (allegedly 16,000) at Moron and the Vikings retreated from Sevilla. Before retreating they ransomed their hostages, taking only clothes and food.

Aside from Viking raids in the Islamic Mediterranean, there were also sustained diplomatic relations between the Vikings (referred to as "Madjus" in Arabic sources) and the Islamic world. The Arab diplomat Al-Ghazal ("the gazelle") was dispatched to the court of the Danish King Harek at

Hleiðra in 844 AD (as recounted in Ibn-Dihya) to make peace with the Danes followed their defeat at Sevilla.

But of course, the Viking raids didn't stop.

The year 859 AD, Danish Vikings sailed through Gibraltar and raided the Moroccan state of Nekor. The king's harem had to be ransomed back by the emir of Córdoba. These and other raids prompted a shipbuilding program at the dockyards of Seville. The Andalusian navy was thenceforth employed to patrol the Iberian coastline under the caliphs Abd-ar-Rahman III (912–961 AD) and Al-Hakam II (961–976 AD).

In 860 AD, a fleet of sixty-two Viking ships led by Hastein and Björn Ironside attacked Galicia (northwestern Spain), the Portuguese shores, and Sevilla. The fleet then crossed over to Africa and again sacked Moroccan state of Nekor. They then returned to the Iberia peninsula, stopping at the Balearic Islands and attacked Pamplona after crossing the Ebru river and capturing the king of Navarra, García Íñiguez.

They were paid a ransom for his release.

Another raid on Lisbon was attempted by Vikings in 966 AD, but was without any success when the Muslim defenders repelled them.

But the Vikings weren't through with the Muslim controlled areas of Spain.

Cadiz, Medina, Sidonia, Niebla, and Beja were plundered. These accounts were written in Annales Bertiniani, one of whose authors was the Spanish

Prudencio, the Bishop of Troyes and also written in the Crónica Albedense.

In some of the Viking raids on Spain, the Norsemen were crushed either by the Christian Kingdom of Asturias or by the Muslim Emirate armies. The Vikings who did stay and settle in these areas in Spain, such as in Al-Andalus, were eventually "Hispanized" into the culture, even though many of them kept their ethnic identity and culture. Many Norse converted to either Christianity or to Islam, depending on where they settled.

Evidence pertaining to the Vikings converting to Islam includes a memoir recorded by the 16th century Persian geographer, Amin Razi who stated that:

"…They [the Vikings] highly valued pork. Even those who had converted to Islam aspired to it and were very fond of pork."

Another written account by Omar Mubaidin, states:

"Vikings would make numerous raids against both Muslim and Christian states in the Iberian Peninsula. Eventually, a community of settled Vikings, who converted to Islam in southeast Seville, would be famous for supplying cheese to Cordoba and Seville."

In Andrew Marr's "History of the World," he commented on how Vikings in Russia (the Rus) also came very close to converting to Islam with their king being unable to initially decide which of the world's religions would suit them best.

It is also reported that there were forced baptisms of Muslims in Sweden in 1672 AD and again in 1695 AD.

This shows that there were Muslims living deep in Norse homelands. This was also a time when many Heathens, Pagans, Jews, and Catholics were baptised and force converted into Protestantism.

Chapter 9 – Norse Religion

It is not known exactly when religion began to form amongst the Norse people, but during the Norse Bronze Age there are suggestions from rock carvings that a semi organized religion began to form during this time. There are depictions of a pair of Twin Gods that were worshiped as well as a Mother Goddess. There is also an association of water sites such as lakes and ponds that were considered holy sites due to items sacrificed and used in ceremonies at these locations such as bronze lurs (a blowing horn without finger holes), jewelry and weapons, animals, and even humans.

There are also rock carvings during the Norse Bronze Age that have some of the earliest depictions of other well known Norse gods, such as a male figure holding an ax or hammer as being the god Thor and others holding spears, possibly depicting the Aesir gods: Odin or Tyr.

One depiction of a Norse Bronze Age rock carving shows a man holding a spear missing a hand which is most probably a depiction of the god Tyr. There is one depiction holding a bow that may be Ullr, the god of bow hunting.

However, it is not known if these are depictions of gods or simply depictions of men holding weapons. Perhaps celebrating a hero in a particular battle or feat that took place.

The religion and beliefs of the Norse people throughout the centuries have deeply rooted their culture into the World around them. Many aspects and influences of their religion and customs exist with us today and have carried into practice with our modern world.

For example, the days of the Week we use today were influenced by Norse religion, customs and beliefs.

Monday, means Moon's Day or Moon Day.

In Old Norse, this day of the week is called: Mánadagr. The first half of the word 'Mána' in Old Norse means 'Moon' and the second half of the word 'dagr' means 'day.' Máni is also the name of the brother of Sól, the Sun. Both who are being chased by two wolves seeking to devour them.

The translation of the Old Norse word *Mánadagr* for day of the week means in English: *Moon Day*. In modern English we've shortened it to *Monday*.

In German it is called: Montag, Anglo-Saxon: Móndæg, and in Norwegian (Norsk): Mandag.

In a sense when you say Monday, you're not speaking English but a form of Old Norse.

Tuesday is from the Norse's *Tyr's Day*.

In Old Norse this day of the week is called: Týsdagr.

The Old Norse word Týsdagr translates into *Tyr's Day*, in honor of the one handed god Týr. In Anglo-Saxon it is *Tiwesdæg* and in English it's *Tuesday*. The Norwegian word is Tirsdag and in Swedish: Tisdag.

Wednesday is for Odin's Day. In Old Norse this day of the week is called *Óðinsdagr*. Odin was also called Wotan in some areas. This would make the same day of the week called Wotan's Day instead. In the Anglo-Saxon dialect of Norse, this day of the week is called Wódnesdæg (Wotan's Day). In English, *Wódnesdæg* became Wednesday. In Dutch it is called Woensdag.

Thursday is named for Thor's Day, the Thunder God himself. Old Norse this day is: Þórsdagr (Thórsdagr). The Norwegian word for Thor's day is Torsdag and in Anglo-Saxon, it is: Þunresdæg (Thunresdæg).

Friday meaning Frigg or Freyja's Day. The Old Norse day is *Frjádagr*. The Norwegian word for the day is Fredag and in German it is: Freitag. The Anglo-Saxon word for friday is Frigedæg. This is suggesting it to be referencing it as Frigg's day, instead of Freyja's day, which became friday in English from the Old English "Frīge's day." It is suggested that Frigg and Freya were possible the same goddess. The reference to the vanir goddess Freyja didn't spread outside of Scandinavia. Norse settlements outside of Scandinavian regions were commonly referring to Odin's wife, Frigg instead of 'Freyja."

Saturday comes from Saturn's Day. This influence was not from Old Norse, but had Latin influences on the Anglo-Saxons after the 10th century from monks. The Old Norse word for this day of the week is: Laugardagr, which means: Laundering Day. Saturday to the Norse was Washing Day. In Norwegian it is called Lørdag and it's called Laugardagur in Iceland. The English word Saturday came from the Christian church's Latin influence on the Anglo-Saxons who called it Sæternesdæg. In Dutch. the day is called Zaterdag.

An interesting fact about the Norse is that they were a particularly clean people. This is contrary to beliefs and myths about how savage and unkempt the northern "barbarians" were and how they lived.

The Norse bathed regularly and combed their hair daily. Saturday was the day of the week that they set aside for bathing and washing. This is the reason it is called Launder Day by the Old Norse. An irony to the common misconception that the so called "barbarians from the North" were considered by the rest of the World as being primitively savage in their ways and severely lacked in hygiene.

But it turns out the Norse were cleaner and cared more personal hygiene than that of their critics. Particularly of the criticism of their cleaning habits as was portrayed by christian monks that complained of the Norse's obsessive over cleanliness and their threat of luring christian maidens.

Sunday is Sun's Day. In Old Norse it was called Sunnudagr and is in Norwegian Søndag. The German word is Sonntag and in Anglo-Saxon: Sunnandæg.

Most of the Norse days of the week were so named after

their gods and customs, such as the practice of washing day. These names of the days of the week carried over into modern languages in use today. The old Norse gods may be forgotten to time, but their names live on and are mentioned at least once a week in many Norse influenced languages.

Like all other religions, the Norse had a beginning story and a prophesied dramatic end to the world around them.

The Norse Creation Story

The Story of creation according to the Norse. In the beginning of everything, there was a realm called **Niflheim** (also known as Neflheimr). Niflheim was located on the northern side of the Great Void the Norse called the **Ginunngagap.** The Ginunngagap was the Mighty Gap of nothingness between realms.

Niflheim was a dark and cold place that consisted mostly of ice and frost. Everywhere in Niflheim there was a mist from which it gets its literal translation of its name, 'Mist Home' or 'Mist World.'

In the frozen mist realm of Niflheim, there's a water spring called "Hvergelmir" from which all the cold rivers originate from. The rivers flow down into the Gininngagap where the cold water would then solidify into dense layers of ice. This explained to the Old Norse as to why the North was so cold. It also explained why the rivers and streams that ran down from the mountains was so cold all year long, regardless of season.

The Hvergelmir Spring was believed to be the place from where all living things originated and where they'd eventually return back to after death. Within the spring, it is believed that many snakes live there and that it's the home of the dragon Nidhogg (Old Norse: Níðhöggr).

On the southern side of the Mighty Gap of Gininngagap was the realm of fire called, **Muspelheim**. From the realm of Muspelheim flowed lava and fire that went into the south side of the Gininngagap.

In the center of the Gininngagap, where the ice from Niflheim and the fire from Muspelheim met, formed the great giant **Ymir**. From Ymir more giants formed. As he slept, he'd sweat a giant from each of his armpits, a male and a female. And from his legs, a third giant formed. These giants were the first frost giants (Jötnar *plural*, Jötunn *singular*).

The giants were breastfed by Auðumbla, a giant cow (aurochs possibly) which had also been created in the middle of the great void of the Gininngagap where the Niflheim ice met the fire flowing from Muspelheim.

Daily the great cow Auðumbla would lick the salt from the ice that formed in the Gininngagap for nourishment. One day when she was licking the salt ice, a human hair formed from out of the ice. She continued licking the salt from the ice and on the next day a human head formed from where the human hair had previously formed.

She continued licking the salt ice and then on the third day, a whole human body emerged. This was the first man to have emerged from Auðumbla licking salt from the ice.

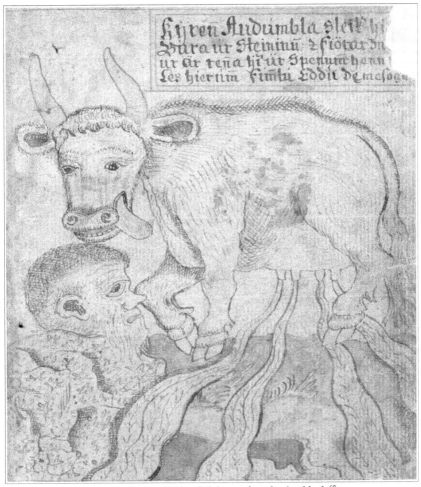

Auðumbla licking Búri out of a salty ice-block.[68]

This first man was known as **Buri** and he was also the first of the Aesir Gods.

Buri had a son called Borr that married a frost giant (jötunn) named Bestla and together they had three sons named, Odin, Vili, and Ve. These brothers were to become the creator gods.

The brothers Odin, Vili, and Ve were greatly disturbed by the fact that the Frost Giants (Jötnar) outnumbered the Aesir Gods. The giant Ymir was constantly conceiving new Jötnar and killing Ymir to stop this from happening was the only solution that the three Aesir gods could come up with to solve the problem.

Ymir being slain by the three Aesir gods; Odin, Ve, and Vili.[67]

So they came up with a plan to slay Ymir; While he was sleeping they would attack him.

As soon as they were sure the great giant was asleep, they ambushed him. The slumbering Ymir was instantly rose from his sleep by the attack and there was a huge battle that ensued. The great giant fought with all of his might, but the Aesir gods emerged victorious.

So much blood flowed from the slain great giant Ymir that it drowned most of the Jötnar. All the frost giants died, except Bergelmir and his wife and they escaped to Niflheim. All Jötnar afterward were descended from this frost giant couple.

The Aesir gods dragged the slain body of Ymir to the center of the great void Gininngagap and then Odin, Vili, and Ve, created the World from the slain corpse. From Ymir's blood, they created the oceans and seas. Then they made the mountains from the giant's bones and used his flesh to make the lands. They formed rocks from his teeth and used his hair to make the grass and trees.

From Ymir's eyelashes, the gods made barriers around the World, "**Midgard** (Miðgarð)," where humans would live, to keep it safe from the Jötnar. The clouds formed when they threw his brain into the air and they formed the sky from the great giant's skull. In the sky, they threw some of the sparks that emitted from Muspelheim and those became the stars.

On the splendid plain of Iðavöllr, they then built their home **Asgard**, which was far from the reach of where both the Jötnar and the humans lived.

While Odin, Vili, and Ve were creating everything in the World, worms began crawling out of the dead body of Ymir. These worms turned into and became the dwarfs (dvergr). Odin, Vili, and Ve told four of the dwarfs to hold up the sky, as they didn't want to risk the sky falling down.

The names of the four dwarves holding the sky were: 'Nordi' (North), 'Vestri' (West), 'Sundri' (South), and 'Austri' (East). The rest of the dwarves made their homes in Nidavellir, which was underground in the rocks and caves where the dwarves became expert craftsman and builders.

Two dwarfs as depicted in the 19th century by Lorenz Frølich.[69]

A Jötunn (frost giant) had two children that were so beautiful that they actually shined. So the frost giant called his bright son 'Mani' (Moon) and his radiant daughter 'Sol' (Sun). The children were admired by the whole world and this was a source of great pride to the Jötnar.

The Aesir gods became furious by this arrogance and took both of them from him and placed them in the sky. Sol (Sun) and Mani (Moon) were then pulled across the sky by horse driven chariots.

"The Wolves Pursuing Sol and Mani" by J.C. Dollman 1909.[70]

To keep the Sun and Moon's motion constant and swift, the Aesir gods placed two other Jötunn children named, Sköll and Hati (Hati Hróðvitnisson) in pursuit behind them. These two Jötunn children in pursuit were both great wolves and they chased Sol (Sun) and Mani (Moon) in a never ending quest to gobble them whole.

Each month wolf Hati was able to take a bite out of the Moon, trying to gobble it up as it caught up to it. But the Moon always got away and grew whole again after a few days. At Ragnarok, the wolves Sköll and Hati would eventually catch the sun and the moon and consume them whole.

Until that time happens in Ragnarok, the Norse end of times, the chase after the Sun and the Moon goes on relentlessly.

The three Aesir gods, Odin, Vili and Ve, were walking on a beach one day when they came upon two logs. One log was from an Ash tree and the other from an Elm tree. From these two logs, the Aesir gods created the first humans.

From the Ash log became the first man, named **Ask** and from the Elm log became the first woman named **Embla**.

The Aesir gods gave them life by each giving them separate gifts. Spirit and life were given from Odin. Ve gave both logs movement, mind and intelligence. And from Vili they were given shape, speech, feelings, and the five senses. The Aesir gods decided that the humans should live in the place they created named Midgard.

Midgard would be the garden of mankind of which the gods had created, both humankind and their world around them.

The first living people, Ask and Embla. Sölvesborg, Sweden.[71]

To the Norse, there were different realms in which different beings existed and ruled over. They believed there were nine worlds that were divided into three levels.

The 1st level:

Asgard (Ásgarðr), home of the Aesir (Æsir) gods.

Vanaheim (Vanaheimr), home of the Vanir (Vanr) gods.

Alfheim (Ālfheimr), home of the light elves (ljósálfar).

The 2nd level:

Midgard (Miðgarðr), home of the humans. Midgard is connected to Asgard by the Rainbow Bridge, "Bifrost."

Jotunheim, home of the Frost Giants (Jötnar).

Svartalfheim, home of the Dark Elves (dökkálfar).

Nidavellir, home of the Dwarfs (Dvergr).

The 3rd level:

Niflheim to the north (underground in Niflheim is Helheim home of the dead).

Muspelheim to the south, home of the fire Giants and Demons.

In the middle of the nine worlds was the massive ash tree called Yggdrasil (The World Tree) which connected them all by its branches and roots. Yggdrasil had gigantic roots which went in three separate directions to wells in different realms.

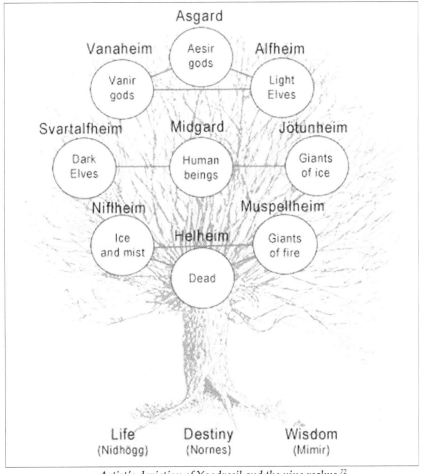

Asgard

Vanaheim — Aesir gods — Alfheim

Vanir gods — Light Elves

Svartalfheim — Midgard — Jötunheim

Dark Elves — Human beings — Giants of ice

Niflheim — Muspellheim

Ice and mist — Helheim — Giants of fire

Dead

Life (Nidhögg)   Destiny (Nornes)   Wisdom (Mimir)

Artist's depiction of Yggdrasil and the nine realms.[72]

The first root from Yggdrasil went to Asgard, the home of the gods. By this root was a well named Urd's well. This was where the Aesir gods held their daily meetings.

The second root from Yggdrasil went down to Jotunheim, the land of the giants, by this root was Mimir's well.

The third root from Yggdrasil went down to Niflheim,

close to the well Hvergelmir. It was here that the dragon Níðhöggr (Nidhug) gnawed on one of Yggdrasil's roots. Níðhöggr was also known to suck the blood out of the dead bodies in Niflheim.

The Norse gods were divided. There were the Aesir gods and the Vanir gods. Additionally, there were the Jotnar (Giants), who were sometimes counted amongst the Vanir gods. The Aesir were generally considered the warrior gods, while the Vanir gods were the gods of fertility and magic.

Here is a short list of some of the Norse Gods, starting with the Aesir Gods.

Odin (Óðinn), the Allfather, also known as Wotan or Wodan.

Odin the Wanderer by George von Rosen. 1896.[73]

Odin was called the All-Father and was ruler of all the Norse gods and goddesses in all of Asgard. Odin wielded a magical spear called Gungnir that never misses its target and he rode an eight-legged horse named Sleipnir.

Odin sits atop his steed Sleipnir, his ravens Huginn and Muninn and wolves Geri and Freki nearby by Lorenz Frølich. 1895.[74]

The origination of the tale of Odin's stead Sleipnir may have come from Icelandic ponies that have a four-beat lateral ambling gait called a 'super tölt' that makes them appear to have eight legs when using this gait.

Odin was a great seeker of knowledge and even sacrificed one of his eyes at Mimir's Well for wisdow and for the secret of the runes, he pierced himself with a spear and hung from a tree for nine days and nights until the runes revealed themselves to him. He shared the knowledge of the runes with mankind.

Odin Hanging on the World Tree. Illustration by Hans von Wolzogen. 1920.[75]

Odin also has two ravens named Huginn and Muninn, meaning "Thought" and "Memory," who fly around World each day and then report all the World's happenings to Odin at night.

Odin is usually represented by the Valknut. The Valknut, also known as the Slain Warrior's Knot, is a symbol consisting of three interlaced triangles that are associated with Odin.

The Valknut – The Slain Warrior's Knot of Odin.

Odin is also the god of war, who often instigates battles by throwing down his spear. Symbolically, in battle Norse have been known to start the conflict by hurling a single spear into the enemy in honor of pleasing the god of war, Odin.

It is Odin, who commands the Valkyries, the shield maidens that collect the bravest amongst the dead to bring them to the Halls of Valhalla or to the Meadows of Fólkvangr.

Odin was often known to sit on the high seat of Hliðskjálf with his wife Frigg and make wagers with her about the outcomes of events as they looked upon happenings in the other worlds.

The goddess Frigg and her husband, the god Odin, sit on the throne Hliðskjálf and wager the outcome of events.[76]

Frigg, also known as Frigga, was the wife of Odin and the Queen of Asgard, the Realm of the Aesir gods. She is known as being the goddess of foreknowledge and wisdom. Although her husband Odin had many other children, Frigg was the mother of Balder, who was a god of light and purity. The day of the week Friday is named in honor after this goddess, Frigg's Day.

Balder, also known as Bald, Baldr, Baldor, and Baldur. He was the god of light and purity was the son of Odin and Frigg. Balder has many brothers, which includes the well known gods Thor and Váli. It had been prophesied that the death of Balder would be a sign triggering the event of Ragnarok, so Balder's mother had all things promise to never harm him. This made the god Balder invulnerable to all weapons. This was of great amusement to his brothers and the other gods that would spend hours of entertainment hurling various weapons at him to watch them bounce off of him harmlessly.

Statute of Balder.[77]

Balder was a well beloved, wise, and gentle god who was accidentally killed when his brother Hod was tricked by Loki into slaying him. Loki had discovered weakness in Balder's invulnerability and used it to trick Hod into slaying him. This event which was a prophesied indication of the coming of Ragnarok. The great war of the gods that would cause the end of times when the World would be destroyed and then recreated.

Thor with Toothgrinder and Toothgnasher.[78]

The god **Thor**, also known as Þórr, Þunor, ðunor, Donar, Thunar, and Þunraz. Thor was a son of Odin and was known as the god of thunder and war. He had red hair and red eyes and was seldom ever without a beard if he could help it. Thor was known as being the strongest of the gods and wielded the hammer, Mjölnir. Thor rode in a chariot that was pulled by two goats named Toothgnasher and Toothgrinder (Old Norse: *Tanngrisnir* and *Tanngnjóstr*).

The hammer wielded by Thor, Mjölnir, was made by the dwarven brothers Sindri and Brokkr. The dwarf brothers were persuaded into a bet by Loki that they couldn't make

178

something better than the things made by the Sons of Ivaldi. The Sons of Ivaldi were the dwarves that crafted special items such as Odin's spear, Gungnir.

The dwarven brothers won the bet by creating Mjölnir, which they presented to Thor. The brothers crafted a fearsome hammer so powerful that it could smash mountains level. The weapon would never fail and if it were thrown, it never missed its intended target. Also when thrown, the hammer would never fly so far that it couldn't return to Thor's hand.

Necklace of Mjöllnir, the hammer of Thor.[79]

The hammer Mjölnir is the religious symbol of Thor and was most commonly worn instead of a cross during a period of resistance by many Norse as a form of defiance against the forced conversions into Christianity.

Thor was revered by warriors, not just because he was a god of war like his father Odin (and some of his brothers), but Thor was one of the strongest gods and was heroically victorious in battle when he fought Jötnar (frost giants).

It was foretold to Odin that Thor would die in the Ragnarök event while battling Jörmungandr, the Great Midgard Serpent. Jörmungandr is the Great Sea Serpent that chases its tail as it encircles Midgard, the realm of mankind.

Circular Symbol of Jörmungandr, The Midgard Serpent.[82]

The symbol of the Midgard Serpent is often depicted as a Serpent chasing its own tail in a complete circle. In Old Norse, the serpent's name is "Jǫrmungandr" and means "huge monster." The venomous serpent is the middle child of Loki and the giantess Angrboða.

Thor had once before encountered the sea serpent Jörmungandr when he was fishing with the reluctant giant Hymir out on a boat. When Hymor refused to give Thor any bait to fish with, Thor chopped off and took the head of Hymir's greatest ox and used that as bait. As Thor was fishing, he caught the great serpent and pulled the beast in with his line as Hymir cowered in the boat of fear.

Thor angling the serpent of Midgard Serpent.81

However as Thor struggled pulling in the beast, the great serpent suddenly broke the line and escaped before Thor could slay it with his hammer, Mjölnir.

Tyr, God of War.[80]

Tyr (Týr), also known as Teiws, Tīw, Ziu, and Tîwaz was also a son of Odin. Tyr was both a god of war and the god of single combat. Tyr was known as the bold one-handed god that lost his hand while tethering the Great Wolf Fenrir. The day of the week, Tuesday is named after this god, "Tīw's Day."

Loki (Luka), also known as Loptr or Hveðrungr, was the son of two giants, Fárbauti and Laufey (or Nál), and was known as the trickster of the gods, His relationship with the Aesir and Vanir gods is a bit hazy as to whether he was a god, a jötunn (giant), or both. Loki is best known for the

mischief he caused among the Aesir gods. He is well
known as the "trickster-god," even though it is debated as
to whether or not he was actually a god or giant.

The Punishment of Loki.[83]

In the Saga "Lokasenna (Loki's Quarrel)," Loki insults
the Aesir gods during a feast, each individually, until they
become so infuriated that as punishment for his insults and
his role in the death of the god Baldr, the gods brought Loki
into a cave. Inside the cave, the Aesir gods took three flat

stones and drilled a hole in each one of them. The Aesir gods then took two of Loki's sons, Váli and Narfi (or Nari) and changed Váli into a wolf and had him tear apart his brother Narfi. The Aesir then took the entrails of Narfi and bound Loki with them over the three stones they had drilled holes in. They bound his shoulders, his waist, and his lower legs to the three stones. Once Loki was securely bound, the lashings that the Aesir gods had made from Loki's son's entrails were turned into strong iron so he could not escape them.

To add to Loki's torment, Skadi (the god Njord's wife) fastened a venomous snake over Loki so the snake's poison would drip onto his face. Sigyn, Loki's wife, sat with him and held a basin beneath the dripping venom to catch it and prevent it from harming Loki. Yet when the basin would became full, she had to carry the poison filled basin away and empty it. During this time, the poison would drip on to Loki and cause him such pain that he would writhe with such violence that all of the earth shook from the force. Norse legend states that result of Loki's writhing in agony from the poison dripping on him is the result in what are now known as earthquakes.

Loki eventually escapes his bonds during the Ragnarok event and leads the army of dead released from Hel against the Aesir gods.

Mimir (Mímir), also known as Mim was the god of Wisdom. Each day, Mimir drank from a Well (Mimir's Well) with a drinking horn that was made from a dragon's foot and gained great knowledge from it. Mimir arranged the truce between the Vanir and Aesir gods during the Aesir-Vanir war. However, he was beheaded by the Vanir gods when they felt that they had been cheated when the two sides had exchanged hostages to seal the peace.

The Vanir gods sent the head of Mimir to the Aesir gods, whereas Odin preserved it and cast a spell on it so it could speak. Odin then carried the head around to gain counsel, wisdom, and learn secrets from it.

Heimdall (Heimdallr), also known as Hallinskiði, Gullintanni, Vindlér, and Vindhlér. He is described as the "whitest of all gods," has gold teeth, and a golden maned horse named Gulltoppr. He possesses the great horn Gjallarhorn, that will be blown to warn the gods of the coming of Ragnarok.

The Norse god Heimdallr blowing the horn Gjallarhorn.[84]

Heimdall possesses great foreknowledge, keen eyesight, and hearing. He keeps watch at the burning rainbow bridge Bifröst, the link between Midgard and Asgard, guarding the realm of the gods from the Jötnar. Heimdall is believed to be the one who created the social classes among humans.

Thor's wife, the goddess Sif.[85]

Sif - Thor's wife and the Norse goddess associated with the Earth and Marriage. Sif is known for falling victim to a prank when Loki cuts off her hair and the angered Thor demands that Loki replace it. Loki manages to replace Sif's hair by having the dwarves, the Sons of Ivaldi, create one made of gold for her. Sif's golden hair becomes the first of the six magical items that were made by the Sons of Ivaldi for the gods.

Hel – Daughter of Loki, she was appointed by Odin to rule the realm of the dead of which is named after her, "Hel" (Helheim), located in the plane of Niflheim. She is easily recognized because of her gloomy appearance and half black / half flesh colored skin. She takes in the dead who have died of sickness or old age. The term, "go to hel" is to die and go to her realm.

The goddess Hel.[92]

Hod (Höðr), also known as Hoder or Hodur. is another son of the god Odin. Höðr was a blind god that accidentally killed his brother Balder with a weapon made from mistletoe when he was tricked by Loki.

Vidar (Víðarr), also known as Vidar, Vithar, Vidarr, and Vitharr. Vider is the Aesir god associated with vengeance. Víðarr is the son of Odin and the jötunn Gríðr (Grid). Vider avenges his father's death by killing the great wolf Fenrir during the battle at Ragnarök.

Freyr, also known as Frey, Yngvi-Freyr, or Fricco. Freyr is an important Vanir god and is the son of the god Njord. He is associated with farming and weather. Freyr presides over Álfheimr, the realm of the Elves.

The Norse god Freyr standing with his sword and the boar Gullinbursti.[87]

Freyr rides the shining boar Gullinbursti and possesses the best sailing ship, known as Skíðblaðnir, which can be folded and carried in a pouch when not in use. Both items were made by the dwarves (dvargr) known as the Sons of Ivaldi.

Gerda (Gerðr), also known as Gerd or Gerth. Gerda is a jötunn, Vanir Goddess, and the wife of Freyr. She is often known as being a beautiful goddess of fertility and love.

Freyja, also known as Freya, Frejya, Freyia, Frøya, Frøjya, Freia, and Freja. Daughter of Njordr and has a chariot that's pulled by two cats. This Vanir goddess is not only associated with love, beauty, and fertility, but also seiðr (magic), death and war. Freyja rules over Fólkvangr and where she receives half of those who died in battle (the other half go to Valhalla, Odin's hall).

She also accepts women that have suffered noble deaths into the halls of Fólkvangr. Frayja is also known for her magical cloak of falcon feathers that allows her to fly. She occasionally loans her cloak of feather to the other gods when they're in need of it.

Freyja's married to the Vanir god **Odr** (Óðr), also known as Óð or Od. He is often referred to as the strange double of Odin.

Njord, also known as Njörðr, Njoerd, Njor, or Njorth. He is the father of twins Freyja and Freyr and is the husband of Skadi. Njord is a Vanir god associated with the wind and sea. This makes him a god of fishing, seafaring, and of all things of the sea. He made his home at the sea and lives in Nóatún, which is either his home or his ship.

Njord is one of the gods that survived Ragnarök. He'd
been one of the Vanir gods that was traded as a hostage
when peace was negotiated between the gods during the
Aesir-Vanir War. Njord was often unhappily married as his
wife Skadi longed to be in the mountains, whereas Njord
long to be by the sea. They had tried to live within each
other's realm, but were both unhappy in the other's.

Njord, being with Skadi in her home in the mountains, desires to be by the Sea.[89]

As an act of reparation for Þjazi's death, the Aesir
allowed Skadi to choose a husband from amongst them.
However, there was a stipulation that she may not see any
part of them but their feet when making her choice. She
expected to choose Baldr by the beauty of the feet she
selected. When she made her choice, Skaði discovered that
she had picked Njord.

Skadi (Skaði), also known as Skaoi, Skade, Skathi.
Öndurguð, or Öndurdís. Skadi is a jötunn and the goddess

190

associated with winter, the mountains, skiing, and bowhunting. She was married to the god Njord, who had married her when the Aesir gods allowed her to choose a husband amongst them in return for her dead father.

Skadi longs for the Mountains when with her husband Njord by the sea.[90]

Skadi's home is in the mountains and she's revered by bowhunters who hope for her blessing in success with their hunts. In the poem *Lokasenna*, she fastens a serpent to drip its venom onto Loki's face when he's bound to rocks as punishment for the death of Baldr by the Aesir gods.

Although she married to Njord, she loved Baldr and was exceptionally bitter towards Loki upon his death.

There are many more other Norse gods, as their children had children and their children's children had children. The Aesir and Vanir gods were a race. They married, reproduced, and even mixed with other races. But they could also be maimed and killed; as could be attested by Odin's one eye, Tyr's missing hand, and the eventual demise of the gods and in the foretold event of **Ragnarok**.

Chapter 10 – Ragnarok: Twilight of the Gods

Ragnarok (Old Norse: Ragnarøkkr), the Doom of the Gods. This is the great event that was foretold to Odin when many of the gods would die in a great battle fought that would destroy the cosmos in which afterward the World would be again re-created.

The Norse gods battling at Ragnarok. [88]

The time when the World would be destroyed and then rebuilt was prophesized by a Völva (Seeress) to the god Odin. He was told when the first events would come to pass and informed the other gods, who started preparing and taking steps to prevent or at least delay its happening.

The Aesir gods had also learned that their foretold doom at Ragnarok was to happen by the hands of Loki and three of his children. This compelled them to take preventive steps against those that would bring about their doom.

One of their preventative steps was to bind and prevent Loki's children from being able to rise up against them. The three children of Loki in question were: the great wolf Fenrir, the serpent Jörmungandr, and the female Hel.

The gods cast the great serpent Jörmungandr into the deep sea that lies around the lands of Midgard. The serpent grew so large that he was able to encircle Midgard and grasp his own tail. This is how he earned the name as the "Midgard Serpent," for his eventual encirculating it.

The gods then sought to bind the great wolf, Fenrir. Their first two attempts to bind Fenrir failed, as the great wolf easily broke the tethers they tried to use to bind him.

The gods began to fear that they wouldn't be able to bind Fenrir,so Freyr sent his vassal Skírnir as a messenger down into the land of Svartálfaheimr to request that the dwarves that dwelt in that realm would make them a fetter that would be strong enough to tether Fenrir. The dwarves constructed the fetter called Gleipnir which they'd made from six mythical ingredients. The fetter was smooth and soft as a silken ribbon, but strong and firm.

It was only on the third attempt that the god Tyr was successfully able to bind him when he wagered Fenrir that he wouldn't be able to break this tether as he had the previous ones. Fenrir didn't trust that the gods would let him go if they tethered him and he failed to break the fetter, so he refused to let him tether him again.

So as a sign of trust, Tyr placed his right hand in Fenrir's mouth as a pledge that if he failed to break the fetter, that Tyr would untether and free him.

Týr with his hand in Fenrir's mouth.[91]

The great wolf Fenrir agreed to allow Tyr to tether him with his other hand. However after Tyr put the tether on he refused to let Fenrir go when he wasn't able to break it, so Fenrir bit Tyr's hand off and devoured it. This is how Tyr became known as the one-handed god.

Odin then cast Loki's daughter Hel to Niflheim and bestowed upon her authority over the nine worlds, in that she must administer board and lodging to those sent to her. Her realm was to take in those who have died of sickness or old age.

Having taken steps to prevent Loki's children from rising up against them, the gods now felt a false sense of security. That is, until the god Baldr began having dreams about his own death. This worried his mother, Frigg, who then went around the world and made everything in the world give oaths to never harm her son Baldr.

The gods became so confident in this, that they'd amuse themselves by throwing weapons (or anything else they could find) at him to watch them harmlessly bounce off him. Nothing they threw at him would harm him and they were convinced of Baldr's invincibility. They were convinced that his invincibility would prevent Ragnarok from happening.

Loki was the trickster of the gods and while amused over Baldr's invincibility, asked his mother Frigg if she'd overlooked anything in the World when she sought out oaths from all things to never harm him. Frigg stated that she didn't bother seeking an oath from mistletoe, because she felt it was too small and rather harmless.

Armed with this information, Loki set off to make a spear (sometimes told as an arrow) from mistletoe. He then convinced the blind god, Hod, to throw it at Baldr for amusement to watch it bounce off of him. Hod threw the spear (or fired the arrow), not knowing what it was made of nor that it would do any harm to Baldr, and pierced Baldr with the mistletoe weapon. The mistletoe weapon killed Baldr.

When Baldr died, he went to the Underworld into the realm of the goddess Hel. The Aesir gods were in anguish and decided to send one of them to the underworld (Helheim) to plead to Hel for the release of Baldr.

Hermod, one of Odin's sons, set to make the journey down the World Tree, Yggdrasil while riding Odin's steed Sleipnir until he reached its roots at the bottom where Hel's realm was located.

Hermod pleading for Baldr's life to the goddess Hel in her realm Hel.[86]

Hermod pleaded on behalf of the Aesir gods for the goddess Hel to release Baldur, but she said she would only release him if they proved that he was as beloved as they claimed he was if the everything in the World wept for him. Everything in the World did weep for Baldr, except one, the giantess Þökk (possibly Loki in disguise).

Þökk's refusal to weep for Baldr was enough to make

198

the goddess Hel refuse to release him from death until the coming of Ragnarok.

The death of Baldr was a major sign of the coming of Ragnarok and forced the gods to believe in the Völva's prophesy. All they could do now was to begin preparing for it. Any god that had any doubts about Ragnarok's inevitable coming had now long lost any uncertainty.

Loki was punished by using the internal organs of his son, Narfi, to bind him on top of three stones in three places. The lashings tethering Loki turned to iron once they were in place.

Thor's wife, Skaði then placed a poisonous snake over him that continuously dripped venom onto his face. Loki's wife Sigyn tried to collect the venom in a bucket to prevent it from dripping on him, but she had to empty it periodically. When she had to empty the bucket, the dripping venom caused Loki so much pain that when the poison dripped on his face, the pain made him convulse so violently that they resulted in earthquakes. Loki was to be miserably bound this way until the onset of Ragnarök.

Odin spent a great deal of time and energy to select the dead that fell in battle. He sought to make sure he had the strongest and bravest to fight with him in the coming battle of Ragnarok. These fallen warriors called Einherjar were brought to the Halls of Valhalla by the Valkyries. Odin collected these Einherjar and built his great army while watching for more signs of the coming of Ragnarok.

There will be three roosters that warn all of the coming of Ragnarok by their crowing:

- The crimson rooster called Fjalar will crow in the forest of Jotunheim to warn the Jötnar (frost giants) living in Gálgviðr.

- The golden rooster named Gullinkambi will crow to Valhalla to warn the Æsir gods.

- The third, a soot-red rooster will crow in the halls of the underworld (Helheim) of Hel to warn the dead.

The decay of humanity is another sign of the coming of Ragnarok. In the realm of humans, Midgard (Miðgarðr), people will lose faith in the gods and begin to abandon their traditional ways. They will break oaths, disregard kinship bonds, and fall into having a general nihilistic outlook on everything. Humans will become absent of any moral values, having no real value in anything or its outcome. They will lose faith that anything in their world now or will there ever be, has any meaning or value to it.

Upon the approach of Ragnarok, there will be a Great Winter called, Fimbulwinter (Fimbulvetr). This is the winter of all winters that will last three years without any summers in between the seasons. The Sun will become useless and will not warm anything. Snow will fall from every direction and freeze everything.

All of mankind will begin to die off from the cold, except two humans that will survive named Líf and Lifthrasir (Lífþrasir). They will be safely hid in the Yggdrasil tree (also referred to as being called "Hoddmímis holt").

An illustration of Lifthrasir and Líf.[93]

It was during this time that the wolf sons of the Great wolf, Fenrir will succeed in their never ending quest of trying to devour the Sun and the Moon. Sköll, the wolf that's been chasing the Sun every day, will finally catch the Sun and devour it. His wolf brother Hati, who chased the Moon will also finally catch the Moon and devours it.

When the Sun and Moon are devoured, the stars will fall

from the sky and the Earth will tremble with the trees becoming uprooted and mountains crumbling. This great trembling causes all binds around Loki to break as well.

Loki is set free and immediately heads to the realm of Hel to collect all the dead in Helheim for battle. The great wolf Fenrir will also break loose from the bond that was placed on him by the Aesir gods when he bit off Tyr's hand.

Fenrir, now free and vengeful, will then charge forward with his mouth agape with the bottom of his mouth touching the Earth and the top touching the sky. He will devour everything in his path while his eyes and nostrils spray flames everywhere.

His brother, Jörmungandr, the Great Midgard serpent will ferociously come out of the sea, causing great tidal waves and he will spit venom into the sky and sea.

While this is all happening, the sky will split in two and from the realm of fire, the sons of Muspell (demons and fire giants) will ride forth. They will be led by Surtr who will be surrounded by flames and be wielding his flaming sword that shines brighter than the Sun.

They will be joined by the great wolf Fenrir, the great serpent Jörmungandr, and all the frost giants (jötnar). Loki will be sailing a ship made from human finger and toe nails called, "Naglfar." The ship will be filled with the dead from Hel's realm and together they will join the others and come to the field of Vígríðr to do battle with the Aesir gods.

Heimdall, the watchman and guardian of Valhalla, will see them coming and sound his great horn Gjallarhorn, warning the gods of the invasion.

The giants will set upon destroying the god's realm and the cosmos along with it. The Aesir gods will move to battle them.

Odin is then swallowed whole by the great wolf Fenrir. Tyr moves to battle the great wolf and also falls to Fenrir. Odin's son Víðarr will step forward and avenge his father's death by tearing Fenrir's jaws apart and killing the great wolf by stabbing it in the heart with his spear.

Thor will meet his nemesis the serpent Jörmungandr in combat and furiously fight the great serpent to the death. Thor will defeat the beast, but Thor dies as well, collapsing after taking just nine steps. Not only do Thor and the sea serpent Jormungand kill each other,

The Aesir god Greyr fights Surtr and falls to the jötunn's flaming sword. Freyr then battles Surtr and they slay each other in close combat.

Surtr and Freyr slay each other.[94]

Heimdall and Loki kill each other while in battle as well.

Many of the gods and giants fall in battle as the flames spread by Surtr burn and devour everything as the ravaged worlds crumble and sink back into the sea and vanish completely below the waves.

Once the flames caused by Surtr have been completely sated, the perfect darkness and silence of the great void Ginnungagap will reign again once more.

The Earth will then re-emerge from the sea and the land becomes more lush and fruitful than it had ever been since it was created the previous time.

Baldr will return from the underworld and the surviving gods, such as the Odin's sons Víðarr and Váli will live in the new temples of the gods and Thor's sons Móði and Magni will possess Thor's hammer Mjolnir.

The two surviving humans, Líf and Lífþrasir, that were hidden and surviving off the morning dew, will emerge and repopulate the Earth. And that concludes the event of Ragnarok, when the World is destroyed and recreated.

Chapter 11 – Hörgr, Altars of Stone

The Norse built many altars of stone called Hörgr (plural hörgar).

A hörgr is a type of cairn, which is an altar or shrine made of stones that are either piled, heaped, or stacked. They are commly used in Norse religion, as opposed to a roofed hall used as a hof (temple).

These stone altars called hörgr are attested to in the Poetic Edda and the Prose Edda, the sagas of Icelanders, skaldic poetry, and its Old English cognate in Beowulf.

The term hörgr is used three times in poems collected in the Poetic Edda. In a stanza early in the poem Völuspá, the völva says that early in the mythological timeline, that the gods met together at the location of Iðavöllr and constructed a hörgr (alter) and a hof (temple):

Old Norse:

> *Hittoz æsir á Iðavelli,*
> *þeir er hǫrg ok hof hátimbroðo.*

English translation:

> *Æsir met on Eddying Plain*
> *they who built towering altars and temples.*

In the third poem in the Poetic Edda, Vafþrúðnismál, Gagnráðr (Odin in disguise) engages in a game of wits with the jötunn Vafþrúðnir. Gagnráðr asks Vafþrúðnir whence the Vanir god Njörðr came, for though he rules over many hofs and hörgar, Njörðr was not raised among the Æsir:

Segðu þat it tíunda,
allz þú tíva rök
öll, Vafþruðnir, vitir,
hvaðan Niörðr um kom
með ása sonom,
hofom og hörgom
hann ræðr hunnmörgom,
ok varðat hann ásom alinn

English translation:

Tenth answer me now, if thou knowest all
The fate that is fixed for the gods:
Whence came up Njord to the kin of the gods, —
(Rich in temples and shrines he rules, —)
Though of gods he was never begot?

In the Poetic Edda poem Hyndluljóð, the goddess Freyja speaks favorably of Óttar for having worshiped her so faithfully by using a hörgr. Freyja details that the hörgr is constructed of a heap of stones, and that Óttar very commonly reddened these stones with sacrificial blood:

> *"Hörg hann mér gerði hlaðinn steinum,*
> *– nú er grjót þat at gleri orðit; –*
> *rauð hann í nýju nauta blóði;*
> *æ trúði Óttarr á ásynjur."*

English translation:

> *He made me a high altar of heaped-up stones: the gathered rocks have grown all bloody,*
> *and he reddened them again with the fresh blood of cows;*
> *Ottar has always had faith in the ásynjur.*

The Norse often made hörgr altars or shrines to use in blóts.

The blót is a Norse pagan sacrifice to the Norse gods and the spirits of the land (wights). The sacrifice is often in the form of a sacramental meal or feast. The verb blóta means "to worship with sacrifice" or "to strengthen or bond."

The blót usually consisted of animal sacrifices followed by a feast at which the animal(s) would be eaten. The animal(s) are killed in a sacred butchering and its blood caught in a bowl (Blótbolli). The priest (goði) or individual presiding over the rite will then sprinkle the rite's participants and the walls of the temple (hof) with the sacrificed animal's blood using a wooden blood rod (hlaut-teinn). The remaining sacrificial blood in the Blótbolli (sacrificial blood bowl) is then poured over a hörgr (stone shrine or altar).

This was how Óttarr earned the favor of Freyja in the Poetic Edda. The he covered hörgr

Traditionally, the sacrificed animal meat is often boiled in large cooking pits with heated stones, either indoors or outdoors. But there's absolutely nothing wrong with using BBQs and smokers too.

In the Prose Edda book Gylfaginning, we are told about how the gods were traveling in midgard on day and at the end of the day they came upon a herd of oxen. Famished, Loki slaughtered one of the oxen while Óðin and Hœnir built a fire to cook it.

The sacred communion continued as the folk gathered to share the sacrificial cooked meat and other offerings.

They would have a meal together with the gods. A blessed drink of beer, mead, or wine was passed around from participant to participant to hail the Aesir, Vanir, or other wights being celebrated or bonded with in the blot.

The sacrificial butchering of animals is still considered normal practice, but there are acceptable alternatives of blessing a hörgr. The blood offering is often replaced with a votive offering of beer, mead, or wine.

There are many other variations, such as non-alcoholic alternatives, for example Norwegian wights known as nisse are known to prefer offerings of porridge with butter and honey on top.

Our information is limited, but it is possible that the Norse also built hörgr when they were away vikingr and far from their home hofs.

An example of this would be all the hörgr at Laufskalavarda Iceland and other locations inhabited by Norse settlers.

The making of many hörgr was depicted in the film, "Valhalla Rising" when the Norse were far away from home in possibly Vinland and are trying to reach out to the gods. The Christians made a wooden cross and the Pagans made cairns (hörgr).

The Inuit, often called Skræling by the Norse, also piled or stacked rocks into what they call Inukshuk.

Inukshuk monuments made of unworked stones that are used by the Inuit for communication and survival. The traditional meaning of the inukshuk is "someone was here" or "you are on the right path."

Chapter 12 – The Sacrificial Blót Ritual

The Blót is a sacrificial holiday held in honor of the Dísir, the Gods, and Ancestors.

Also called a Dísablót (deese-a-blawt), which is two words, 'dísir' (or 'dís') and 'blót'.

Meaning, it is a "Dísir's Blót" or "Blót for the Dísir."

A Blót is a sacrifice offered to the Norse gods and/or the spirits of the land, homestead, or clan. The blót sacrifice is often offered in the form of a sacramental drink, meal, or feast which is usually placed or poured over a hörgr (stone altar), vé (shrine), lund (grove), haug (sacred mound), or other sacred location such as a hof (temple).

The Dísir (singular: dís, meaning "lady", plural dísir) are female spirits or 'beings' that are associated with fate and act as protective spirits of individuals, households, and entire Norse clans. The dísir play various roles throughout different Norse poems, legends, and sagas that resemble those of fylgjur, valkyries, vættir, and norns. The term 'dísir' is a broad and collective term for these different types of female spiritual or unseen beings. The term even includes the Norse goddesses.

- *a fylgja is a spirit who accompanies a person in connection to their fate, often thought to be the spirit of an ancestor.*

- *a valkyrie ("chooser of the slain") is one of a host of female figures who choose those who may die in battle and those who may live. In Poetic Edda, Helgakviða Hundingsbana I, when the hero Helgi Hundingsbane first meets the valkyrie Sigrún, the poet calls her "dísir suðrænar," meaning "dís of the south"or simply, "the southern maid."*

- *a norn is a female being who appears at a person's birth in order to determine his or her future destiny (not to be confused with the Three Norns: Urðr, Verðandi, and Skuld).*

- *vættir are nature spirits (house wrights, brownies, nisse, tomte).*

One of the most comprehensive descriptions of a blót sacrifice in the North can be found in Hakon the Good's Saga, which was written by the Icelander Snorri Sturluson in the 1200s.

Sigurd Håkonsson, like his father, frequently made sacrifices. It was the common practice that all farmers from the area gathered at the temple (hof) to sacrifice. All were given food throughout the celebration.

Many different animals were sacrificed, especially horses. The blood from the sacrificed animals was collected in bowls and twigs were used to spatter the blood on altars, walls, and cult participants. The meat was cooked and then eaten by all in attendance. It was boiled in cauldrons that hung over a fire in the middle of the hall. Full cups of beer were carried around the fire and the magnate, who was the pagan priest, then blessed the meat and the cups.

Toasts were then made. The first was in honour of Odin, "to the king and victory". Afterwards the cups were emptied for Njörd and Frej in the hope of securing a prosperous and peaceful future. Then the participants emptied their cups with a personal pledge to undertake great exploits, in battle, for example. Finally toasts were made for kinsmen resting in burial mounds.

Snorri writes that Sigurd Håkonsson was a very generous man and supplied the whole feast, which he was long remembered for.

The sacrificial rituals of the Vikings ranged from great festivals in magnate's halls to offerings of weapons, jewelry and tools in lakes. Humans and animals were also hung from the trees in holy groves, according to written sources. The Vikings repeatedly used certain sacrificial sites, because they believed that there was particularly strong contact with the gods at these locations. From the accounts of the Christian missionaries we know that the Vikings sacrificed to statues, which stood out in natural surroundings or in cult buildings.

Some believe that there were four fixed blót sacrifices a year. These blóts were at the following times:

- *Winter Solstice (also Midwinter, Yule, Longest Night, Jól, Jul, Hibernal Solstice, December Solstice, Winter Festival. Winterfest) – Usually December 21-23*

- *Spring Equinox (also Vernal Equinox, March Equinox, Northward Equinox) – Usually March 19-21*

- *Summer Solstice (Estival solstice, Midsummer, St John's Day, Midsummer's Eve, St. Hans Day, Longest Day, June Solstice, Feast Day) – Usually June 20-22*

- *Autumn Equinox (September equinox, Southward equinox) – Usually September 21-24*

These four seasons are represented by a variety of symbology in different cultures. Most commonly as a four points.

The Zia Sun Symbol represents the Four Seasons on the New Mexico flag.

Have you ever wondered why the "swastika" was adopted by so many cultures through the ages? It is because it symbolizes the position of the Big Dipper during each Solstice/Equinox. This is excluding certain racist groups and a defeated political entities that abused the symbol and corrupted it to mean something else.

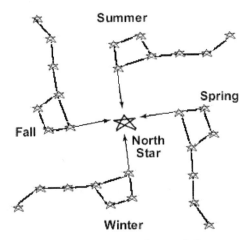

Big Dipper position of the stars during different seasons.

Here is the symbology most often used in Nordic, Celtic, Gaelic, and Western Germanic Cultures.

When specifically blóts took place is uncertain.

Some argue it eight times a year as is practiced by many Gaelic and Celtics, as well as many Wiccans. This is both Solstices, both Equinoxes (Jul, Litha, Eostre, Mabon), and the day marking between each cycle (Imbolc, Beltane, Lughnasadh, Samhain).

Others argue just four times a year, Winter Solstice (Midwinter), Spring Equinox (Eostre), Summer Solstice (Midsummer), and Autumn Solstice (Mabon).

The problem is, calendars and astronomical knowledge were not wide spread, so blots varied place to place, as did the customary practices and times.

220

The Vikings also held additional blót sacrifices, for example, if a crisis arose that required help from the gods. Before a battle most importantly.

The Arabic traveler al-Tartuchi describes how the Viking town of Hedeby celebrated the winter solstice.

"They celebrate a festival, at which all come to worship the god and to eat and drink. The one who slaughters a sacrificial animal erects stakes at the entrance to his farmyard and puts the sacrificial animal on them. This is so that people know that he is sacrificing in honour of his god."

The sacrifices might be followed by a communal blót feast – a feast at which the participants ate and drank together. Sacrifices of animals were not the norm, but were primarily associated with magnates and kings.

The dísablót is mentioned in the Hervarar saga ok Heiðreks (The Saga of Hervör and Heidrek), in the Víga-Glúms saga (Sagas of the Icelanders), Egils saga, and the Heimskringla.

In the Hervarar saga, the dísablót was held in autumn and was performed by a woman. The saga tells of the daughter of King Álfr of Álfheim (Elf realm), who "reddens the hörgr (stone altar) with sacrifices" and is subsequently rescued by Thor after she'd been abducted.

In the Víga-Glúms saga, it was a large gathering for friends and family which was held at Winter Nights (Old Norse: vetrnætr) at the onset of winter.

Winter Nights or Vetrnætr was a specific time of year in medieval Scandinavia that referred to "the three days which begin the winter season." The term is attested in the narrative of some of the Fornaldarsögur (Legendary Sagas). Vetrnætr is mostly used to express passage of time, such as,"when autumn turned into winter."

Picture of the Lofotr Viking Center

Odin's Law for Blót

In the Ynglinga saga by Snorri Sturluson (part 8, Odin's Law Giving), the exact term "winter nights" is not mentioned when he mentions the three great sacrifices of the year, but it is implied when he states one as being, "at the beginning of winter":

- Þá skyldi blóta í móti vetri til árs,

  There should be a sacrifice at the beginning of winter for a good year,

- en at miðjum vetri blóta til gróðrar,

  and in the middle of winter for a good crop,

- hit þriðja at sumri, þat var sigrblót.

  the third in summer day, that was the sacrifice for victory.

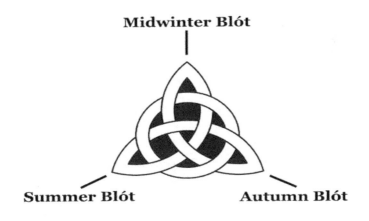

223

The Autumn Blót was performed in the middle of October (about four weeks after the autumn equinox), the Winter Nights, indicating the beginning of winter.

The great Midwinter Blót, or Yule, took place in the middle of January.

The Summer Blót was undertaken in the middle of April (about four weeks after the spring equinox).

Blōtmōnaþ (blót month)

For the early Anglo-Saxons, November was known as Blōtmōnaþ, as this later Old English passage points out:

Se mónaþ is nemned on Léden Novembris, and on úre geþeóde blótmónaþ, forðon úre yldran, ðá hý hǽðene wǽron, on ðam mónþe hý bleóton á, ðæt is, ðæt hý betǽhton and benémdon hyra deófolgyldum ða neát ða ðe hý woldon syllan.

Which translates as:

The month is named in Latin November, and in our speech Blót-month, because our forefathers, when they were heathens, always blóted in this month, that is, that they took and devoted to their idols the cattle which they wished to offer.

Specific sacrifices held at the beginning of winter during the Old Norse period were álfablót and dísablót.

Of these, dísablót came to be a public sacrifice, according to the Ynglinga saga performed by the king of Sweden. In western Scandinavia, dísablót appears to have been a private observance; even the large gathering in Víga-Glúms saga was for family and friends.

By contrast, álfablót was a sacrifice held at each homestead separately for the local spirits, under the explicit exclusion of any strangers.

In the poem Austrfararvísur (c.1020), the Christian skald Sigvatr complains of not being able to get into to any of the farms around the area of Sweden where he visits because of the diligent celebration of a sacrifice in honor of the elves (tomte/nisse).

that was administered by the lady of the household. Álfablót or the Elven sacrifice was a pagan Scandinavian sacrifice to the elves towards the end of autumn, when the crops had been harvested and the animals were most fat.

The Álfablót was a sacrifice made after a successful harvest to the vaettir of the homestead to show appreciation for their contributions.

In Kormáks saga (Icelanders' sagas), there's an account on how sacrifices were done to the elves in order to heal a battle wound:

Hún segir: "Hóll einn er héðan skammt í brott er álfar búa í. Graðung þann er Kormákur drap skaltu fá og rjóða blóð graðungsins á hólinn utan en gera álfum veislu af slátrinu og mun þér batna."

"A hill there is," answered she, "not far away from here, where elves have their haunt. Now get you the bull that Cormac killed, and redden the outer side of the hill with its blood, and make a feast for the elves with its flesh. Then thou wilt be healed."

Unlike the sacrifices described by Sigvatr, this one appears to have been a sacrifice that could have been performed at any time of the year.

So how do modern practitioners of the Old Ways have blót?

Well, the answer is: it depends.

Most practice blóts four times a year on the Solstices/Equinoxes. The blót ritual varies person to person and family to family, along with varying religious practices and observances.

Most families only observe a single blót a year on Jul/Christmas time when they leave out a bowl of porridge with butter, honey, and cinnamon out for their Julnisse / tomte.

Some people only celebrate a blót on Memorial Day when they remember loved ones who have passed when they place flowers and other tributes on their grave sites (or mound sites from the Late Stone-Early Bronze Age through after the Viking Age when burial practices changed). Some people only practice blóts in remembrance of a family member, fallen comrade, or brother-in-arms.

Many just make a seasonal blóts in remembrance of their ancestors and make an offering in gratitude. Followers of Ásatrú and Norse heathenry will make these blót offerings to their favored Æsir–Vanir gods and ancestors.

The method of a blot varies person to person as well.

Many leave out offerings from the fruits of their labor, such as a farmer leaving some of the best of apples from their orchards or the best steaks from their cattle. In a Christian example, this would be similar to the offerings made by the brothers Cain and Abel (which led to murder – same with the Egyptian Set and Horus).

Some people simple leave out portions of their personal favorite food or drink. This would be something they consider special and don't prepare often except on special occasions, such as: Christmas, Thanksgiving, or when Grandma comes over to visit for example.

The blót practice is a practice of kindred by sharing food and drink as they would with visiting kin, or even with the gods themselves if they came to visit. A blót is a 'toast of remembrance'.

In Christian practices, the Eucharist (Communion) is a form of Blót

The blót is an observance of remembrance and it is not religiously tied, except when the blót is used in a religious ceremony or context. It is a practice which began before the Ása belief system and before Judeo-Christianity. It is a practice which has prevailed in all religions and belief systems throughout the world in many forms and practices.

Paganism and heathenism is a matter of definition by the beholder and is often misunderstood or misinterpreted because of ignorance and cultural bias.

We already know many 'heathen' practices were carried over to modern mainstream religions (Christmas, Easter, etc.). This is no different with the practice of blót.

One doesn't have to be a heathen to celebrate a blót. You are not making an offering to the devil (unless that's your thing). You're making an offering to your God or Gods. You're making a tribute to loved ones who've passed on. It's an offering to your ancestors and to those who were here before you.

Some people make blót offerings such as food and/or drink, while some (especially Christians) offer prayer to loved ones – as do many pagans and heathens.

Chapter 13 – The Nordic Concept of the Self

The Hugr is part of the Old Norse concept of the self.

Most people, regardless of their religious beliefs, have a general concept of the "self" in terms of it having three components:

The Body, the Mind, and the Soul or Spirit.

The Old Norse and Germanic folk had a similar concept of the self:

- the Body, called the **Líkami,**

- the Mind or Will, called the **Munr,**

- and what can be best described as the very essence of their being called the **Hugr,** which is much like a Soul or Spirit.

The mind (munr), although a separate concept, is part of the very being called the hugr, which would be best described as a soul or spirit. The hugr was the very essence of an individual's being that could be separated from the body at will and returned.

The mind (munr) stayed with the spirit/soul (hugr) when it left the body (líkami). The hugr, with the munr attached, left the body upon the death of the body (líkami).

The will of the Norse appears to be very strong.

Strong enough for them to draw their hugr back to their own body and reanimate it so they can walk amongst the living again.

Even the gods and goddesses have Hugr, because even the gods and goddesses can die.

There are three primary places where the dead are perceived to go:

- Helheim (Old Norse Helheimr, "the home of the goddess Hel"),

- Valhalla (Old Norse Valhöll, "the hall of the fallen"), and

- Folkvangr (Old Norse Fólkvangr, "the field of the people" or "the field of warriors").

The Halls of Valhalla and Folkvangr are not halls of the dead for all eternity. They are merely training grounds and housing for those deemed worthy by the Vanir and Aesir gods to defend them at Ragnarok.

It appears that all beings, gods and humans alike, die and eventually go to helheim. The gods and that of all men can experience death, a second death, or even a third, and sometimes final death after Ragnarok.

Valhalla and Folkvangr are side roads to Hel. All upon death, all make their journey to Hel, it is those chosen to go to Valhalla and Folkvangr that may not have to make the journey all the way to Helheim. At Ragnork, even Hel releases her hugr to Vigrid. After which, Helheim, Valhalla, Folkvagr, and the rest of the worlds will cease to exist then the world will be renewed.

Hel is a place where all, humans and gods, must go after their death. We know this because the god Baldur was killed and had to go to the Realm of Hel.

Hel was given control over all in death, her realm would be the final journey.

> *"For there is a time when every man*
> *shall journey hence to Hel."*
> *- Fáfnismál 10*

Baldr died and went to Helheim when Loki gave the mistletoe spear to Baldr's brother, the blind god Höðr, who then inadvertently killed Baldr with it. Odin and the giantess Rindr then gave birth to Váli who grew to adulthood within a day and slew Höðr.

(Speculation: could Höðr have been Baldr's Hugr?)

Thus, two gods were killed. The gods can die and when they die, they go to Hel's realm.

Upon his death, Baldr's Líkami (body) was ceremonially burnt upon his ship, Hringhorni, the largest of all ships.

The dwarf Litr was then kicked by Thor into the funeral fire and burnt alive. Yeah, Thor was a bit of a dick at times and apparently, Dvergr (dwarves) can be burnt to death as well. No word if Litr went to Helheim or not.

> *"Then Thor stood by and hallowed the pyre with Mjöllnir;*
> *and before his feet ran a certain dwarf which was named Litr;*
> *Thor kicked at him with his foot and thrust him into the fire, and*
> *he burned."* —Gylfaginning

Nanna, Baldr's wife, the goddess Nanna also threw herself on the funeral fire to await Ragnarök when she would be reunited with her husband. She must have gone to Helheim as well.

*Alternatively, Nanna died of grief and then her body was placed on her husband's funeral pyre.

Thor kicks Litr onto Baldr's burning ship, illustration by Emil Doepler (1905).

Baldr's horse with all its trappings were also burned on the pyre.

Meanwhile, Hermod rode nine nights through ever darker and deeper valleys on his quest to rescue the part of Baldur (his "Hugr" (spirit/soul)) that had been sent to Hel. However, Baldur's Hugr remained with Hel in her realm Helheim until Ragnarok.

That was one incident, in which two gods (Baldr and Höðr) and a goddess (Nanna) died and went to Helheim. When the Líkami (body) dies the Hugr is drawn to Hel when it leaves the body.

Odin's Ravens

The Norse god Odin has two ravens, named Muninn and Huginn.

Each day the ravens, Huginn and Muninn, fly over Midgard (Earth) and then later return to bring Odin information about the happenings of that day.

In the Prose Edda book Gylfaginning (chapter 38), the enthroned figure of High tells Gangleri (king Gylfi in disguise) that two ravens named Huginn and Muninn sit on Odin's shoulders. The ravens tell Odin everything they see and hear. Odin sends Huginn and Muninn out at dawn, and the birds fly all over the world before returning at dinner-time. As a result, Odin is kept informed of many events.

Although the ravens fly out each day, Odin fears that one day they may not return.

In the The Poetic Edda: Grímnismál, a disguised Odin expresses that he fears that they may not return from their daily flights.

Benjamin Thorpe translation:

> *Hugin and Munin fly each day*
> *over the spacious earth.*
> *I fear for Hugin, that he come not back,*
> *yet more anxious am I for Munin.*

Henry Adams Bellows translation:

O'er Mithgarth Hugin and Munin both
Each day set forth to fly;
For Hugin I fear lest he come not home,
But for Munin my care is more.

The Norse concept of the self includes:

The personal consciousness or personality. The Mind, called the Munr

The energy which is the astral body. The Spirit or Soul, called the Hugr

And the physical body. The Body, called the Líkami

When the body dies, the spirit (hugr) leaves the corpse and moves on to the afterlife. The mind (munr) or consciousness stays with the spirit or soul (hugr) when it leaves the body (likami).

Are Odin's ravens, Muninn (Mind or Munr) and Huginn (Spirit or Hugr), representative of his mind and soul leaving his body as he astral projects himself?

Astral projection (or astral travel) is defined as an out-of-body experience that assumes the existence of an "astral body" separate from the physical body and capable of travelling outside it.

Are Odin's ravens, Huginn and Muninn, actually symbolic to his well known shamanic practices. Odin's ability to send his "spirit" (Huginn or Hugr) and "mind"

(Muninn, Munr) to the trance-state journey of shamans.

The Grímnismál stanza tells us that Odin worries about the return of Huginn and Muninn. This concern of his mind and spirit not being able to return to his physical body would be consistent with the danger that a shaman faces on the trance-state journey.

It is noted in the Prose Edda book, Gylfaginning, that Freyja often weeps tears of red gold because her husband Óðr (possibly another name for Odin) would go off "traveling" for extended periods. Perhaps she fears for him while he's in a trance-like state that he may not be able to return to his body. She also mentions that he travels frequently. Odin's Ravens go out each day. This would mean Odin goes into a trance each day.

Odin was a practitioner of seidh (old customs), which is known for the shamanistic practice of astral journeying.

Seiðr was an exclusively female elite matriarchal order of seiðkonur, led by a chief-shaman sorceress-seeress, who bore the title of 'Wōtan', from which the name Oðin was later derive, Seiðr has its origins in the Nordic Stone Age

In the Viking Age, the practice of seid by men had connotations of unmanliness or effeminacy, known as ergi, as its manipulative aspects ran counter to masculine ideal of forthright, open behavior. Perhaps it was seen as ergi or unmanly to get into a fight (holmgang) and then cheat by using the practice of seiðr to shift into the shape and strength of a bear. It is a but unfair to pull out a handgun when in a fist fight, it's considered a bit unmanly or ergi by modern standards.

Old Norse literature is rich in stories of shapeshifting. Some of the shapes most common in Old Norse literature include: bear, wolf, swan, seal, mare and hare, but it can take almost any animal form.

Perhaps the best known story of such astral travel is that of Boðvar Bjarki, who fought in the form of a bear (spirit-bear) while his lich, or Líkami (body), lay in trance (Hrólfr Kraki's Saga)

Freyja and many of the other goddesses of Norse mythology were seiðr practitioners.

Perhaps the shamanistic seidr practice of astral traveling (the mind (munr) and spirit (hugr) outside of the physical body (likami), was how all the gods got around. Odin's two ravens Muninn and Huginn, Thor being charioted by Tanngrisnir and Tanngnjóstr, Freyja's chariot pulled by two cats, etc..

Chapter 14 – Vörðr, the Norse Warden Spirit

The Old Norse believed that the Vörðr was a warden spirit that followed them everywhere from their birth to their death.

The word vörðr means: "warden," "watcher," or "caretaker." In Old Swedish, the word is varþer and in modern Swedish it is vård. The English word "'wraith" derived from the Norse word vǫrðr, while "ward" and "warden" are cognates.

The belief in them remained strong in Scandinavian folklore up until the last centuries.

The vörðr is also believed to be the soul (hugr) of every person.

The mind (munr), although a separate concept, is part of the very being called the hugr which would be best described as a soul or spirit. The hugr was the very essence of an individual's being that could be separated from the body at will and returned. The mind (munr) stayed with the spirit/soul (hugr) when it left the body (líkami).

The hugr, with the munr attached, left the body upon the death of the body (líkami).

The combination of the hugr (spirit/soul) and munr (mind) may be what the Norse called the vörðr.

In the Poetic Edda Grímnismál, when Odin was disguised as Grimnir, he mentioned his ravens Huginn and Munin and how he feared them not returning back to him one day.

> *I fear for Hugin, that he come not back,*
> *yet more anxious am I for Munin.*
> *(-Odin disguised as Grimnir)*

Odin feared losing his mind (munin or munr) and spirit/soul (hugin or hugr), also defined as his mind and memory.

Are munin and hugin, symbolized as ravens, together his Vörðr? Was he leaving his body in his vörðr and feared not being able to return one day?

The Old Norse weren't specific as to what a vörðr was and if it were the hugr and munr combined or something completely different.

Odin was also known for his astral projection and the fear of not being able to return to his body may have been the root of his fear.

The Vörðr can sometimes be seen.

On occasion, the warden spirit or vörðr revealed itself as a small light (orb) or as the shape (hamr) of the person. The perception of another person's warden could cause a physical sensation such as an itching hand or nose, as a foreboding or an apparition. The warden could arrive before the actual person, which someone endowed with fine senses might perceive.

The vörðr of a dead person could also become a revenant and haunt particular spots or individuals. In this case, the revenant warden was always distinct from other undeads, such as the draugr.

Under the influence of Christianity, the belief in wardens or vörðr changed into becoming more akin to the Christian concept of a Guardian Angels and spirits.

In comparison to Judeo-Christian-Muslim faith and beliefs, the Norse vörðr would be considered as being a lessor angel.

Chapter 15 – The Fylgja, The Norse Spirit Animal

Fylgja are familiar spirits that are sometimes referred to simply as "familiars," "spirit guides," or "spirit animals".

They are supernatural entities believed to be in the spirit realm that would assist shaman, seiðr (witch-seeress) and other folk in tune with the spirit world and nature, such as vættir. The Norse believed the natural world and the spirit world were tied together.

In Norse mythology, a fylgja is a spirit who accompanies a person in connection to their fate or fortune. Most of the time they remain in spirit form, unseen by the physical world.

The Norse believed that a fylgja would take on the form of the animal and show itself when a baby is born. It was believed that the fylgjur revealed itself in the form of the animal which represented the character of that person.

A bear would be symbolic for strength. A fox for cunningness, or an owl for wisdom, for example.

Turville-Petre discussed in his studies about commonalities in symbolism represented between the various animals such as an evil wizard or sorcerer's fylgja being that of a fox because they are sly and hiding something, or that of an enemy being depicted as a wolf.[248]

In the "Story of Howard the Halt" (*Hárvarðar saga Ísfirðings*), Atli has a dream about eighteen wolves led by a vixen running towards him. A 'dream-vision' fair warning him that an army led by a sorceress was going to attack him.

Fylgjur could also mark transformations between human and animal or shape shifting. In Egil's Saga, there were many references to both the characters Egil and Skallagrim as transforming into either wolves or bears, as well as examples of shape shifting in the Saga of King Hrolf Kraki, where Bodvar Bjarki turns into a bear during a battle as a last stand. These transformations are often hinted to when sagas discuss berserkers who transform into animals or imitate animalistic characteristics.

Fylgjur usually appear in the form of an animal or a human and commonly appear during sleep, but the sagas relate that they could appear while a person is awake as well, and that seeing one's fylgja is an omen of one's impending death. However, when fylgjur appear in the form of women, they are then supposedly guardian spirits for people or clans (ættir).

Female fylgja were often considered as being a "dís", which is a spirit or nature goddess that is attached to their fate.

A noted parallel between the concept of the hamingja, the personification of a tribe, family, or individual's fortune, and the fylgja is in the Icelandic saga of Gísli Súrsson (*Gísla saga Súrssonar*).

In the saga, Gisli was visited by two beautiful women. One of them tried to bring good fortune and the other tried to edge him towards acts of violence. These two women relating to the idea of the hamingja and fylgja, whereas the hamingja represented his good fortune and the other represented the violent nature his fylgja.

Much like cats, ravens, and other animals who are often considered to be familiar spirits of witches in most folktales. The fylgja is generally perceived in an animal form by those with 'second sight' able to see in the spirit realm. It's an attendant spirit whose well-being is intimately tied to that of its owner. For example, if the fylgja dies, its owner dies as well.

In a sense, this helping spirit can be seen as the totem of a single person rather than of a group.

Usually a totem is a spirit being, sacred object, or symbol that generally serves as an emblem of a group of people, such as a family, clan, lineage, or tribe.

The word fylgja literally translates as "follower," but contrast to its name it is usually depicted by seerers as traveling ahead of its owner and arriving at the intended destination before its owner. They are also said to appear in the dreams of someone who will meet the owner the fylgja the following day.

Interesting enough, the term is also applied to the afterbirth. Perhaps the ancient Norse believed the fylgja to have been in the placenta while the person was in the womb.

Chapter 16 – Christianization of the Norse

The Christianization of the Norse took place between the 8th and the 12th centuries. It was a gradual process that took considerable effort by Christians. Christian clergy attempts to convert the Norse proved to be difficult. The Norse people were quite content with their own gods and simply did not wish to be converted. In many cases, conversion was only achieved by force.

Prior to Christianization, the traditional religion of the Norse people was firmly in place. The Norse religion wasn't just a form of worship, it was a part of their culture and way of life. A belief system that was so deeply rooted that it made the concept of the original sin and other Christian beliefs just too hard for the Norse people to understand or believe.

Because of hard core Norse beliefs, converting the Norse was a task that took Christendom a relatively long time to achieve. As far as the Norse were concerned, their gods had brought them nothing but success in battle and they had absolutely no reason to embrace the Christian god.

This led to the Christians to seek Norse conversion by any and all means possible, including converting existing Norse beliefs, practices, and cultural beliefs into Christian ideology. This was often practiced in order to introduce Christian beliefs in a way that the Norse could relate to in comparison to the gods they already knew well.

So to help convert the Norse to Christian ways, many pre-existing Norse practices and customs were converted into Christian practices, such as the Christening of a child for example. The missionaries adopted the name-fastening ceremony practiced by the Norse pagans and adopted it into their own religious ceremony know today as a christening ceremony.

When a child was born, there was a great deal of ceremony conducted by the Norse. For example, a newly born infant would be placed on the ground and then remained there until he or she was picked up by their father (or next of kin in his absence) and placed in the folds of his cloak. This act of picking up the infant by the father ceremoniously acknowledged the legitimacy and acceptance by the father as his offspring.

The father then examined the infant for any abnormalities and judged whether or not it had a future. This process decided the fate of the child as to whether it was to live or be left exposed to the wilderness to die. A custom commonly known to be practiced by the Greek Spartans.

If the child was free of defects and deemed to live, a sacred religious rite called the *Ausa Vatni* was preformed.

This ceremony was conducted by either sprinkling or pouring water over the child and then naming the child.

This ceremony was an ancient sacred rite of the Old Norse religion that predates Christian baptism. To expose a child after this ceremony was preformed was considered murder. The rite of Ausa Vatri was also practiced by some of the Northern Frankish tribes. Some forms of Christian baptism are based on this rite and only changed it in name by early Christian missionaries who made it a part of Christian practice.

There is also record of the sacred rite being practiced in the Norse Sagas. One example is the birth of Sigurd, who was the son of Ragnar Lothbrok. Ragnar's wife, Kráka (also known as Aslaug) bore Ragnar a son and they carried the child to Ragnar to see him. Ragnar took the boy and placed him in his cloak and gave him the name Sigurd. In addition, it was customary to give a gift to the child during the naming ceremony. In the Saga of Ragnar Lothbrok, it is said he took a gold ring and gave it to his son as a "name-fastening (Old Norse 'nafnfesti')."

The gift given to a child during the nafnfesti (name-fastening) rite varied from either rings, weapons, and other tokens, to even such things as entitlement to farms, or lands.

In addition to the *Ausa Vatni* rite and *Nafnfesti* ceremony of giving a gift while naming the child, it was also customary practice to give a child a gift when they cut their first tooth. This practice later evolved into modern day's practice of the "tooth fairy."

Another well known ancient Norse practice worth mentioning that was taken into Christian practice was the celebration of Yule. The pagan holiday of "Yuletide" became what we in the modern day know as Christmas. The Scandinavians still use the word "Jul" or "Yule" for Christmas. This celebration was originally a fertility rite used to ensure good harvests in the following seasons. The Old Norse practice of receiving a blessing from spirit of the farm that guarded and protected it was later substituted by receiving blessings from a Christian priest.

However before Christianization, each Norse farm was believed to have its own land spirit or protector which the modern Danes and Norwegians call a "Nisse" ("Tomte" in Swedish). The Nisse spirit was replaced with the Christian St. Nicholas or Santa Claus. However, the conversion attempt wasn't completely successful by the Christian missionaries and to this day on Christmas Eve many children in Scandinavia who aren't waiting for Father Christmas, instead await a Nisse or Tomte to arrive with gifts.

Once the Norse had a better understanding of Christian concepts as they were compared to their own established religion, they eventually were able to accept Christianity and its beliefs. Many early successful conversions of the Norse was done by relating Christian concepts as closely to Norse practices as possible.

However, most conversion attempts were done by means of entire communities converting as a whole rather than individual conversions. Mass conversions were carried out by methods such as demanding conversions through subjugation. The subjects of a leader would be forced to convert.

Typically, the Norse leader or King would convert to Christianity and as an opportunity to solidify their power, they would force all their subjects to convert as well. Peace treaties formed with other Christian monarchs were often only achieved if the Viking leader converted to Christianity and had their men do so as well. Even when at the Norse's mercy and being demanded silver payments to release cities conquered by Norse raiders (Vikings). They managed to buy the Norse off with caches of silver and an agreement of Christian conversion.

So instead of trying to convert individuals to become Christians, the community would be ordered to convert by their leader. This made the clergy's job easy as entire regions would become converted by order of their King.

Not all agreements went as planned for Christian monarchs and clergy when they ordered their followers to convert. There were instances, such as when Jarl Haakon was in Denmark. Harald Bluetooth forced him to accept being baptized as a Christian and to take clergymen with him to Norway in order to spread Christianity in Norway. Haakon had no choice by to accept, but when favorable winds allowed Haakon to set sail and leave, he commanded the clergymen off his boats to return ashore as he and his men left.

Haakon ordering the clergymen off his boats.[38]

Once an area was ordered by their leader to convert, missionaries, priests, and monks would then come in to finish the process. Once the people were converted, the old gods and practices would be outlawed. Entire communities would be baptized and swear oaths to forsake the old gods and take in Christ as their only god.

Further subjugation took place through instruction and discipleship training by christian missionaries that would be set up. Even still, foreign missionaries did get resistance, often for no other reason than distrust of them simply because they were foreigners.

The English missionaries were more successful in their attempts at spreading Christianity because most of them came from England. It was as simple as that. English missionaries were more trusted because they were from conquered areas that were under subjugation by the Norse.

The Norse had already gotten used to the English people and their customs. The Norse weren't as suspicious of the English missionaries, militarily or politically, as they were the missionaries from other Norse lands, such as the Germanic Kingdoms or Francia.

One attraction to Christianity was that Norse pagans were impressed and tempted by the sheer materialistic power of world of Christendom. Christian lands, especially to the south, were rich with bountiful crops. This led many Norse to believe that the Christian god was more caring and generous.

Their pagan beliefs and faiths were mostly focused by gaining material prosperity through specific gods that gave attention to specific things. For example, they worshiped gods of agriculture because they wanted their crops to grow. Please the gods that favored cattle so that they would produce more milk. The Norse gods weren't particularly concerned with the human plight and were very hard to please.

When these Norse pagans looked at the wealth and power coming out of Christian Europe, they were impressed. Obviously the Christian God would deliver the goods and gave greater concern towards humankind. The Christians built bigger buildings and formed wealthy cities. Christians possessed more and it was of greater beauty and quality. The Christian crops were bountiful, so it was obvious to the Norse that the Christian god was more generous.

This was why when the Norse did begin converting,

some pagans had no problem converting to Christianity. They had the hope that conversion would give them material prosperity that was nonexistent with their current gods. The Norse gods didn't seem to care about them, but perhaps the Christian god will.

However, a majority of Norse converts would often continue with their pagan practices. Norse paganism was also a part of their culture and was very hard to simply cast aside. But thankfully for the Norse, strict Christianity wasn't enforced. Besides, the Norse were polytheistic and had many gods, accepting a new god alongside their already many existing gods wasn't that hard for them to do or accept. They didn't exactly convert to a new god and discard the old ones, they simply added another one to the count.

Polytheist pagans have lots and lots of gods. Gods for everything: gods of weather, of harvest, of the sea, of the sky, of beer making, of battle, and so forth. The Christian god was simply another god to them. The concept of a monotheistic faith of having only one god didn't sink in very well at first. This is why even after being converted, it took a very long period for Christians to wash away the Norse belief in many gods, goddesses, spirits, fairies, elves and giants from coexisting with faith in Christ.

The image of a "Victorious Christ" frequently appears in early Germanic and Norse art, suggesting that Christian missionaries presented Christ to the Norse as a figure of strength and as a victor in battle. Using the Book of Revelation that tells of Christ's victory over Satan to play a central part in the spread of Christianity among the Vikings, who looked to Odin and Thor for such attributes.

Even still, completely converting the Norse to true monotheistic Christianity was an extremely difficult task. The Norse never had anything against the Christians or their religious beliefs. The notorious Viking attacks on monasteries were due to the fact that they were rich and poorly defended. These raids were nothing more than opportunities for a Viking raid and had nothing to do with the Christian religion itself. The Christian monasteries were easy pickings.

Many Norse monks didn't take the whole religious life all that seriously. Becoming a monk at the time was seen more as a means of acquiring an education and learning to read and write. The strict conversions did not take place until later, especially when the age of Protestantism was sweeping across Europe.

For the most part, Christian conversions weren't taken seriously at all by the Norse. Missionary monks that came into Norse areas trying to convert them simply were ignored and tolerated because they were regarded as peaceful and harmless.

The first serious conversion attempts began somewhere between 710 AD and 718 AD, when a Anglo-Saxon monk named Willibrord had made unsuccessful attempts to convert the Danes. This took place during the reign of King Ongendus (also known as King Angantyr). Unfortunately, his efforts to spread the Christian faith were simply not appealing to the Norse Danes.

Not one to give up, in 725 AD, Willibrord made another attempt and led another mission to Denmark in hopes of conversions. Yet even though he was well received by the king, his mission once again had little effect on the general populace.

This failure did not stop the missionary monks from trying, as they were usually sent and backed by the Frankish King (Holy Roman Emperor) Charlemagne and other rulers in the Kingdoms bordering south of the Norse. Church missions were strategically built where they could make attempts to convert the populace.

However, even after a church was established they were sometimes later targeted by pagans. In the Netherlands, a church in Deventer was sacked and burned by a Saxon expedition in January of 772 AD. This act gave the Frankish King Charlemagne the justification (Casus belli) to wage war on the Saxons.

The war began with the Franks invading Saxon territory. They conquered and subjugated the Engrians and destroyed the sacred symbol "Irminsul" at Eresburg (near Paderborn, Germany). The Sacred Symbol "Irminsul" represented "Yggdrasil," the pillar tree that supported the skies and cosmos and was considered sacred to Odin and the gods. Which made it extremely sacred to the Norse. Its destruction was a grave insult to the Norse.

The destruction of Irminsul by King Charlemagne.[40]

When the King of the Franks, Charlemagne, chopped down the Irminsûl, the sacred column or holy tree of the Saxons, it began the Viking Age and relentless raids on Frankish lands. The retaliation was ruthless. In a series of several ambushes, Charlemagne had also assassinated around 5,000 Saxon nobility and effectively decimated the Saxon's ability to further resist his armies any longer. This allowed further subjugation and forced conversions into Christianity of the Saxon Norse.

Unfortunate for the Saxons, the methodology used by King Charlemagne was to convert his enemies by essentially defeating and killing them. After they were dead, he'd have a priest say some words in Latin and sprinkle some water over them and thus they were converted as Christians.

These were the events that influenced the Norse in Scandinavia to finally cease all hostilities against each other and focus their attention on a mutual hatred and thus began to wage war and attacks on Christianity. This was part of what started what we know as the Viking Age, as anything Christian was considered by Norsemen as a legitimate and justified target to raid.

Prior to this event in 772 AD, the kings of Norway were at war and allied against the Danes with Charlemagne. However, when the Frankish King had the Irminsûl cut down and the Saxon Nobles assassinated, the various kings of Norway switched sides, uniting with their Norse brethren (the Danes) and went to war against Charlemagne.

This effectively put a damper on any attempts by missionaries with their efforts to convert the Norse into Christianity.

It was later, after Charlemagne, in the 820's AD and onward that the missionary Ansgar and his followers, with the support of the new Frankish King, Louis the Pious were able to establish missions in both Denmark and Sweden. Even though the missions were made with the support local Norse rulers, once again the missionaries had made little to no influence on the population as a whole.

The missionary Ansgar converting the Norse.[39]

It was in 826 AD, that Harald Klak, the King of Jutland, was forced to flee Denmark by the Danish King Horik I. King Harald was forced to go to King Louis I of Germany and seek his help in getting back his lands in Jutland. King Louis I offered to make Harald Duke of Frisia if he would give up the old Norse gods and convert to Christianity. Harald agreed to this proposal. He, his family, and the 400 Danes that were with him were all then baptized as Christians.

When Harald returned to Jutland, the missionary monk Ansgar was assigned to accompany him and oversee Christian adherence among the new Norse converts. It was when King Horik I once again forced Harald Klak from Denmark that the monk Ansgar left Denmark and focused his efforts in Sweden instead. In 829 AD, Ansgar established a small Christian community in Birka, on the island of Björkö in Sweden. By 831 AD, the Archdiocese of Hamburg was founded and assigned the proselytizing responsibility for converting the Scandinavians from their traditional Nordic beliefs to Christianity.

Regardless of the mass conversions spreading through Scandinavia, Sweden did face a pagan reaction in the mid-11th century and Christianity did not become firmly established there until in the 12th century.

The greater increasing numbers of converts was because from the 11th to the 14th century, Christian society in Europe became less tolerant of other religions and beliefs. This was the time period when the Christian hammer slammed down on pagans and heretics. This is also when we see the persecution of Jews and the crusades against Muslims happening. At this time, forcible conversion became widely accepted, especially in Scandinavia and the Baltics, the only European region that remained resistant and unconverted.

When the Protestant Reformation began, it spread through Scandinavia like a wildfire. Protestantism took hold easier that did the earlier Catholic Church's attempts.

All of Scandinavia had ultimately adopted Lutheranism over the course of the 16th century, because the monarchs of Denmark (who also ruled Norway and Iceland) and Sweden (who also ruled Finland) converted to that faith and required their subjects to convert as well. The Scandinavian having a firmer grip on their subjects than ever before, had an easier time converting their people from Catholicism to Protestantism.

In Sweden, the Protestant Reformation was spearheaded by Gustav Vasa, who was elected King of Sweden in 1523 AD. Swedish national conversion to the Protestant faith led to the discontinuance of any official connection between Sweden and the Papacy. Four years later, in 1527 AD, the King of Sweden succeeded in forcing his dominance over the national church. This was when the king took possession over all church property and church appointments required royal approval. The national church and clergy were now subject to civil law, along with Lutheran Protestant ideas and views which were now to be taught in the schools and churches.

Under the reign of King Frederick I in 1523 to 1533 AD, Denmark remained officially Roman Catholic. King Frederick initially persecuted the Lutheran Protestants, but later he began protecting the Lutheran reformers. Due to this religious tolerance of Protestantism, conversions to Lutheranism grew significantly among the Danish population.

King Frederick's son, Christian, was openly Lutheran. When King Frederick died, his Lutheran son was prevented from succession of the throne because of the Catholic hold still in place in the nation. It was when the National Assembly terminated the authority of the Roman Catholic Church in 1536 AD and after his victory in the "Count's War" the following year that he was crowned as King Christian III of Denmark and Norway. At this point he was able to continue the reformation of the state's church and began to enforce Lutheranism in his kingdom. The resistance to this religious change nearly escalated to the point of civil war.

It was also during this time of the Protestant Reformation that Iceland had also adopted Lutheranism in place of its earlier established Roman Catholic religion. However, the Protestant Reformation in Iceland proved to be much more violent than in most of the other lands ruled by Denmark. Iceland had to be converted by force.

It wasn't until Lutheranism was firmly in place that Catholicism was outlawed by Icelandic law. It was outlawed to the point that for more than three centuries no Catholic priest was permitted to even set foot on Iceland.

Chapter 17 – Norse Language

The language used by the Norse people was *'Old Norse'* It was the primary language used in settlements up onto the 14th century when the language eventually developed into the modern North Germanic languages.

The transition period of this language transformation is approximate, because *Old Norse* was still found in written form well into the 15th Century. This was eventually phased out by the church, who preferred Latin text when writing.

Primitive Norse, or *Ancient Norse* (also called Proto-Norse) was the language of the Scandinavian people prior to the first centuries AD. *Ancient Norse* developed into the characteristic northern Proto-Germanic dialect that attests to the Elder-Futhark inscriptions from the 3rd and 4th centuries. During the Iron Age *Ancient Norse* eventually evolved into the *Old Norse* language used at the beginning of the Viking Age during the 8th Century.

There were three distinct dialects of Old Norse: *Old East Norse, Old West Norse,* and *Old Gutnish*.

The *Old Icelandic* language was essentially identical to Old Norwegian used. Together, the Old Icelandic and Norwegian formed into the *Old West Norse* dialect. This dialect was spoken in the Norse settlements of: Ireland, Scotland, the Isle of Man, and in the Norwegian settlements of Normandy.

The *Old East* dialect of the Norse language was spoken in Denmark, Sweden, and spread as far as to settlements located in Russia. Many Norse followed the Volga river and reached the Black Sea and Caspian Sea to open up trade with Easterners.

This Old Norse dialect used by the Danes was also used in England and in the Danish settlements that were located in Normandy. Gotland and various other settlements in the East spoke the *Old Gutnish* dialect of Norse.

Due to Norse expansion and trade, *Old Norse* was the most widely spoken language in Europe in the 11th century. The Norse language influence ranged all the way to Vinland and Greenland in the West to the Volga River in Russia to the East (which lasted well into the 13th century there).

This map shows the range of Old Norse dialects used in Viking settlements. The language spread the most near coastlines and rivers where Norse built trade settlements and ports. Many reaching further into the country mainland as settlements grew and expanded.

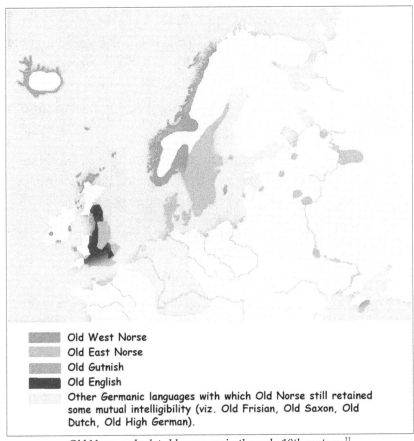

Old Norse and related languages in the early 10th century.[11]

The modern descendants of the Old West Norse dialects spoken today are: Icelandic, Faroese, Norwegian. There are also the now extinct Norn language that was used in the Orkney and the Shetland Islands.

The Danish and Swedish languages are the modern descendants of the Old East Norse dialect. Even though Norwegian is descended from Old West Norse, it has been heavily influenced by Old East Norse Dialect used by the

Danes and Swedes during the Kalmar Union from 1397 to 1523 AD. Then by the Danes during the Denmark–Norway union in 1524 AD. From 1536 to 1814 AD, the Norwegian kingdom was formally dissolved and integrated into Denmark. This period heavily influenced the Norwegian Language.

Among these Norse languages, Icelandic and Faroese (spoken mostly on the Faroe Islands) have changed the least from Old Norse in the last thousand years.

Much like the Norwegian language, Danish rule in the Faroe Islands had influenced the Old West Norse Faroese dialect with the Old East Norse Danish dialect.

Old Norse also had an influence on the English language and that of the Lowland Scots, both of which contain many Old Norse loanwords. Old English and Old Norse are closely related, which is why it shouldn't be of any surprise to an English speaker that Old Norse words look and often sound familiar.

Here are a few examples Old Norse words carried over in English:

they (þæiʀ), their (þæiʀa), them (þæim), flat (flatr), happy (happ), ill (illr), likely (líklígʀ), anger (angr), bag (baggi), bait (bæit), band (band), egg (ægg), gap (gap), husband (húsbóndi), cake (kaka), kid (kið), knife (knífʀ), leg (læggʀ), sale (sala), scrap (skrap), seat (sæti), sister (systir), skin (skinn), skirt (skyrta), sky (ský), slaughter (slátr), snare (snara), steak (stæik), are (er), blend (blanda), call (kalla), cast (kasta), get (geta), give (gifa/gefa), hit (hitta), lift (lyfta), raise (ræisa), take (taka), want (vanta).

Note the Norse use of the letter *"thorn"* or "þorn" (Þ, þ). This sound carried over into use in the Old English, Gothic, and Icelandic alphabets, as well as some dialects of Middle English. It is still used today by Icelandic speakers.

Thorn(þ) is sometimes still used in writing to give it a "Medieval" or "Olde English" feel to it. Most often, this example is used in business signs and logos.

Th eventually replaced the written *Thorn*(þ) sound, especially in writing. *Thorn*(þ) is replaced by th in several words, such as: the (þe), they (þæiʀ), their (þæiʀa), that (þetta) and them (þæim).

Thorn (Þ) is often mistaken as being a **Y** by modern English speakers. For example, the **Þ** in *Þe Olde English* is commonly mistaken as being: *Ye Olde English.*

The letter thorn þ is most easily mistaken when written in Middle English as *Winn* Ƿ. The Middle English *Winn* Ƿ has a greater chance of being mistaken as being a Y.

It's easy to see how"Ƿe Olde Tavern (**The** Olde Tavern)" can be mistaken as "**Ye** Olde Tavern."

The picture below displays comparison examples of the letter thorn being hand written and how easily it is mistaken as a Y.

Capital Thorn   Lower case

Þ   þ

Other variations that make it look
like a "Y"

Þ þ Þ ⇢Y

An example from an old written text.

A business sign in England, whereas it
gets mistaken as a "Y". The sign reads,
"The Olde Chippy" not "Ye Olde Chippy."

Examples of Thorn þ where it is mistaken as a "Y."

Old Norse also influenced the development of the
Norman language. Many of the Norse settlements that
eventually founded Normandy were mostly either Dane or
Norwegian and heavily influenced the language used.

There are also a number of other languages, while not
closely related, that have also been heavily influenced by
Old Norse: the Norman dialects, Scottish Gaelic, Waterford
Irish, Russian, Belarrusian, Lithuanian, Finnish, German, all
the Scandinavian languages, and Estonian as a few
examples.

The language influence stretches over an area that covers the northern half of Europe in general. Most of these languages have a number of Old Norse loanwords just as the English language does.

The Icelandic language is the closest to original Old Norse that was spoken by the Vikings. In fact, because modern written Icelandic comes from the Old Norse phonemic writing system; Icelandic-speakers can read Old Norse, only varying slightly in spelling, semantics, and word order. However, this is only written Icelandic, as in verbal Icelandic pronunciation the vowel phonemes have changed as much as in the other Northern Germanic languages used today influenced by Old Norse.

Written Norse is called the **Futhark**, more commonly known as the **Runic Alphabet**. The Norse Runic Alphabet is said by the Ancient Norse to have been given to them by god Odin himself.

Odin had learned *the Runic Alphabet* after hanging himself upside down from the Yggsdrasil tree and then pierced himself with a spear. He peered below into the shadowy depths below for nine days at the edge between life and death until the Runes revealed themselves to him. It is said, they not only showed him their forms but their secret meanings. Odin was a seeker of knowledge and wisdom, who even sacrificed one of his eyes for wisdom.

The **Elder Futhark** (Runic Alphabet) is named after the initial phoneme of the first six runes: F, U, Th, A, R and K, The Elder Futhark consists of twenty-four runes, which are arranged in three groups of eight runes called ætts.

This graphic shows the Elder Futhark Runic Alphabet.

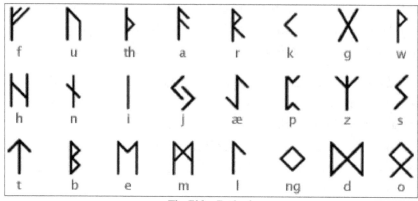

The Elder Futhark

It is generally agreed among scholars that the Runic Alphabet originated sometime in the 1st century AD. Some estimates place it about the 1st Century BC.

The Norse Runic Alphabet had somewhat altered in around the 9th Century AD in Scandinavia into what's called the **Younger Futhark.** The Alphabet was reduced to only 16 characters from the Elder Futhark's original 24. This is probably because of language changes made from Proto-Norse (Ancient Norse) into the Old Norse that was used from the 8th to 12th Centuries.

However, use of the Runic Alphabet had drastically declined in the 12th Century. After the Christianization of Scandinavia, most writing was done using the Latin Alphabet favored by the Roman Catholic Church.

But before then during the Viking Age it was the Younger Futhark Alphabet that was used predominately by the Norse and was known as the "Alphabet of the Norsemen" in Europe.

The Younger Futhark Alphabet divided into two branches: The Swedish/Norwegian Short twig and the Danish long branch. There is debate as to why there are differences. One argument claims that the Danish long branch was used for inscription purposes, such as stone inscriptions for records and that the Swedish/Norwegian short twig was for inscribes on wood for private or official messages in everyday use.

This graphic comparison shows the differences in the Danish long branch and the Norwegian short twig with their Latin letter equivalents.

The Younger Futhark: Danish long branch (top), Swedish/Norwegian short twig (middle) and Latin letters (bottom).

Runic characters survived in marginal use after the Christianization of Scandinavia in the form of the **Hälsinge Runes (Staveless Runes)** used in the 10th through the 12th centuries. The *Staveless Runes* seem to be a simplification of the Swedish/Norwegian short twig runic alphabet, being that they are staveless and are lacking vertical strokes.

Although staveless, the alphabet retains the staves of the Younger Futhark runes.

Here is an graphic example of the Staveless Runes or Hälsinge Runes.

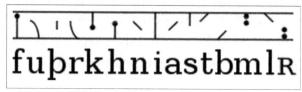

Hälsinge runes (staveless runes).

During the Middles Ages use of the Younger Futhark had expanded along with the expansion of the Norse. The language was becoming more complex and writing more in common use, the Runic Alphabet evolved into the **Medieval Runes (Futhork)** Alphabet during the end of the Viking age in the 11th century and becoming fully formed by the 13th century.

This graphic compares Medieval Runes, or what is known as Futhork, and their Latin alphabet translations.

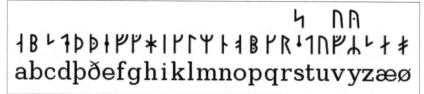

Medieval Runes

Most probably, the Medieval Runes had evolved with the competition of the Latin Alphabet which was fast expanding with the Christianization of Europe and Scandinavia. The Latin Alphabet could be copied into Norse easier with this expanded Medieval Rune (Futhork) alphabet.

By the 13th Century, the Runic Alphabet had mostly fallen out of use in favor the Latin alphabet, except still being in use by artisans, farmers, and traders who continued to use it to communicate and mark items. As the use of Latin became the standard for writing throughout Europe and Scandinavia, Runic writing was rarely used. A few hundred years later, the use of the Runic Alphabet became almost extinct and nearly forgotten.

Chapter 18 – Norse Life

Daily life for the Norse was not much different from that of anyone else. Notably, they did live a slightly tougher life given the more rugged terrain and weather experienced in the North. But adaptation to the climate and terrain was the key to successful survival. The Norse were innovative and made the best out of what they had. Their way of life reflected these traits and evolved over time as needed.

During the Viking era, most Norse families lived on a farm in a longhouse. A longhouse was a large, hall-like building that sometimes were up to 30 meters long. Longhouses were built with walls made from timber or stone and a thick turf roofs to retain heat. In the center of the typical Norse longhouse was the hearth, providing warmth and light for the occupants inside.

Originally, longhouses were just large single room halls, housing members of the family, farm workers (the thralls) and even the livestock together under the same great roof. It was later that the longhouse became divided, having several separate rooms which would usually include bedrooms and kitchen area. A longhouse was the typical setup for those living on farms.

Those living in the towns and settlements had houses that generally were either made of wood or made of wattle and daub (a lattice of wooden stakes covered with sand and clay) type of construction.

Typical of living in most towns or settlements, the houses were built closer together. Although houses built in town were smaller, they still had enough room for their own rubbish pit, yards and a workshop. The workshop was important, as living in town generally meant you were an artisan or smith of some form.

Cleanliness was important to the Norse. Contrary to the dirty image of a savage and barbaric people the Vikings tend to be portrayed as in film, archaeological evidence proves that this as a myth and false stereotype.

Perhaps the most telling comment about Norse cleanliness comes from the English cleric, John of Wallingford. The cleric John had bitterly complained about the Viking men of the Danelaw because they combed their hair, took a bath on Saturday, and changed their woolen garments frequently.

He claimed that they performed these unchristian and heathen acts in an attempt to seduce high-born English women.[12] He blamed their habit of bathing, combing their hair daily, and because they regularly laundered and changed their clothes, that they were able to undermine the virtue of married women and even seduce the daughters of nobles.[13]

Besides being clean, the Norse also wore well made clothing. The typical Viking or Norse person was usually dressed in garments made from wool. Typically during the Viking Age, most textiles were made of worsted wool in twill patterns. These wools were carefully woven, supple, and were attractively textured and often dyed in bright colors.

Having a decent weaver in the extended family was a necessity if one wanted to be smartly dressed. Another necessity for the well dressed individual was jewelry. A typical decorative ornament and symbol of status worn by many Viking men was an armring.

In Viking times, armrings or béag were given by powerful lords to secure allegiance from their followers. Bestowing such gifts was a demonstration of wealth and power by Viking lords and were worn with pride by those that followed them. These armbands were also symbols of coming of age, when a boy became a young man and swore an oath of loyalty to his lord. They were not only seen as a token of manhood, but as acceptance by their lord and peers.

10th Century Wendover Arm-Ring (British Museum).

Both Norse men and women took great pride in their appearance, and besides the armring worn by men to show their allegiance, both women and men also wore a variety of ornately bejeweled gold and silver brooches, rings and necklaces. Ornate combs were also one of the most common artifacts that are uncovered by archaeologists at Scandinavian settlements.

Personal hygiene items are some of the most common finds. The Norse were a very clean people. Not only were many types of combs found, but also such things as ear spoons.

Another common stereotype of the "Viking" is one of them all having blonde or red braided hair. It is true that the Norse favored light colored hair. Ahmad ibn Fadlan, an Arabic emissary that had contact with the Norsemen of the Rus Tribe, noted that the Norsemen would bleach their beards to a saffron yellow color.

Although it is not documented, it is most probable that they bleached their hair as well. The Norse bleached their hair using a predominately basic soap mixture they made from goat fat and beech wood ashes which had excess lye in it that caused the bleaching action.

The Roman, Gaius Plinius Secundus (better known as Pliny the Elder) also mentioned the Norse practice of bleaching their hair among the Germanic tribes he had contact with. He also pointed out that he felt that the men were more likely than women to bleach their hair.

Hair styles among the Norse varied according to an individual's preference and needs. Usually only thralls (slaves) wore their hair very short, a hair style that marked their status as a thrall.

However contrary to the long braided hair depicted of the Viking warrior, the average Norseman wore his hair about collar or shoulder length. An individual's beard was kept as long as was comfortable for him. In fact, a Viking warrior might make their choices of hairstyle based on minimizing the hazard of having their hair or beard grabbed in combat. Combat was an extremely violent confrontation and any means to win a fight were used, even grabbing hair or articles of clothing to bring your opponent down.

Clothing choices for combat differed than those of everyday wear. We know of the different kinds of armor worn by Viking warriors, but seldom is it ever mentioned about what they wore on a daily basis. This is because actual artifacts of Norse clothing of the Viking era are hard to find. The reason being is because cloth and fabric tend to decay quickly over time, but there have been a few items of Viking era clothing found.

In York, named Jorvik during the Viking Age, boots and shoes have been discovered made of calfskin or goatskin. But even these finds were decayed, making it hard to tell exactly what the Norse people wore during the Viking Age. So to fill in the gaps, we must rely upon poems and artwork of the time to piece it all together. From these poetic and artful depictions. We know that Norse women wore either woolen or linen smocks that were fastened with brooches and pleated underdresses.

The smock layer actually differed in cut and design from one archeological site to another and from one time period to another. For example in the 9th century, the Norwegians wore a unpleated smock that was cut in a wide oval or "boat" neckline in the tunic fashion.

In Denmark during the 10th century, the Danes wore a unpleated smock that was refined with set-in sleeves, shoulder seams, and gores. In Brika Sweden, they wore long sleeved pleated smock underdress that was made from a lightweight undyed linen during the 10th century.

These underdresses were often covered by another full length tunic-like gown with long sleeves and then there was an apron dress pinned over that.

Much care was put into these full length gowns. On the sleeves and torso of the outer layer gown (and often the apron dress over it) they would have had elegant ornamentation in the form of embroidery, appliqué, silk trimming, and tablet-woven bands.

The apron dress worn over the outer smock or gown is often called a "Viking apron." This garment was not a typical apron as worn today when cooking, but a complete over garment, so the descriptive name "apron-dress" is more befitting for this garment.

The Viking style apron-dress was worn over the shoulders and secured in place by a pair of brooches that were hooked through narrow loop straps. In addition to the gowns and apron dresses worn over them, married Norse women also wore scarves on their heads.

Reconstruction of the Køstrup apron-dress.[14]

During the Viking era, men worn woolen tunics over trouser type leg coverings. There were at least two types of leg coverings: a wide, knee-length, baggy type and a narrow, fitted full-length type of trouser.

Several finds of trousers dating to the Migration Era at around 400 to 800 AD tell us that the narrow full length types of trouser were worn by the Norse way back then. A site at Thorsbjerg Mose in Denmark, trousers found more or less intact, had the sophisticated Migration Era that required three separate pieces cut for the crotch gusset alone.

These trouser finds alone disprove any claims made that early period garments worn by the Norse were simple and untailored. The leggings of the Migration Era Thorsbjerg trousers even extended into foot coverings, just like children's pajamas.

The remains of a pair of trousers found in Birka, Sweden were probably of the short and baggy style. These trousers were made from linen and had little metal eyes set into their lower edges. The accompanying leg stockings were made from wool with little hooks sewn on to them. The woolen leg stockings were hooked to the lower edges of the linen trousers just below the knees.

The little hooks used to connect the trousers to the leg stockings were called "garter hooks." Even the Vikings had issues with their socks falling down.

Along with trousers, Norse men wore an under tunic and smock. During the Migration Era, a jarl at Evebø Norway wore two tunics, one over the other. He wore a knee-length red wool undertunic that was trimmed at the neck, wrists, and finished edge hems. His undertunic also had complex wool tablet-weaving patterns with various depictions of beasts in yellow, red, and black. The under-tunic's cuffs were secured with bronze wrist clasps, a feature fairly common in period.

The smocks discovered that were worn at the Danish-Northern Germanic Norse settlement at Hedeby were of two basic types. Both types have a rounded neckline with rounded armholes for set-in sleeves and had separate front and back panels sewn together at the shoulders. However, they differed in their side-seams: one type had narrow, slit sides, while the other type was wider with inserted gores for fullness at the hems.

Most were made from wool and some were even dyed. The sleeves on the smocks were tapered at the lower arm, so at the wrists they fit fairly snugly and they could also be cut in more than one piece to achieve a more complicated taper.

Some of the smocks from the Birka, Sweden area had keyhole style necklines rather than Danish rounded ones. The front and back panels were cut in one piece and weren't sewn together with shoulder seams.

On top of the tunics worn, the Norse wore an over-tunic. An over-tunic at Evebø, Norway belonging to a jarl was dyed blue, made of wool and was decorated at the neck with tablet-woven wool bands patterned with animals in two colors. The over-tunic also had silver clasps, however it's unknown whether they were cuff clasps or clasps for the front of the over-tunic.

It is most probable that the clasps fastened in the front on the chest like a coat. However, the over-tunics were not coats, as they had actual coats that were worn on the outer layer as weather demanded.

There were two basic coat layer types during the Viking Era that were most commonly used by the Norse. Basically not much different than today, there was the "jacket" and the "coat." The jacket was lighter and wrapped around without a fastening device, while the coat was heavier and buttoned securely closed.

Viking era jackets have been found in several spots in the Norse-dominated world and appear to have been a very old tradition.

We have a good idea of coat styles from a helmet that was found at the "Sutton Hoo" ship burial site. It had human figures depicted on it who were dressed in what look like bathrobes or large coats. This depicted coat consisted of a short tunic open all down the front with diagonal, overlapping flaps.

The Sutton Hoo helmet.[95]

Saxon graves in parts of England and Europe also have a coat layer of this design type that were ornamented on the lapel and down the front with gold-brocaded tablet weaving.

Fragments of a jacket found at the Hedeby trading site were made of plain 2/2 twill. Although incomplete, the jacket is believed to have been hip-length and trimmed with fake fur made of wool along the hem and down the front edges.

A type of Norse coat known as the "caftan" or "Rus riding coat" may have been an explicitly eastern Norse concept of the Swedes and Viking Rus tribes during the 9th and 10th centuries. This type of coat was a long over-garment that buttoned from neck to the waistline and was decorated with specialized and elaborate metal trimmings.

There have been five remains of these kinds of overcoats found and each of them had a row of cast metal shank-buttons. Several other coats have been identified which had the right sort of elaborate trimmings, but hadn't the associated buttons. Nevertheless, this does not mean that they didn't have buttons or other kinds of fasteners, because organic items such as wood or bone buttons disintegrate over time and leave little or no trace in a burial site. So it's very likely that these coats had buttons, even though none were found at the sites.

The Norse also wore cloaks and caps in the wintertime. The basic Viking cloak was rectangular cloak and was fastened with a cloak pin.

Cloak pins were usually of the pennannular brooch type or ring-headed pin types. Cloaks came in a variety of weights and weaves that ranged from lightweight patterned twills to the "rogvarfelðr" types that were heavy cloaks napped with "fake-fur" made from wool.

A cloak found in Evebø, Norway was an elaborate lightweight rectangular cloak that had fringed edges. It was red plaid with blue and yellow stripes in a 12x12cm repeat. At the edges of the cloak were tablet-woven bands of either blue or green with beasts in either yellow or red.

At a site in Jorvik (York), Fragments of red and undyed tufted wool have been found. Remnants of a heavy cloak with blue and red pile loops as long as a thumb have been found in Birka, Sweden.

Burial sites at Birka, Sweden have included cloaks worn on the body in the grave or were deposited near the body. These cloaks worn were usually thick, heavy blue ones that were either pinned at the shoulder or the hip. Several burial sites included a cloak that was deposited near the body. There were five men's burial sites that dated to the 9th century and all had cloak pins at the shoulder. Several cloaks from the 10th century were found pinned at the hip rather than the shoulder.

The Norse also wore a variety of woolen hats, caps, and other head wear. Some partially silken peaked hats with and without metal buttons have been found as well. Hats were worn for fashion as well as functionally such as keeping one's head warm and dry.

Belts rarely survive time and generally deteriorate, leaving little to no evidence. Although a variety of belt buckles have been found in many sites, most of them are simple in design. Shoes and boots, also made of leather that deteriorates, are also difficult and rare finds. However, some examples have been found.

The shoes found dating to the Viking Era were either made with separate soles that were stitched to the leather uppers or were "hide" shoes that had the upper and sole cut in one piece and then stitched to itself.

Most shoes types found were either half-boots or ankle shoes. There were some shoes that were slip-ons, while some were tied with leather lacing, and some that used lappets with cylindrical leather buttons. The materials and leather most often used for making shoes, were usually goat hide, deerskin, calf, sheep, and cowhide.

A Viking Male – reconstruction.[15]

We know that life for the Norse was hard considering their climate. Their struggle led them to expanding their culture to reaches further than most any of the cultures in the world. We normally depict them as a hard working, hard fighting people who were masters in trade and innovation.

But all work and no play makes Thorvald a dull and bored Viking.

As with other cultures, the Norse people not only worked hard but also set aside time for leisure activities. Most leisure that we know about were in the forms of celebrations whereas they held feasts celebrating successful raids, trade expeditions, and marriages. This is in addition to holidays and community Thing meetings.

Norse banquets, there would be a variety of meats served including beef, pork, lamb, fish and other seafoods, wild game, and goat. A variety of other foods as well, such as breads that consisted of various seeds that gave it flavor. And most notably the Norse people drank large quantities of wine, beer, and mead.

Life was well blended with a combination of leisure and labor.

Consistently practiced were the craft skills which played an important part in Norse society. Skilled weavers made woolen cloth which was not only used for clothing, but also for the sails on the masts of their ships. Smithing was a well known skill of the Norse, who not only created items of metal but were able to repair their weapons or farming tools as needed.

A variety of craftsmen made items that were carved with ornate figures and patterns. Musical instruments have also been excavated from Norse settlements such as flutes and panpipes.

The typical Norse life was filled with music and as much pleasure as it was filled with the daily drudges of life's daily struggles.

Chapter 19 – Norse Marriage

Marriage was important to the Norse people because they centered their lives around kin and kindred.

Family and community were among the most important aspects of Nordic life. The Norse held a family and community bond of that extended into the afterlife.

This is contrary to the modern popular belief that 'Vikings' desired nothing more than to die in battle and go to Valhalla, this was not the typical Norseman's desire.

Upon death the typical Norseman was hoping to go to places such as Helgafjell (the "holy mountain") where they could join their ancestors, family, and friends in the afterlife. Valhalla (Odin's Hall of the Slain) was a different concept and is most often misunderstood.

The "Nordic Dream" was not dying heroically in battle, but more akin to marrying well and raising a family.

For example, the 'Viking Expansion' had more to do with a great need for land in order to farm and raise a family. Popular culture made the Norse appear as nothing more than robbers and raiders, but this is far from the truth. The truth is that there was no land at home. Word spread about the Roman collapse and the Norse, who'd previously been pushed and squeezed into the far North for centuries by the Romans, seized upon the opportunity. It's not as glorious as we love to portray them, but it's the simple truth.

One had little choice but to dream of going on a viking expedition in search of lands to migrate their families to and start new lives.

Being the very core of the family, marriage was the most important social institution in Scandinavia.

One's personal sexuality did not matter, it was more important to marry and reproduce by having children. After that, nobody really cared what you did, as you accomplished your duty for clan, tribe, and family.

A wedding was an important matter, not only for the couple, but also for the families involved. You didn't marry your spouse, you married into each other's families. You were part of a family clan. A marriage was a binding legal contract which established many things beyond inheritance and property relations. The wedding ceremony and celebration itself was only the formalization of a pact in which the joining families promised to help each other.

The couple didn't just become tied to each other, thy formed alliances, not only in warfare and defense, but also in farming and trade.

It took an entire clan or village to survive, especially through harsh winters.

Families needed each other as solitude was certain death in such a harsh climate.

A marriage was usually negotiated and the legal codes reflect the enormous amount of the Norse concerned themselves over the matters of family and marriage.

One dares say, love for one another as a couple was least important. Dowries were required among many other things. Getting married and not being able to take care of your family was something considered. Being able to produce dowry demand was one way to prove you had the ability to support your family. For most, it wasn't that high of a price.

A typical dowry for an Icelandic wedding was in the region of eight ounces of silver, while the Norwegians set the figure at twelve. The minimum figure of twelve ounces of silver was known as the "poor man's price".

For a wedding to be considered legal and the children to be classed as legitimate in the marriage, the dowry must have been paid.

The dowry was paid by the groom to the family of the betrothed. This wasn't party money for selling off your daughter, this money was classed as being the soon-to-be wife's property and was usually used as an inheritance for the newlywed's future offspring.

If the marriage was without heirs, then the dowry sum was passed over to the closest kinsmen of the bride.

As with many negotiations, those who sought a marriage often took with them a person of prestige, power, and/or wealth to act for them as a negotiator when making the proposal of marriage to the family. This person was not a 'match-maker' as was common in many cultures, but that of a 'match negotiator' or broker. Much akin to hiring an attorney to get the best deal possible.

Such sponsors not only acted as witnesses to the handsal *(handshake)*, but the promise of their support and political influence formed a part of the inducement for the bride's kinfolk to accept the proposal. Once it was agreed that an alliance between the two families would be satisfactory, the next step was to negotiate the bruðkaup or 'bride-price'.[244]

The bride-price usually consisted of three payments:

From the groom would come the *mundr* and *morgengifu*, while the bride's family provided her dowry *(heimanfylgia)*, which was the bride's inheritance from her father and paid to the groom. Note: both families are paying a form of dowry, not for the couple or their families, but for the future of the offspring they are expected to produce from the union.

As a prologue to marriage, the family of the groom sent the groom and several envoys to the family of the bride to formally propose marriage. It was during this step in the process that the actual date of the wedding ceremony was set.

Weddings were held on Friday or "Frigga's-day" to honor Frigga, the goddess of marriage.[242]

For some Norse families, the date of the wedding were often further limited by weather and seasonal conditions. These were the people from *"the land of ice and snow"* and it does tend to snow and freeze up with a vengeance at sometimes.

Travel for all the extended family members, guests, participants from both the groom and bride's side to the wedding location would have been difficult or even impossible during the winter months. The wedding celebration was typically a week-long affair, although many times running through the entire moon cycle.

Copious amounts of food and drink to meet the needs of those gathered for the wedding had to be available. Besides weather, the harvest time to meet these needs also affected the wedding date.

It's of no wonder that often times many weddings would take place at the same time, sharing the costs of the feasts.

The legal requirements for a wedding included the stricture that the bride and groom would drink together the bridal-ale or mead, which meant that plenty honey needed to be available to brew the mead. Large quantities needed to be available, not just for the wedding feast, but so that the couple could share the honey mead together over the month following the wedding.[243]

Thus the name "honey-moon".

This lasted for a period of one moon, or 28 days.

Taking into consideration all these needs for the wedding and honey-moon, most weddings were probably planned to take place towards the end of summer into the early part of winter, after the harvests when things were plentiful.

This wedding proposal with planning a wedding date was the first legally binding step between the families. The occasion was used to negotiate the inheritance and property rights of the couple, as well settle the dowry *(heimanfylgia)* and wedding present *(mundr)* from the groom's family.

Those were to become the personal property of the bride.

Usually the bride's family were less wealthy than than that of the groom's, but in most cases the difference was not great. Thus the dowry was an investment by the bride's family that made it possible for her to marry into a more powerful family.

When an agreement on these matters had been reached, the deal was sealed at a feast.

These conditions of marriage were reserved for the nobility and that of karls *(freemen)*. The remaining population of thralls *(slaves)* and some contracted freed-men *(people who were thralls purchasing their freedom on contract)* were not free to act in these matters without approval of their master.

A wedding was a long and collective process subject to many ritual rules, which unfortunately have been lost to time or erased from record and practice as a result of forced christianization.

We do know from hints in sagas that procedures had to be followed for the gods and goddesses to sanction the marriage and avoid a disastrous marriage afterwards.

The wedding *(brudlaup)* ceremony was the most important single ritual in the entire process, which included a feast.

It would be the first gathering of the two families and consisted of a feast that lasted for several days. Anything less than three days was considered was considered petty and trivial.

The guests witnessed that the wedding process and rituals had been followed correctly.

A seated bronze statue of Thor (about 6.4 cm) known as the Eyrarland statue from about AD 1000 was recovered at a farm near Akureyri, Iceland and is a featured display at the National Museum of Iceland. Thor is holding Mjolnir, sculpted in the typically Icelandic cross-like shape.

As mentioned, our current sources tell us very little about how a wedding's ceremony and what rituals were related to the gods and goddesses. There aren't any descriptions about the actual wedding ceremony directly or of any worship rituals or blóts which took place – *save we know they had them.*

It is known that during the ritual the goddess Vár was called to witness the couple's vows, legitimizing them. We also know that a symbol of Mjölnir would be placed on the lap of the bride asking Thor to bless her. Most scholars believe Mjölnir was used as a phallic symbol of fertility.

And we also know that Freyr and Freyja were often called upon in matters of love and marriage.

We get this part of the marital ceremony about placing Mjölnir in the lap of the bride from the Poetic Edda Þrymskviða (*Lay of Thrym*). In this saga, we are told how the jötunn Þrymr (*Thrym*) steals Thor's hammer Mjölnir and demands Freyja as ransom for it, desiring the goddess as his own wife.

Instead of sending Freyja, the Æsir gods trick the jötnar (giants) and dress Thor as the bride and Loki as the bridesmaid. Now disguised, the two travel to Jötunheimr to meet the jötnar for the "wedding".

Thor's identity is comically hinted at throughout the
reception, such as when Thor eats an entire ox on his own.
Loki provides weak explanations the entire time which the
giants somehow accept for the odd and unladylike
behavior. One example was when he claims that the bride's
immense hunger for eating the entire ox was because she
hasn't eaten for the last seven days because of her
excitement over the wedding.

As part of the wedding ceremony, Mjölnir is eventually
placed onto Thor's lap which allows him to strike down the
giants and return home victorious with his hammer.

Additionally, we know from some sources that there was also the traditional marriage ritual of leading the newly wedded couple to a decorated bridal bed.

On the night of the wedding ceremony, the couple would be ritualistically led to a ceremonial bed by witnesses carrying torches and the 'consummation' was then witnessed.

Because the couple's wedding had to take place within a set period of time, the wedding ceremony generally took place within the bride's homestead or some other prominent mutual acquaintance.

A traditional Norse pagan wedding went on much longer than a traditional Christian ceremony. The celebrations were very much inclusive of large quantities of alcohol with many blessings of the new union by all who had gathered. Within the pagan ceremony many rituals were performed to ensure fertility and to remove any evil spirits or intentions by anyone else.

The term "honeymoon" has it's origins from the Norse traditional drinking ritual after the marriage ceremony with mead being part of the marriage ritual. The bride and groom were provided with enough mead to last one full moon cycle of 28 days. They were encouraged to consume this sweet wine to instill good luck in their marriage and it was also believed to promote fertility and virility.

The adoption of christianity into the culture saw many of these pagan traditions replaced or borrowed by the new faith. Many ceremonies that Norse christians practiced afterwards were a mixture of their ancient heathen beliefs and that of the new christianity.

Chapter 20 – Homosexuality in the Viking World

The Norse Sagas and poems have absolutely no mentioning of any homosexual relationships whatsoever.

But that does not mean that there weren't any gay or lesbian relationships amongst the people of the North.

It also does not mean that gay, lesbian, or bisexual relationships weren't tolerated either.

Christian influence, along with other male dominated cultures that came into the Norse world, frowned greatly upon homosexuality in any shape or form. This stigma has carried itself into the present day as there continues to be a tendency for people to retain some of their prejudices and attitudes towards homosexuality. A prejudice which has continued in the beliefs of many Muslims and Christians today which has heavily influenced modern European culture.

We already know this. It's obvious if you haven't had your head in the sand.

So why aren't there any records when we know that

LGBT individual and relationships existed in every culture on every part of the World throughout time. Well, first you must ask the question: why would they bother documenting a LGBT relationship? They didn't even document heterosexual marriages unless there was a significant reason to do so. Such a reason would be that of an heir who was significant enough worth mentioning marrying someone else significant enough worth mentioning.

The regular recording of marriages and births didn't occur until later when the local churches began to keep records of this information. Prior to that, hardly anything was recorded and all that we have of that time period are fragments of brief hints or mentions of forgotten kings and heroes. As far as LGBT relationships, there would be no reason to record them unless it influenced a significant event in history, and even then the record may cease to exist anymore.

The Ancient Maya and Ancient Norse share a commonality; most of their histories were burned and erased by forced religious conversion and indoctrination. Our information on these cultures, to this day, is very vague at best. If any records of LGBT relations were made, they had long been destroyed. Since then, only modern records exist.

They may be keen to record such relationships today, but not hundreds of years ago when the lack of piousness would cost you and your family's life.

The medieval era and its wars for religious dominance were unkind to any that did not follow the doctrine.

So what do we know of Old Norse views of LGBT relationships back then?

317

Jenny Jochens, in her research mentions, 'Norse who attempted to avoid marriage because of their sexuality were penalized in law'. The Roman historian Tacitus had described punishment in his De Origine et situ Germanorum when he mentioned cowards and homosexuals being drowned in bogs.

Is there more to the story of the famous bog bodies found from the Iron Age?

Jochens goes on to explain that this (punishments) was not only because of Christian influence and other male dominated cultures coming into the Norse world, but also because of the need to produce population. It was necessary to build your family and the clan or tribe you belonged to also needed to grow. Remember, it wasn't until the 20th century that we stopped having large families and raised the help to operate a simple family farm. There weren't any Wal*Marts around back then or very many clean water sources either for that matter. This led to shunning those who avoided marriage and reproducing.

A man who shunned marriage was termed fuðflogi (man who flees the female sex organ) while a woman who tried to avoid marriage was flannfluga (she who flees the male sex organ).

What about after someone had married and reproduced?

We simply don't know.

Lagertha portrayed as a bi-sexual in the television History channel series "The Vikings".

The social stigma of being LGBT was never emphasized in any records or sagas. The only records are of a social stigma placed upon those that did not reproduce and on those considered to be weak. As far as someone having a LGBT relationship who had already married and reproduced, we simple don't know.

What about the real Lagertha, was she LGBT?

Although the popular television series, "The Vikings" has recently introduced LGBT characters, the Norse Sagas do not mention any LGBT individuals or contain any stories of any gay or lesbian relationships whatsoever.

So, again, was Lagertha LGBT? We don't know and we will never know. In all truth, we really don't know all that much about her.

She, like almost all characters in the Norse Sagas, faded away and disappeared into history. It is quite possible that she could have been, which is probably the reason the television series "The Vikings" cast her as later being LGBT.

But it must not be forgotten, the television series is a historical fiction, which allows them to throw in the "what-ifs" where history hasn't any recordings or is very vague.

What about Old Norse name-calling and labels for LGBT individuals?

There is no direct reference to any LGBT individuals in any of the Sagas, but they do contain several instances of revenge enacted by men accused of being a passive partner in intercourse. This act was considered as being "unmanly" behavior and thus was a threat to a man's reputation as a leader or warrior.

(Note: There is no mention of those who didn't care what others thought.)

Although we haven't a known word for homosexual, we know a stigma was placed upon a male for being 'unmanly' if he played the role of a female.

Here is a reference used for "unmanly' behavior:

Ergi and argr are two Old Norse terms used to insult which denoted effeminacy or some other behavior considered unmanly. Argr (also ragr) is "unmanly" and ergi is "unmanliness". To accuse another man of being argr or ergi was a legal reason to challenge the accuser to a holmgang (a Viking duel).

Again, there is nothing mentioned about those who didn't care about what others thought or said. Being called

Argr was considered a legal reason to challenge someone to holmgang if you felt insulted by it, but it wasn't a requirement.

So what else do we have on the subject?

It has been suggested by Saxo Grammaticus, in his "Gesta Danorum," that Freyr, a Norse god of fertility, may have been worshiped by a group of homosexual or effeminate priests. This ties to the magical practices of the Vanir gods which were mocked by the Aesir gods, which they considered as being unmanly. Odin is mentioned as being a practitioner of seiðr, a form of magic considered shameful for men to perform, so was reserved for women. It is possible that the practice of seiðr involved passive sexual rites and Odin was taunted with this fact.

Additionally, some of the Norse gods were capable of changing sex at will, for example Loki frequently disguised himself as a woman. In one myth, he turned himself into a mare and after having sex with the stallion Svaðilfari, he gave birth to a foal which became Odin's eight-legged steed Sleipnir.

We have LGBT behavior in the Sagas and mythologies, but what about the view of the common Norseman? This is were we come back to the mentioning by the Roman historian, Tacticus.

The Roman historian, Tacticus, when describing Germanic law and offenses said that "moral infamy (cowardice and homosexuality) was punished by throwing the condemned into a bog."

When Tacticus wrote: 'ignavos et imbelles at corpore infames,' the 'corpore infames' part is translated as "unnatural prostitutes." This translation is believed to be how Tacitus referred to male homosexuality (unnatural prostitutes). He'd pointed out the differences in punishments whereas murderers and such would be publicly hanged and cowards and homosexuals drowned and/or buried. He explained the "glaring iniquities" must be exposed in plain sight, while "effeminacy and pollution" should best be buried and concealed.

So in this record, we know the Norse persecuted homosexuals during the Iron Age.

In Celtic mythology, there are no direct representations of any gay or lesbian relationship. Ancient Greek and Roman commentators attribute sexual activity between males, including pederasty, to pre-Christian Celtic tribes.

However, Peter Chicheri argues in Celtic sexuality: power, paradigms, and passion that homosexual affection was severely punished in Celtic culture due to influence from Christianity and suggests that any non-procreative sexual experience was subsequently expunged from mythic tales.

Which again brings us back to the fact that because of the bias doctrine of the recorders towards such relationships, there were no records made of them.

So where does that leave us on the subject?

We simply don't know what the average Norse individual thought on this subject. We know pre-Christian Norse were only concerned about reproducing and having descendants. We know that it was considered unmanly by men who were the submissive ones in a homosexual relationship. However, once someone reproduced there is nothing said of what they did with their lives afterwards.

After the christianization of the Norse, the rules of Christian doctrine at the time dominated social thinking and practices.

What about being called, 'Argr'? Doesn't that imply 'faggot' or 'queer'? Meaning they didn't like homosexuals,so as an insult they called you a faggot or argr?

No, argr means unmanly and is more like calling someone a 'wimp' or 'snowflake' in today's comparison with American English slang. For example: Are you going to be able to help me lift this, or do I need to go get my daughter to help me because you're too Argr to lift it?

Were there LGBT individuals during the Viking Age? Yes and before and after the Viking age until mankind ceases to exist. We know this because we know why more about human nature than we used to - that answer is obvious.

Were they persecuted for being LGBT? An individual that married and reproduced, we know nobody gave two bits of silver what they did. For those that avoided marriage and reproducing, we know they were shunned. Not because of sexuality, but because of not reproducing. Roman records give us an account going both ways - 1 attributing it to early non-Christian Celts and another describing it as being punished by death (bog drowning).

And this is all we know about it historically and from Norse Sagas.

Chapter 21 – Norse Trade

For as long as history can trace, the Norse have been well known as great traders. Their trade reach extended all the way to the Far East, through Russia and the Black Sea, to the Middle East. Regular trade thrived throughout Europe and in the Mediterranean. The Volga trade route along the Volga River connected Norse tradesmen all the way to the southern shores of the Caspian Sea to trade with Muslim countries, sometimes as far as Baghdad through the Euphrates and Tigris Rivers trade routes. The reach of the Norse was extensive.

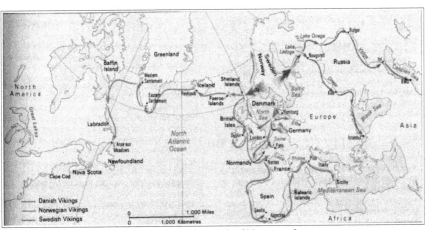

Map showing the reach of Norse trade.

Norse trade settlements were everywhere and even some scholars argue that during the Viking Age if many Norse traders were mislabeled in history as being marauding Viking raiders rather than the welcomed peaceful traders that most of them were.

In fact a great many modern cities throughout England, Scotland, Ireland, and across Europe actually began as welcomed peaceful Norse trading settlements, rather than the result of conquered entities. Skilled craftsmen and smiths were drawn to and even relocated to these trade centers as well.

The Norse had established regular ports and settlements where trade was held for the bartering of wares peacefully without any fear of molestation. Booths were built in these places so that native and foreign merchants alike could come and trade goods such as: furs, dried meats, skins, garments, grain, slaves, weapons, metals, and just about everything and anything. Götland was regarded as a major trade center for the North.

The trade ships heading to trade ports were free from Viking attacks, as plundering merchant vessels seems to have been considered unmanly. The Vikings, although having a reputation for raiding targets of opportunity, were not pirates.

Kaup-skip (trade ships), unlike the longships and other war vessels, were easily recognized as being ships of trade. Kaup-skips didn't have shields on the sides or war pennants and dragon ornaments of the war ships. The Viking longships stuck out as raiders or obvious vessels of war, whereas the knarrs and other merchant ships were obvious.

St. Olaf mentions trade ships having red and white striped sails to clearly identify them as peaceful trade vessels.

Replica Merchant Knarr with red and white striped sail marking it a trader ship.[96]

Traders (Kaufman) were respected and trading considered as a high calling. Even the sons of kings became famous warriors, seafarers, and traders.

Kings made trade agreements with traders and controlled some trade to an extent, such as domestic grain which was forbidden to be exported during hard years. Incentive was always made to keep traders coming and importing goods they couldn't get otherwise. This also allowed exportation of local goods, which opened the door for profit and taxes.

The Norse had a greater value for silver than they did for gold as far as trade standards were considered. The Norse used a monetary standard of what is called a 'Bang.' A 'Bang' was a spiral ring of silver that was used for trade before the regular presence of silver coins as a standard.

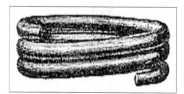

Drawing of a Norse "Bang" (ring).

The Bang values were measured by marks and aurar. One mark equaled eight aurar (1 oz.), one eyrir (singular for aurar) equaled eight ortugar, and one ortug (singular for ortugar) equaled ten (or sixty) penningar (singular penning, German: pfenning).

It was customary to weigh the medium of exchange by scales. With all things being equal, trust was a limited commodity. Even when the bang fell out of use, the new silver coin standards were weighed by scale to verify their weights when used in trading.

Chapter 22 – Norse Law and Government

The Norse had a class structure to their society. They had kings, priests, jarls and lords, freemen and slaves (thralls). Before the formal organization of the Scandinavian countries, the Norse were considered as a single people consisting of various family clans. Nordic society was set and organized with a deliberate means to the ends.

Norse social stratification was layered like most other cultures of the World. The Kings and royal families were at the very top of the class structure. Kings were generally placed and chosen by birth, as being the heirs to current kings in power over petty kingdoms.

Next down the social layer were the **Jarls**, who were the chiefs of the clans. The united family clans were ruled by Jarls until the end of the Viking Age when the separate Scandinavian nations emerged and became ruled by centralized kings. The Jarls were the chieftain landowners and warrior noblemen that pretty much controlled everything within their realms.

In the middle of the social layer cake were the **Karls**,

these were some of the freemen that owned large farms and owned slaves (thralls). Some of the Karls (freemen) worked as fishermen, craftsmen or boat builders as well. The typical Norseman was a Karl or freeman. At the coming of age, a young Karl will usually pledge their allegiance to the local Jarl and receive an arm band.

The lowest on the social layer were the **thralls** (slaves), who were considered as property and were often traded for large amounts of silver and gold. In most cases, about the value of a cow. In Norse terminology, "thralls" were male slaves and "ambátt" was the term for a female slave.

The mark of a thrall was to have closely cropped hair and they were to wear a white vadmal or kulf (coat) to distinguish themselves from freemen. Thralls and ambátts generally wore used clothing and clothes made from undyed cheap cloth. Colorful garments and embroidery was generally reserved for free Norse and nobility. The best to those who could afford it.

War captives from expeditions were the chief supply for slaves and they came from places such as: the European mainland, mostly from the various Frankish Kingdoms, Britain, Ireland, Scotland, Spain, and even from the various shores along the Mediterranean. Thralls were acquired from everywhere, the Norse did not discriminate.

However, thralldom wasn't a permanent placement in life if one could help it. Sometimes a thrall would be fortunate enough to be able to buy their freedom from their master. Those who belonged to wealthy masters were often allowed to work for themselves and eventually be able to acquire the means to buy their own freedom.

It was more commonplace for a slave to buy their freedom from their masters than to be set or made free. They either paid the full sum and became a freeman at once or paid part of the sum down and the rest owed by working off the debt for their master as an indentured servant. Freedmen enslaved by debt, so to speak.

Norse Law

Law and order is a necessity among all civilized people in order to peacefully live amongst each other. The Norse, like all other people, made their own laws to uphold peace and justice between them. At a gathering, they made their laws and passed their judgments on the law breakers at an assembly called the **Thing**.

The Thing (þing) was a public assembly of which all freemen would have a say in the governance of the land and people. The old Norse clans formed the Thing as a balancing structure for the leaders and freemen of the country to meet at least once a year, or as needed to settle matters.

The gathering of karls and jarls at the Thing dealt with electing or recognizing other jarls, clan leaders, or even kings. It was at the Thing meetings they made and enacted laws. This was also when they made judgments following the law before a law-speaker. A law-speaker was someone who memorized and recited the law to ensure it was followed.

The thing, although not consistent, held much of the same laws throughout the Norse world and weren't written but memorized by the Law-Speaker. It wasn't until the Christianization of the Norse was when the laws began to be written down.

A Thing assembly typically met in each region for a week during the Spring and Autumn. From around 902 AD onward in Iceland, of which there wasn't a king or centralized ruler, they held a meeting called an **Althing**.

The Norse Althing is considered to be Northern Europe's first national assembly, much like the centralized assemblies held by the Roman Senate in the Southern portion of Europe. However, unlike the Romans who only gave voice to the members of the Senate, the Norse Althing gave voice to all freeman.

The mutually agreed recognized powers bestowed to the Thing allowed it to set taxes, decide and confirm who was king and even argue and negotiate property disputes and marital affairs. It was also at the Thing that murders and other crimes were investigated.

An accused murderer might call upon the support of twelve men to swear his or her innocence, similar to what we consider a jury today. If the assembled freemen at the Thing meeting found the accused person to be guilty of murder, then the guilty person might be required to pay a fine (weregild) to the victim's family.

The concept of "Weregild" was a system of value that was placed on all humans and property. This was usually the value paid to affected families or owners of lost or damaged property. This is similar to a modern civil lawsuit today when a victim or a victim's family sues for monetary damages.

Sometimes a murderer would be found guilty and sentenced to death, or be banished and outlawed from the country for a set period of time (as was found with Erik the Red). The relatives of the victim could also demand that the wrongdoing be settled with a duel to the death, called a Holmgang.

Germanic Thing depicted by Marcus Aurelius (AD 193)[16]

Although the assembly of a Thing was often dominated by those with the most power and influence within the clans, such as chieftain jarls, kings, and the wealthy. The purpose of the Thing was to maintain universally recognized laws and try to give an equal voice amongst the people.

The very existence of the Thing was necessary to prevent social disorder and tribal feuds. Not an easy task as it was customary with the Norse that every member of a clan was obligated to avenge the injuries against its dead and mutilated. The Thing assembly prevented wars by allowing disputes to be peacefully heard and the demand for reparations be settled by means other than outright blood feuds between clans.

There were various levels of Thing assemblies, starting from the smaller local Things to the larger high leveled Althings where the local Things would be represented. Much like a representative congress or parliament, at the Althing a representative of the clan would attend and speak on behalf of their clan before the other clan representatives.

The location of a Thing assembly was often held at a religious site or other well known trade location. They were held at locations that were well known or near landmarks of the day so they could be found by distant members.

The Thing eventually evolved into Parliaments and still reflects the original concept that the Norse had for a representative government. The 'Storting' (Great Thing) is the name of the Norwegian Parliament. The Swedish speaking people of Finland are represented by the 'Folkting' ('Folks Thing' or Thing of the People) and the Sami are represented by the Sameting ('Sami Thing' or Thing of the Sami).

Disputes settled by Holmgang.

Not everything could be settled by talks and negotiation. This is when justice demanded the blood of another. A **Holmgang** was a duel and a commonly recognized way to settle disputes by the Norse. The word "holmgang" translates to "Island Walk" which refers to a hide or cloak which was about three meters long on each side that was staked to the ground of which was the boundaries that the participants had to stay in during the duel.

Egill Skallagrímsson engaging in holmgang with Berg-Önundr.[17]

Just like a duel, regardless of social status, a person could be challenged to settle a dispute by means of the Holmgang. The duel usually took place within three to seven days after the challenge and if one didn't show up, then the other was considered the winner of the dispute by default.

If it was the challenger of the holmgang that didn't show up, then they would be outlawed and labeled as a 'niðingr' (a coward that had no honor and was beneath everyone else – the lowest of low).

In some cases, a capable warrior could stand in behalf of a clearly outclassed participant of a holmgang. A person's more capable son or someone from their clan to champion on their behalf.

The results of a holmgang was not considered murder and thus a weregild was not required to be paid by the victor, even though it was seen in the film "The 13th Warrior," the victor of a dual had paid weregild after winning a duel.

Chapter 23 – Norse Warfare

The Roman Tactius wrote his observations on Germanic and Norse warfare practices. He made his observations from a gathering of collected tribes that were a mix of Germanic tribesmen and the Norse that had joined them. They had gathered to face the Roman Legions and Tactius made note of their methods and weaponry.

He wrote that he could tell by their weapons that iron wasn't plentiful. During their time of conflict with the Romans, that swords or broad lances were seldom used and that they generally carried a spear. Tactius noted that their spears had an iron blade that was short and narrow, but so sharp and manageable that they employed them either in close or distant fighting.

A spear and a shield were all the armor of their cavalry as well. Each man in the infantry had several missile weapons that they hurled at an immense distance. The warriors were either naked or lightly covered with a small mantle. There was no uniformity amongst the warriors and their shields were the only things decorated with the choicest of colors.

Few warriors were equipped with a coat of chain mail, and scarcely here and there was an individual wearing a helmet.

Their horses were not remarkable, having neither beauty nor swiftness and they were not trained in various formations as those practiced by the Romans. The cavalry either charged straight forward or wheeled once to the right in compact formations so that none of them were left behind.

Their principal strength relied on their infantry and in engagement would be intermixed with their cavalry. The agility of the foot soldiers proved that they were accustomed with the nature of equestrian combat. The most agile selected of their youth from the whole body and placed in the front of the lines.

Their battle lines were set up in wedge formations (boar formations). When they gave ground, as a prudent strategy rather than cowardice, they rallied and reformed. Fear was nonexistent in their ranks.

The greatest disgrace that can befall them is to abandon their shields and run from battle. A person branded with cowardice is neither permitted to join in religious rites nor enter assemblies. A coward after having escaped from battle is put an end by hanging.

Generals and warband leaders commanded less through the force of authority than by their own examples of valor. If a leader is daring, adventurous, and stood out in action, then they procured obedience by the admiration of the men they inspired.

Obedience in battle was not an act of military discipline, but by the instigation of the god who they believed to be present with warriors and watching them. They even carried certain images and standards taken from their sacred groves that represented their gods with them to the battlefield.

Tactius pointed out that their squadrons and battalions are not formed by men haphazardly collected, but by the assemblage of families and clans. One of the principal incentives to a warrior's courage is that they keep their families within hearing distance. This was particularly true with the Norse that came down to aid the Germanic tribes united. The incentive of victory was promised lands to resettle. For the Norse warriors that brought their families with nowhere else to go, it was victory or death.

The yells of their women and the cries of their children keep them brave and are also the most revered witnesses of each man's conduct in the face of the enemy. The women offer encouragement to those who are fighting and will even bring them food. To prevent the men from wavering in combat, the women rallied them by crying out as to what would happen to them and their children if they fail, such as being slain or enslaved by their opponents. This forced the warriors to fight even more ferociously, fighting to the death.

These women also tended to the relief of men's wounds with neither dread to the number of wounds nor searching out the gashes. They carried off their slain even while the battle remained undecided.

Chapter 24 – Norse Battle Tactics

The Norse had no formal standing army nor were they drilled in maneuver like the Roman Soldiers were. They did not fight in regular battle formations and weapons training started when they were youths as a regular part of life. The Norse were a warrior and ax culture. War was apart of their regular life and aspiring warriors would normally be armed by their lords or be rewarded by weapons by their lords. Lords waged war frequently to maintain a following and to maintain power against rivals.

A standard formation universally taught in preparation for battle was that young warriors would line up and interlock their shields to form a shield wall for protection. Typically a veteran warrior would have the younger inexperienced men form a shield wall on either side of them as they directed them in battle.

The leaders would have a special bodyguard, either hurscarls, ulfhednar, or berserkers. These were men consisting of their best veteran warriors that would stand behind the younger warriors and give support, direction, and encouragement.

In medieval Scandinavia the armies were formed by means of the 'leidang' (leiðangr in Old Norse). The leidang was a levy of free farmers that were conscripted into coastal fleets for seasonal excursions and in defense of the king or jarl's realm. The name 'fryd' was used by Germanic invaders and later. The fyrd were the conscripted men that filled the ranks of a local militia in which all freemen had to serve. The Anglo-Saxon army's ranks were the able-bodied men called into action within the realm of a king or jarl. Those who refused military service were probably executed for cowardice, but the laws claimed that they would be subject to fines or loss of their land. The ability to buy one's way out of going to battle hugely depended upon one's ability to pay such a sum.

The battle was usually began by throwing a spear over the enemy's line which was dedicated to Odin and then this was followed by a shower of spears, arrows, and a variety of other assorted missiles at the enemy line.

After a thorough missile barrage, the Norse would then try to break through and rout the opposition off the battlefield, which included trying to capture or kill the opposition's leader.

One of the battle formations that Norse warriors formed to break through the enemy's lines was called the **"svinfylking" (boar formation)**. The svinfylking was a battle formation where a group of heavily armed warriors (usually 20 to 30) would interlock their shields to form a wedge that had the center pointing towards the enemy's formation. The triangular wedge tapered back on each side from the center point to make a tight spearhead.

The Viking warriors would get in a "boar formation" wedge and then charge forward in this tight interlocked formation, spearheading into the enemy's line and breaking through by sheer force alone. Much like a boar's charge.

The sheer force of this charge was tenacious enough that the wedge would punch a hole right through the opposing force's shield wall or line formation. Spearheading through the enemy's formation in this "boar formation" would spread panic in the enemy and break their lines, turning the battle in favor for the Norseman. Several boar wedge formations could also be grouped side by side forming a zigzag line pattern against the enemy's line and break through their ranks.

Use of the "svinfylking" (boar formation) was unique to the Norse and early Germanic people at the time, as the Romans did not document this as a tactic used by the Saxons or any other culture they had come against.

The successful use of a formation of this type most probably required training and considerable practice. It was probably taught and practiced enroute to the battlefield by experienced warriors with irregular troops, as most called up Norse armies were levied (conscripted) and were usually farmers by trade. Although it is also likely to have been learned earlier, as most Norse men were taught and practiced the use of weapons and tactics from boyhood.

Often the Boar formation not only consisted of warriors

interlocked to form the wedge, but would have archers inside the formation behind the warriors on the front line protecting them. They would fire arrows and throw spears at the enemy as the formation bashed its way through.

The Svinfylking formation also would usually thwart cavalry charges on it because the horses and riders would be pushed aside from the wedge's center point and then attacked by the outer wedge's warriors with spears causing complete chaos among the cavalry's horses.

The Svinfylking formation's basic weakness was being flanked by the enemy, because the formation were based on its frontal point by sheer forward force. Additionally, if the boar formation didn't immediately break the enemy line from its forward wedged charge, then the men in the formation wouldn't hold very long and would be forced to break off and reform.

The Norse also formed the standard shield wall formation of the day as well. When in the shield wall, most attacks against your opponent are made overhead. The overhead attack is an attempt to hit over the top of the enemy's shield while aiming at their head and trying to bash or split them in the head, neck, or shoulders. Most thrusts while in a shield wall formation would go against the enemy's shield and open yourself up to similar attacks as you must open a small gap in the wall to allow you to thrust.

Spears are generally used effectively with two hands while thrusting at the enemy chest and waist level. Spears were best used by warriors behind the shield wall that were thrusting and targeting enemy warriors that were involved in another fight. However, this move also exposed a spearman to similar attacks from the opposing side using similar methods. A shield wall was essentially shoved, hacked, and stabbed down by sheer force.

Once the shield wall was broke down, individual fights ensued and were most likely settled by using opportunistic wounding blows that left an opponent disabled but not dead – out of the fight and no longer a threat.

Quite often, legs and arms would be the only exposed targets that would be easy to hit. Obviously the limbs were the most tempting target against a warrior that was wearing a mail shirt or other body armor that would also be protected by their shield. The head was usually crowned with a helmet, so the exposed legs, arms, face and neck would be the best areas to target.

Many of the fallen warriors are usually found with major leg injuries where they were incapacitated and then left behind to bleed to death on the field as the battle went on to be decided. It was a common practice of the day for the victor to return and slay the enemy's wounded that remained.

Beyond special formations and tactics, the Vikings also had special troops that would reap fear into the enemy and instill encouragement on the friendly side. One kind of these special warriors were the infamous **berserkers**.

Berserkers were warriors that would work themselves into a battle frenzy so much that they ignored pain and injury. Often, there would be many berserkers formed into groups and would be set loose on the enemy as shock troops. The berserkers believed that the god Odin would personally protect them from harm and so they often wore no armor into battle.

There is only speculation as to what a berserker really was, as there are no accurate records of them. The word berserk comes from two words, 'ber' meaning bear and 'serk' meaning shirt. This probably means that these battle frenzied super warriors more likely wore bear skin shirts to battle as a symbol of their status.

Another special kind of warrior were the **Úlfhéðinn** (plural **Ulfhednar** or in Old Norse *Úlfhéðnar*), meaning **"wolf's head wearer."** These elite Norse warriors had attributes similar to that of a berserker. These warriors were also sometimes described in Norse Sagas as being special warriors of the god Odin himself.

The Ulfhednar were identifiable by the pelt of a wolf or a wolf's head that they wore on their heads when they went into battle. Just like berserkers, these elite Ulfhednar warriors would whip themselves into a fearsome battle frenzy and were often used as the personal bodyguards of a king or jarl chieftain.

Another special warrior worth mentioning were the **Huscarls** (Húskarlar in Old Norse). They were "household troops" that were often the most experienced and best equipped warriors around. These special warriors were usually of freemen (Old Norse 'Karl' or Old English 'Carl') status who had sworn loyalty oaths to be professional warriors in the service of a jarl or king, typically as personal bodyguards.

It was normal for them to be placed in the front of battle ranks or used as shock troops. Their presence would bolster the morale of the other warriors as they also gave battle guidance with their experience. They're also used as completely separate units that operated behind the main battle lines and provided an instant reactionary force to the army's flanks or reinforcing areas on the battle line which may be weakening on the front. It fell to the Huscarls the task of defending the battle standard and the army's leader.

With all these tactics and methods of using special shock troops, a Viking Age leader was expected to lead his army from the front. After having achieved the respectable position of leadership by their skillful use of weaponry and battle tactics, a Viking leader was expected to stand in the amidst of a battle, personally leading the charge.

The Norse were a superstitious people and would depend on the leader's personal fortunes and favor of the gods. If the leader fell in battle, it was likely that his army would withdraw or rout from the field, although his personal bodyguard (the huscarls) were expected to stand over him and die with their leader.

It was also normal for the leaders of Viking Age armies to seek each other out on the battlefield and achieve a quick victory by slaying and cutting off the head of the opposing army's leader. Although this tactic wasn't usually successful, there have been several cases where the huscarls of one army would charge and breach the enemy's shield wall and slay the opposing side's leader. This was presumably part of a charge that was led personally by the earl or king. A Viking king or jarl led by example, not by title. If they were not brave and battle worthy, they would not be followed.

Chapter 25 – Glíma, Viking Martial Arts

Viking warriors had the skills to survive against various forms of warfare and combat.

The reason for the Vikings fighting prowess is found in the way they trained both with and without weapons. For combat without weapons, the Norse had developed a martial arts system called Glima.

Glíma, the ancient wrestling style.

To be a good fighter and survive the unpredictability of combat, a warrior must know how to defend themselves unarmed against an armed opponent.

The Norse developed Glima, which is a self-defense system that employs throws, blows, kicks, chokes, locks, pain techniques and some weapon techniques. It is comparable with the best martial arts systems from all around the world. The word glíma in Old Norse means "glimpse" or "flash," which describes the system's techniques...speed.

The Viking martial art is so named because the methods bring down their opponents with lightening quick moves and tricks using both feet and hands.

This style of combat training helped develop the strength, reflexes, endurance and courage that Viking warriors needed to survive in combat. Glima also builds self confidence and for Norse children, Glima training usually began at around 6 or 7 years of age.

Glima self-defense training was the foundation of a Viking warrior and these techniques are still practiced today in Scandinavia, Europe, North America, and South America.

Glima is mentioned in the Prose Edda in the book of Gylfaginning when the Æsir god Thor took his journey to Utgards-Loki and was defeated in a wrestling match by the female jötunn Elli (Old Norse "Elli" means "old age").

Yes, Thor was beaten by an old woman in hand to hand unarmed combat...but there's more to the story as to why.

In Gylfaginning, Thor and his companions Loki and
Þjálfi are in the hall of the giant Útgarða-Loki where they
meet difficult challenges testing their strength and skill.
Thor has just been humiliated in a drinking challenge and
wants to get even.

*Then said Thor: 'Little as ye call me, let any one come up now
and wrestle with me; now I am angry.' Then Útgarda-Loki
answered, looking about him on the benches, and spake: 'I see no
such man here within, who would not hold it a disgrace to wrestle
with thee;' and yet he said: 'Let us see first; let the old woman my
nurse be called hither, Elli, and let Thor wrestle with her if he
will.*

*She has thrown such men as have seemed to me no less strong
than Thor.' Straightway there came into the hall an old woman,
stricken in years. Then Útgarda-Loki said that she should grapple
with Ása-Thor. There is no need to make a long matter of it: that
struggle went in such wise that the harder Thor strove in
gripping, the faster she stood; then the old woman attempted a
hold, and then Thor became totty on his feet, and their tuggings
were very hard.*

A depiction of Elli wrestling Thor (1919) by Robert Engels.

Yet it was not long before Thor fell to his knee, on one foot. Then Útgarda-Loki went up and bade them cease the wrestling, saying that Thor should not need to challenge more men of his body-guard to wrestling.

Glima is so important to Norse society, Thor is also the god of wrestling.

As with people of every age and nationality, the Norse loved sports.

Glima was not just used for self defense and combat, but was also a sport. Wherever Vikings gathered, Glima was a big part of the entertainment. It was the most widespread sport in the Viking Age and there were several variations of Scandinavian folk wrestling, such as: Lausatök, Hryggspenna, and Brokartök.

Glima is practiced by men and women of all ages.

The original Norwegian settlers in Iceland took Viking wrestling and the Glima combat systems with them, according to the Jónsbók law book from 1325 AD. In the Icelandic medieval book of laws known as Grágás (Gray Goose Laws), which refers to a collection of earlier Norwegian laws, there were rules for wrestling. The Icelandic populace has taken very good care of their Norwegian heritage, and Glima there is almost unchanged since Viking times.

Water wrestling was a wrestling match in the water and was the most popular form of swimming competition. The idea was to keep the opponents head under water until he gave up, and such matches could last for hours.

The skilled variants of Glíma wrestling, called Brokartök, Hryggspenna, and Lausatök, have complex rules with competitors divided into several classes based on strength and skill.

Brokartök (Trouser-grip)

Brokartök is by far the most widespread form of glima in Iceland and Sweden and it is this version of glima that is Iceland's national sport.

Brokartök Glima wrestling

The Brokartök form of glima favors technique over strength. Each of the two wrestlers wear a special belt around the waist and separate additional belts on the lower thighs of each leg, which connect to the main belt with vertical straps. A fixed grip is then taken with one hand in the belt and the other in the trousers at thigh height. From this position the glima-wrestler attempts to trip and throw his opponent. In this style of glima, a thrown wrestler may attempt to land on his feet and hands and if he succeeds in doing so he has not lost the fall. The winning condition in this type of glima is to make the opponent touch the ground with an area of the body between the elbow and the knee.

There are four points that differentiate Brokartök from other forms of wrestling:

The opponents must always stand erect.

The opponents step clockwise around each other (looks similar to a waltz). This is to create opportunities for offense and defense and to prevent a stalemate.

It is not permitted to fall down on your opponent or to push him down in a forceful manner, as it is not considered sportsman-like.

The opponents are supposed to look across each other's shoulders as much as possible because it is considered proper to wrestle by touch and feel rather than sight.

The core of the system are eight main brögð (techniques) which form the basic training for approximately 50 ways to execute a throw or takedown.

Brokartök glíma is different from all other ethnic grips in three ways:

- Upprétt staða - Pursuers shall remain upright. The positioning in many of the ethnic grips sports often resembles a setsquare but in Brokartök glíma that is called ousting or "bol" and is banned.

- Stígandinn - Brokartök glíma involves steps, which involves contestants stepping forth and back like they are dancing in a clockwise motion. Stígandi is one of the characteristics of Glíma and designed to avoid a standstill and create opportunities for offence and attack.

- Níð - It is forbidden in Brokartök glíma to tail your opponent to the floor or push your opponent down with force. That is considered to be unsportsmanlike and opposing the nature of Glíma as a sport for honorable sportsmen and women. The Brokartök glíma sportsman or sportswoman shall conquer his or her opponent with a Glíma grip so well implemented that it suffices in a "bylta", which forces your opponent to fall to the ground without any further action. The concept "níð" does not exist in other ethnic grip sports.

Hryggspenna (Backhold wrestling)

Hryggspenna is more similar to other styles of wrestling and is considered to be more a test of strength than of technique. In Hryggspenna the opponents take hold of each other's upper body and whoever touches the ground with any part of the body except the feet has lost.

Lausatö (Loose-Grip or Free-Grip)

Lausatök is the most widespread form of Glima practiced and there are regular competitions of this form of Glima, such as the Norwegian Glima Championship. In Lausatök Loose-Grip wrestling, the contestants may use the holds they wish. Lausatök, or Løse-tak in Norwegian, is quite aggressive and differs in many ways from the other styles of Viking wrestling. This style was banned in Iceland for a period of about 100 years before being taken up again recently, within the last generation.

Lausatök, or Løse-tak in Norwegian, is quite aggressive and differs in many ways from the other styles of Viking wrestling. Lausatök comes in two forms: A version for self-defense or combat and a version for friendly competition.

In both, all kinds of wrestling techniques are allowed, but in the friendly version they are still taught to be executed in a way so they won't cause the opponent injury. In such a friendly match the winner is considered the one who is standing tall while the other is lying on the ground. This means that if both the opponents fall to the ground together the match will continue on the ground by the use of techniques to keep the other down while getting up.

Excessive use of techniques aimed at deliberately injuring an opponent is frowned upon in sport Lausatök glíma. It is enough to use glima techniques that send an opponent to the floor, to inflict 'pain' on the floor, to 'slap' and opponent as opposed to 'punch' and kicks aimed at shocking an opponent rather than breaking bones. Such actions are considered níð; unsportsmanlike and opposing the nature of Glíma as a sport for honorable sportsmen and women. The concept "níð" does not exist in other ethnic grip sports.

Old Norse: níð (Old English: níþ) was a term for a social stigma implying the loss of honor and the status of a villain. A person affected with the stigma is a níðing (Old Norse: níðingr, Old English: níðing, níðgæst).

Surrounding glima is a code of honor called drengskapur that calls for fairness, respect for and caring about the security of one's training partners. You do not injure your opponent in the training and glima as a sport.

Lausatök glima for combat and self-defense was the basis for the Vikings fighting expertise and also includes techniques against weapons. In order to have a structured form of unarmed combatives against striking weapons, the Vikings had to know how to use a variety of weapons, such as sword, axe, spear, seax, long seax, stick and knife. The foundation for the use of these weapons is found in Lausatök combat glima.

As Brokartök is the most widespread form of Glima in Iceland and Sweden, Lausatök is by far the most widespread form of Glima practiced in Norway, Europe and North America. There are regular competitions in this form of Glima such as the Norwegian Glima Championship.

In Lausatök Loose-Grip wrestling, the contestants may use the holds they wish and it is practiced both outdoors and indoors year round in Scandinavia.

Glíma as a sport has also gone by the name of Scandinavian Wrestling and Viking Wrestling (Vikingbryting).

Chapter 26 – Norse Armor and Weaponry

So how did the Norse arm themselves? What we know of Norse weaponry and armor is from what we've found predominately in grave sites from the early periods. Additionally, we get information from depictions that were carved on stones, tales in the Sagas, and from legal texts written in the later periods which give us a general idea and paint clues for us to piece together about how Norsemen armed for combat during the Viking Age.

During the time the laws made by the Gulating (Old Norse: Gulaþing) in Norway, Denmark, and Sweden required that every able-bodied man should own weapons according to his status.

In Norway, a sword or ax, spear and shield must be owned and maintained. In Sweden and Denmark, this was a sword, spear, shield and iron helmet that was to be for each man. Additionally, it was common for some laws to required a mail shirt or protective jerkin and a bow and 24 arrows be provided for each bench seat in a ship or that a local chieftain be required to provide these items.

As part of a coming of age ceremony, a Norse freeman

would receive an armring from his lord, pledging his loyalty and service to that lord. That is, a pledge to come to war or raid when that lord called them to. This was a standard practice and a part of Norse culture. Bearing an arm ring was also a status symbol. Some lords would also reward their new subjects awarded arm rings that had sworn oaths to them with weapons. The use of weapons was also apart of life. From an early age, a lad would train in the use of weaponry as a part of everyday life. This was a common practice and custom among the different Norse clans.

So what were these weapons? The Shield, the Ax, and the Spear. Proficiency with the bow was a bonus and a skill most likely already being mastered and in use for hunting.

Chapter 27 – The Shield

There is Skaldic poetry that is specifically dedicated to shields. They are known as the "shield poems." The shield was as much a part of Norse culture as was the ax. It was well developed and one of the best shields made.

The Viking shield was very different from that of the shields used around the World. The shields were made from wood with a metal center and were colorfully painted. Upon first glance, there doesn't seem to anything special about these shields but you'd be very wrong to think so.

The shield designed by the Norse was a superior and well thought out concept. It was not made from solid wood as were the other culture's shields of the day. This is in contrast of what you would think you wanted from a shield. Something solid enough to block hits from weapons and arrows. Something durable enough to protect you. Something strong enough to protect you from the swing of a sword, thrust of a spear, or an arrow with your name on it.

The Viking shield was a brilliant concept and ahead of its time. It was actually made from what we would think of as soft and flimsy wood like fir, alder and poplar. Norse shields were not made from heavy oak or other known solid woods. In the Sagas, it is written that they were to be made from 'flexible' woods such as linden, lime, or basswood. Wow, that's a flimsy wood to be making a shield from. Why would the fierce Vikings use such a flimsy wood, instead of hard woods like their opponents?

The Norse chose this flexible wood because, unlike the hard woods such as oak, Viking shields weren't inclined to split so easily upon a successful hard impact. When there was a successful split of the Norse shield by a weapon, the fibers of the wood tended to bind around blade which prevented them from cutting any deeper unless a lot more pressure was applied. Something you definitely didn't want to be wasting your time doing in combat. Hesitating in attempts to finish splitting your opponent's shield gave your opponent the opportunity to split your head open.

Another characteristic about the wood the Norse chose to use for their shields was the fact that instead of bearing the blunt of a solid hit, which would also cause the shield to split or shatter, the 'flimsy' wood of the Viking shield would bounce and absorb some of the impact. This made the shield more effective.

They also reinforced their shields with leather quite frequently and occasionally had iron around the rim for added strength.

The shield wasn't made of a single sheet of wood, but of

planks. The shield from the Gokstad ship was about 3 feet in diameter and shows us clearly how the shield planks were laid. The planks were tightly formed running along the grain of the wood. This caused blows against the grain to bounce back, adsorbing the energy and blows along the grain would grip the weapon.

A drawing of a shield from the Gokstad ship.[18]

An addition to the flexibility of the Viking shield that helped repel hits was that it was painted. It wasn't painted for looks or uniformity like the Greek or Roman shields were with identical markings and color to identify them to their lord or unit. The Viking shield was painted specifically for a function other than identification. One thing you'll notice about a Viking shield is that in a band of warriors, they all had different color shields with different markings. Markings that were painted on their shields that had no real significance in relation to marking who they were or who they belonged to.

This was because the Viking shield was painted for a reason that had nothing to do with units or cohorts. It was painted for the sole purpose of hiding the grains of the wood of the shield. If an opponent were able to see the wood grains on a shield, they'd be able to figure out where to hit it in order to split it.

The Viking shield was intentionally painted to conceal the wood grains, it was not painted to look pretty or to mark their loyalties. The cleverness of this was when their opponent went to strike the shield, they had no hint as to the shield's most vulnerable place or where to strike or hit it.

Add the fact that the Norse shield was flexible and would absorb the hits and even would bounce their opponent's weapon back at them. If an attacker did get a lucky hit along the grain of the shield's wood, then their blade would most likely get caught in the wood's fibers and instantly give the shield wielder an advantage over them.

There is one more clever thing about the Viking shield, the center part of it called the shield boss was made of metal. Usually the shield boss was made of iron and was concave with the shield and had a handle inside of it.

The advantage of this was that it was like having a fist made of iron. You could bash the enemy with it and even use it to parry and block blows.

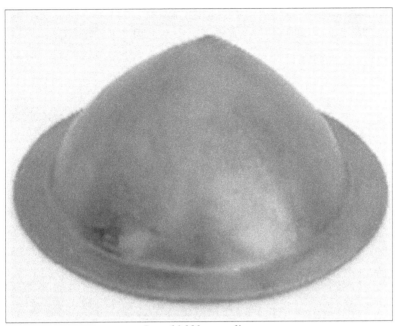

Iron shield boss replica.

The shield center was the primary place where the wielder would use to repel and block strikes against them. The shield boss having a handle made it easier to wield as it fell upon the natural place in the hand and would also serve as an iron fist, so to speak, to strike an opponent with the shield.

With the wood being light weight and the handle also being in the center and formed with iron, the shield was easier to wield and use than the shields used by other nations. Other nations such as the Greeks and Romans, strapped their shields to their forearms which made them difficult to wield in melee combat.

Modern replica of a Viking Shield.[19]

Viking shields were also heavily used in defensive and offfensive formations. The skjaldborg (shield fort) was a main defensive formation where Norse warriors would create a line of interlocked shields and thrust their spears at their opponents. And of course, the previously mentioned Norse shield formation called the "svinfylking" (boar formation), where warriors created a wedge formation and charged forward to burst through the enemy's front line or even thwart an enemy calvary advance on them.

Chapter 28 – The Ax

The ax is probably the most characteristic weapon of the Vikings. One cannot think of the Vikings without thinking about the ax. The Norse evolved into an ax culture during their Stone Age period. Axes of several types have been found in many burial sites, as the ax was not just a weapon but also a tool. It was a common item among the Norse. Axes have even been found in female burial sites. Depictions of the ax are also shown on several carved stones.

The head of the ax was generally formed from wrought iron with its sharpened edge made from steel. It took less skill to forge an ax, so even the poorest of the Norse could afford one. An ax was needed for simple daily life such as wood cutting and splitting. So in a time of need for battle, even a wood ax could be used for battle if the need arose.

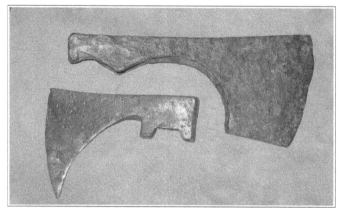

Viking Bearded Ax (top), German Horseman's Ax (bottom).[20]

Axes specifically meant for battle were designed and made differently than those of farm and woodsman axes. Battle axes were designed to cut and smash through a man. Even designed to bash apart shields and split through a helmet. Some battle axes evolved into long handled, two-handed axes that could smash through shield and armor.

Contrary to the fictional stereotype and as cool looking as they are, double headed battle axes were not made by the Norse. Almost all axes forged by the Norse were single bladed.

One of the more popular battle axes was the Dane Ax (Danish Ax). It was an ax that consisted of a wide, thin blade that was 'pronounced' at both the toe and heel of the bit with the toe swept inward for better shearing power.

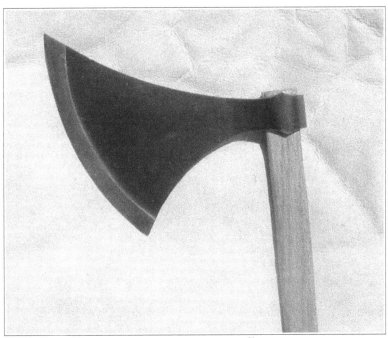

Replica Danish ax head.[21]

The cutting surface of the battle ax varied between 20 centimeters to 30 centimeters (8 to 12 inches) and the average weight was around one kilogram to two kilograms (two to four pounds). It was lightweight and resembled more of a meat cleaver than a wood ax that had devastating cutting ability.

The half (handle) of the ax ranged from 0.9 meters to 1.2 meters (3 to 4 feet) long. This enabled a powerful and controlled swing with the edge of the blade just right to cut through whatever it hits.

Dane Ax on Bayeux Tapestry.[22]

The Bayeux Tapestry shows us exactly the size of a two handed Danish Ax in comparison to the size of the wielder. The battle axes were shoulder level in length with slightly curved handles giving the blade edge a better cutting angle.

Chapter 29 – The Bow

The Norse used bows (Old Norse: bogi) predominately for hunting and in many cases for battle, especially in battles or attacks at sea.

Even though nautical battles were not common to the Norse who preferred to fight on land, bows were indeed used in sea battles. They could use their bows to fire at an enemy awaiting them on the beach as they tried to land. They used the bow to attack other ships by firing arrows and throwing other missiles from their ship at the enemy's ship as they tried to clear the decks of men so the ship could be taken.

Ólaf's Saga describes the bow being used in a fight at sea in the Battle of Svölðr in 1000 AD. Einarr Þambarskelfir, an archer of King Ólaf, shot an arrow at Jarl Eirik who was in an opposing ship and hit the tiller above his head so hard that it penetrated the wood through to the arrow's shaft.

Another shot followed with an arrow that penetrated all the way through his stool with the barbs coming out of the other side. The Jarl then ordered a man on his ship named Fin to fire back at the 'tall man by the mast,' whereas he did and hit Einarr Þambarskelfir's bow and broke it in two.

It is said that King Ólaf's ship was eventually overtaken and that King Ólaf of Norway, rather than die in the hands of his enemy, jumped over the side of the ship in full armor and drown.

One of the land battle tactics commonly employed by the Norse was to hurl and fire various missile weapons at the enemy line prior to charging. After of course, throwing a single spear over the enemy line in the name of Odin first. Gaining favor of the gods was an important ritual of battle to the Norse.

Vikings often used bows to effectively fire arrow volleys at their enemy. At short ranges it is said that a Norse arrow could pierce mail armor, but at longer ranges they only threatened the warriors not wearing armor. But fighting the enemy at a safe distance wasn't a concern to the Norse, who would much rather get within melee range.

The Norse used short bows that were made of yew, elm, or ash and varied in size from around 1 meter to about 2 meters long. Some late examples have been found of Norse composite bows that had been strengthened with either horn or iron. At Hedeby, an important Viking trading settlement that flourished from the 8th to 11th centuries, a complete bow measuring 1.92 meters long made of yew was found. It is estimated that this war bow had a draw weight of well over 100 lbs. Most replica bows of this period have a draw weight of 100 to 130 lbs.

On average, Norse bows were able to shoot an arrow up to 200 meters. The distance an arrow traveled in a single bowshot was a commonly used unit of measurement in Viking Age Iceland. For example, in the medieval Icelandic law book, Grágás, it was required that when the court confiscated an outlaw's property, that it be within an ördrag (the distance of an arrow in a single bowshot) of the outlaw's home. The Grágás later defines an "ördrag" to be 200 "faðmar" (approximately 480 meters or about 1575 feet).

Norse arrowheads were usually of iron and made in a variety of shapes and sizes as well. Many arrowheads have been found at several Viking Age Icelandic house sites that varied in design and size, even a forked arrowhead that was probably used for bow fishing. The average lengths of Norse arrowheads ranged from 10 to 15 centimeters (4-6 inches).

Most arrowheads had a tang that allowed it to be driven into a hole of a hardwood shaft and then secured in place with cord and pitch. It is estimated that the arrow shafts were probably 70 to 80 centimeters (28 to 32 inches) long and about 10 millimeters (3/8 inch) in diameter.

Njáls Saga tells of the use of a bow by the Icelandic hero, Gunnar Hámundarson that single-handedly defended his home against an attack led by Gizurr hvíti. The hero Gunnar used his bow from a loft in the upper level of the house, to kill and wound ten of his opponents before his bow string was cut by one of the attackers. It is said that he asked his wife Hallgerður for a lock of her hair to mend the bow, but Gunnar had slapped her previously so she vindictively refused. He was then forced to fight his attackers off in hand to hand combat where he was killed.

Chapter 30 – The Spear

The spear was the favored weapon of the Norse all-father and god of war, Odin. Odin had a spear that was made from the World tree Yggdrasil named Gungnir. The Prose Edda says that Odin will carry his spear Gungnir and lead the bravest that had fallen on the battlefield and had been taken to the Halls of Valhalla. These fallen warriors from Valhalla are called the Einherjar and Odin will lead them to the battlefield during the Ragnarok event.

The spear held great symbolic importance to the Norse warrior and was the most common weapon during the early Viking Age. Spears were also cheap and easy to produce because they could be made with inferior steel. Notwithstanding, they were a very effective weapon that required minimal skill or training to use.

Most Viking spearheads were long and thin and ranged from 30 to 50 centimeters (12 to 20 inches) long. The Norse used a length of a bladed spearhead that is generally reserved in modern times for boar hunting.

Although many spears would be thrown into enemy lines, they were just as useful when employed as thrusting or slashing weapons. The length of the spear shafts averaged from 2 to 2.5 meters (6 ½ to 8 feet) long and were usually made of strong durable ash. A typical Norse spear was a long bladed spearhead mounted on a sturdy shaft.

Spearheads with wings are called krókspjót (hooked spears) in the sagas. Some larger spearheads that could be used for cutting were called höggspjót (hewing spear).

The Norse used a variety of spear types for varied kinds of combat fighting methods.

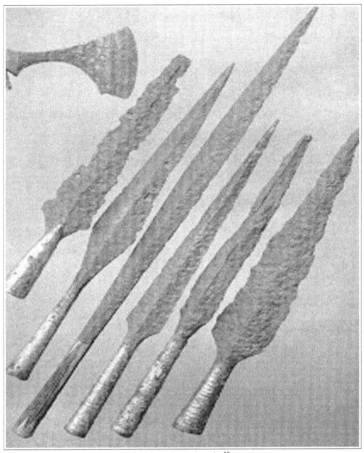

Viking Spearheads.[23]

It is likely that such spears were used in two hands. Although it has been suggested that these could be used in conjunction with a shield, it is perhaps more likely that they were used without a shield once the combat closed beyond the area in which missiles could be useful.

Lighter weight, shorter spears with narrower spearheads were used as javelins in the opening rounds of a battle. Some of these throwing spears were barbed as well. The smaller throwing spears have been found in large numbers by archeologists as the Vikings would hurl a salvo of missiles at their enemy as the lines closed.

The Viking Sagas tell of many heroes removing the pin that held the spearhead in place before throwing it, so the enemy couldn't reuse the weapon. These smaller spears could have also be used as a single-handed weapon with a shield. While the longer spears with the broader spearhead were probably used with two hands.

Chapter 31 – The Atgeir

The Atgeir was a 'spear-like spear' that was used before and through the Viking Age. One reference to the atgeir comes from Icelandic Sagas about the Viking hero Gunnar Hámundarson who used an atgeir in Njál's Saga that would "sing" by making a ringing sound when it anticipated 'bloodshed' when it was used in battle.

The atgeir, sometimes referred to as a "mail-piercer" or "hewing-spear," was a type of polearm used throughout Scandinavia and Norse occupied areas during the Viking Age.

In English it is described as a kind of "halberd," but it more likely resembled a bill or glaive. The word 'atgeir' is often used to describe some typical European halberds. Additionally, some multipurpose spearheaded staves of the time period are called atgeirsstafir.

Kampen ved Rangaa.

Gunnar Hámundarson fights his ambushers at Rangá.[24]

Beyond description from old records and sagas, there have not been any atgeirs discovered by archeologists to get a clear picture as to what one was beyond the assumption of it being a spearheaded type of polearm.

Chapter 32 – The Sword

A good sword was the obvious weapon of choice by the Viking Age warrior who could afford one. Swords were found throughout Europe and it was common for a sword blade to be imported from a Frankish workshop with the hilt fittings made locally.

The most coveted of all Viking swords was a sword with the letters ULFBERHT inlaid into its blade. These very well made, high quality blades were often called an Ulfberht sword. The secrets behind the making of this special sword had long been lost for a 1000 years and they were only produced from around 800 AD to 1000 AD. The Ulfberht sword was made of the best craftsmanship and had a sharpness and strength that was unmatched. It literally was the best sword ever made in Europe and it was a Viking sword.

The typical viking sword of the day had impurities, such as slag which made it weaker including the fact that it was forged with low carbon. This made the sword soft and brittle. The steel was of poor quality and would break in battle. The typical early blacksmith of the day didn't make slag free steel. They couldn't get their fires hot enough to over 3000°f which separates the slag and allows more carbon to mix in evenly.

However, the Ulfberht sword had three times the carbon content of other medieval swords and were relatively clear of slag, making them what's called crucible steel. Crucible steel required very high heat temperatures that nobody in Europe knew how to do at the time. The method behind forging the Ulfberht sword was a closely guarded secret.

There is no archeological evidence anywhere in Europe that shows that this type of steel production was carried out. However, the Norse, especially in the Viking Age had a trade reach like no other culture and it is assumed that this steel was traded for from the Far East, possibly in Central Asia.

There have been Buddhas and rings with the name Allah inscribed on them found in Viking digs. So we know that the Norse had established trade in the Far East along the Volga Trade Route due to these objects being in Scandinavia during this time period. Some believe the steel may have originated from Iran and was traded and brought back to Norse blacksmiths who made the sword under secret conditions.

The word Ufberht actually had two crosses in it, one before the word and one at the ending before the "t." Whereas it actually spelled "+-U-F-B-E-R-H-+-T." Archeologists have not been able to determine the meaning behind the word, *Ufberht*. It is unknown if it was the name of the designer or meant something entirely different.

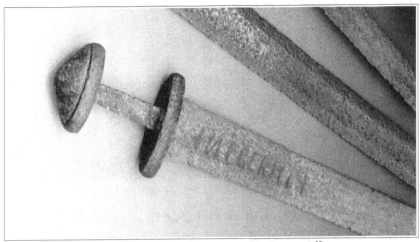

Remains of an +Ulfberh+t sword in Denmark.[25]

Getting your hands on a real Ulfberht sword was difficult and extremely expensive and there were many counterfeits.   Most swords of the time were made from low carbon steel by means of pattern welding. A method where the central section of the blade was made from twisted rods of iron and pounded together forming a strong and pliable core, then a harder (but more brittle) edge was then welded to the core.

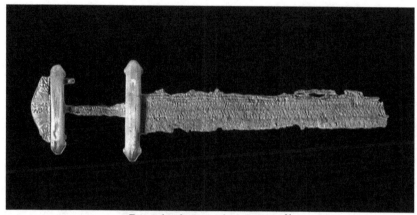

Example of pattern forged sword.[26]

When the quality and knowledge of iron smelting improved, in addition to purer and more regular sources of iron becoming more readily available, the method of pattern welding was discontinued.

Chapter 33 – Viking Armor

The Norse warrior often wore chain mail armor whenever he could get his hands upon a set. Although chain mail wasn't as common as one may think. This was due to the amount of iron needed and the time it took to make the armor in the first place. This made chain mail expensive and was generally only wore by those who could afford it.

Chain mail grew more available when iron became more readily available and smelting techniques significantly improved. It would still take many hours upon hours of chain mail pattern linking to make a complete chain mail shirt.

The speed of chain mail manufacturing improved with the wealth of the blacksmith, as he'd have plentiful access to iron and many skilled thralls tasked to linking the mail. A task that was tedious at every step, as rod had to be first made from iron scraps. Then countless numbers of chain links cut from the rod to be shaped into rings and then 'knitted' in a precised pattern to create the unique and superior chain mail only the Norse made.

There's a fragmented, yet mostly complete example of a Norse chain mail tunic that's been found at the Gjermundbu burial site. Although many partial examples of chain mail exist and there are several historical recordings of Norse use of chain mail; The chain mail found at the Gjermundbu site is the only nearly complete set that's ever found.

Brynja or coat of chain mail, found in Thorsberg moor, Germany.[27]

The Norse mentioned chain mail in their Sagas which they called, 'byrnie' or 'brynja.' These were long tunics of

410

chain mail armor that reached below the waist to protect the wearer from sword cuts.

Of course chain mail armor alone wasn't enough protection. It was essential to wear thick padding underneath the mail to absorb the force of a sword or ax blow. You also needed protection from spear and arrow strikes.

Reindeer hide is said to have been worn by the Norse underneath chain mail and was used alone as armor as well. Reindeer hide was reputedly said to be more effective even than chain mail. Quite often, reindeer hide would've been worn under chain mail for padding and to serve as additional protection. More correctly though, the Norse warrior would have wore reindeer hide armor with chain mail over it as additional protection.

Some examples of viking era chain mail are made up of interlocking rings that were riveted together. But the better chain mail shirts were of alternating slag rings and riveted rings. This made the chain mail armor stronger. A tribute to Norse ingenuity.

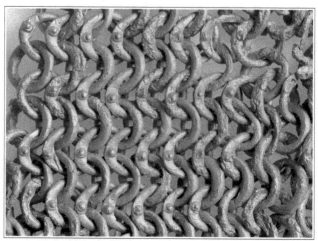
Chainmail sample found in Gjermundbu, Norway.[28]

Scale armor or lamellar armor was occasionally obtained from the East and had been replicated by Norse armorers by using either leather or metal scales. Pieces of scale or lamellar armor have been found at Norse burial sites in: Birka, Sweden, Kertch (Crimea), Ukraine (dated 5th century), and Krefeld-Gellup, Germany (dated 6th century) and Niederstotzingen, Germany (dated 7th century).

Viking warrior in replica lamellar armor, spangenhelm with attached chainmail.[29]

The lamellar armor found at the burial ground from Krefeld Gellep was at least a two-piece set and resembles the lamellar armor found at Niederstotzingen, Germany. A leather or reindeer coat was probably worn underneath the armor to absorb the blows.

Chapter 34 – Viking Helms

Contrary to the popular belief that Vikings wore horned helmets, there is no evidence that this ever happened. The horned and winged helmets were an invention of 19th century art and theater. If you think about it, as cool as a horned helm looks would be extremely impractical. It would not deflect blows, but rather 'catch' them. The horns would catch everything a wearer walked past. Wearing a horned or winged helmet would be a nightmare.

The real Norse / Viking helm was usually made from four plates of iron in the shape of a rounded cap in the **spangenhelm** pattern with an iron "spectacle" visor that formed around the eyes and over the nose.

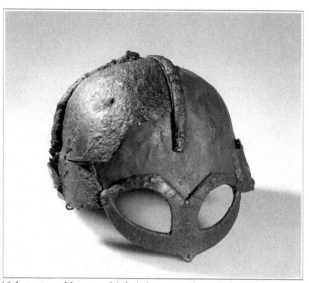

From a 10th century Norway chieftain's grave, the only known complete helm.[30]

Some Helms were made of a simpler pattern with a peaked top and had just a piece of iron as a nose guard, instead of a full visor. This style of helmet was more practical and functional. The Norse helm had a peak and was smooth, this would deflect a blow much better. The nose guard protected the face. A helm wasn't worn by itself but you generally had padding to absorb blows and a chain mail coif to protect the neck and sides of the face from slashes.

Some spangenhelms had a chain mail coif attached to the sides of the helm that would drop down to protect the wearer's neck. This was for those not wearing a full chain mail coif underneath the helmet. This was in addition to a thick cap worn under the helm for padding to absorb the shock of any blows to the head.

416

Replica Spangenhelm with nose guard .[31]

418

Chapter 35 – Norse Longships

The Norse longship is perhaps one of the most recognizable cultural icons of the Vikings. No one else had ships like these and these ships were ahead of their time. The Longships were deeply rooted in Norse culture and their way of life. They were a necessity that enabled the Norse to not only survive, but thrive in their tough terrain.

Much of Scandinavia was of mountainous terrain with fjords and inlets everywhere along its coastlines. This is where the majority of the Norse lived, along the rugged coastline. Inland trade was difficult, cumbersome, and outright dangerous. Movement by ship was really the only feasible way. This led to the incredible high degree of technology and innovation that the Norse put behind designing their ships.

The hjortspring boats from the Norse Pre-Roman Iron Age were designed as a large canoe which evolved from the Umiak type of canoe that was also used by the Inuit (Eskimo) people. The early Norse used this type of boat very similarly as did the Inuits in a sense of hunting and "getting around" locally.

Norse boats were later built in a way where the edges of the hull planks overlapped in a construction method known in shipbuilding as the "clinker" method.

The planks were joined end to end into a 'strake,' which is part of the shell of the hull that runs longitudinally along the ship's sides. This technique was developed in Northern Europe and the Norse used it very successfully.

Longship displaying the 'clinker' construction method of overlapping planks.[32]

It has also been found that the clinker built planks helped hydroplane the ship as it moved and literally glided it across the water. This design made Norse ships faster.

420

The longship was a design that evolved from the umiak canoe design from the Stone Ages to the graceful longships used during the Viking era. The longships were very lightweight, sleek and graceful. They were designed to have a narrow hull which made them not only faster, but they were able to navigate shallow rivers and even permitted beach landings.

The longships were also double ended like a canoe, which allowed it to reverse direction without turning the boat around. The ship's high maneuverability was a useful trait to have in the northern waters where sea ice and icebergs were present. The longship was fitted with oars all along its sides and the later models were also fitted with a large rectangular sail. Norse sails were made from rough wool cloth that were hung on a single mast that would replace the rowers or supplement them. The typical speed of the Longships was around 5 to 10 knots, with a top speed of 15 knots under favorable conditions. A speed on water that was lightning fast in comparison to any other seaworthy vessel of the day.

Longships were highly prized items that were usually owned by farmers and fishermen and then were commissioned by Kings and Jarls for use in warfare during times of conflict or for use in viking raids. The longships were not warships, but would be used as troop transports to carry men.

In that very rare instance that longships were ever used in battle on water, the ships would be tied together to create a steady platform for infantry to fight and archers to fire missiles from. Javelins and spears would be thrown too.

The Longships evolved into such seaworthiness that they were able to be used to navigate across the ocean. The longship has even reached Greenland and the New World, a place which the Norse called Vinland.

This was not only an attribution to the Norse Longship, but to Norse navigation that allowed them to reach such great distances at will.

Navigation at sea, particularly in the North sea where fog and overcast skies that last days long can hide the Sun. This makes finding the direction one is traveling to be an undertaking that would seem nearly impossible. Nothing is worse than being completely lost at sea. However, the Norse were able to overcome this obstacle with an object called a **sunstone**. The sunstone was a transparent crystal that refracted the Sun's light and revealed its position.

Iceland spar, perhaps the medieval sunstone.[33]

This once seemingly mythical object has been found in ship wreckage and has revealed itself to be a real object. The object had been spoken about being used to help Norse seamen navigate the Northern seas which can at times be impossible to navigate by using the sun or stars. Especially when you cannot see the sun or stars and have no idea which way you're going.

Previously, such a glass or crystal that could be used to find the sun in dense fog had never been found. It was assumed that its existence was a myth, such as sea monsters the Norse wrote about. But one has been found in a wreckage and it actually works!

The sunstone was a crystal called an Icelandic Spar or Calcite Crystal. What this object did was refract the light and reveal the Sun's position, in fog, haze, overcast and even after the Sun had just dipped below the horizon. This was the navigational device that allowed such far reaching seafaring conducted by the Vikings.

Chapter 36 - The Norse and Native Americans

When the Vikings reached the New World, they called the native inhabitants (American Indians or Native Americans), "**Skræling**." There has been much debate as to what exactly this word or label meant. Some translate it as "skin wearers," which may be true as to how they described them. The Norse generally wore woolen or linen clothing and North American Natives generally wore animal skins.

There was one thing that is puzzling about the Norse describing their interactions or meeting the Skræling. The Viking explorers weren't curious or baffled by these new people. They acted as if they'd come into contact with people like this before and their way of life. This is significant because it tells us that the Skræling were a fairly or at not unusual sighting by the Norse.

For example, 500 years later when other Europeans had come to the New World (The Americas), they were ultimately curious of these strange new people they had never seen before. They were curious of their ways and everything about them. But not the Norse, they didn't appear to be curious at all and merely noted interacting with these people. The Norse reaction seems to hint that they'd come into contact with people like this on a fairly regular basis.

This is because the Norse did in fact have regular contact and knowledge of these people. The Skræling and Thule people were commonly referred to by the Norse. The island of Thule, which is now called Qaanaaq, is located in northwest Greenland towards Canada and is part of the Kingdom of Denmark. It is believed the Thule people are the ancestors of the modern Inuit (Eskimo) as they are linked biologically, culturally, and linguistically.

The Vikings were in regular contact with the Thule people, particularly in the 11th century when they explored Greenland and the edges of Canada where they referred to these people as both "Thule" and "Skræling." During the occurrence of the "Little Ice Age" from 1650 AD to 1850 AD, the climate changed and caused the Thule communities to migrate. These people scattered and resettled in different areas. They later became known as the Eskimo and then later became known as the Inuit People.

Another very significant group of people that the Norse were in continual contact with were the Sami people (Sámi or Saami). The Sami are an indigenous Finno-Ugric people who inhabit the Arctic area of what's called "Sápmi" today.

The area of Sápmi encompasses much of the northern halves of Norway and Sweden along with the far northern portion of Finland including the Kola Peninsula of Russia.

Map of the Saami Homeland by Rogper, 4 May 2004.

The Sami languages are a part of the Uralic language family, a language family that is associated with native speakers of Estonian, Finnish, and Hungarian. Language regions today that are also traditionally known to be areas that were either part of or in contact with the Norse.

The first mention of a Uralic people was in Tacitus's Germania, mentioning the Fenni (usually interpreted as referring to the Sami) and two other possibly Uralic tribes living in the farthest reaches of Scandinavia.

In recent times, linguists often place the Urheimat (*Urheimat is a term that refers to the original homeland of the language*) of the Proto-Uralic language in the vicinity of the Volga River, west of the Urals, close to the Urheimat of the Indo-European languages, or to the east and southeast of the Urals.

427

Related to this Uralic language is the language of the North American Eskimo. The Eskimo–Uralic hypothesis associates the Uralic languages with the Eskimo–Aleut languages. Uralo-Siberian is an expanded form of the Eskimo–Uralic hypothesis. The hypothesis associates the Uralic languages with Yukaghir, Chukotko-Kamchatkan, and the Eskimo–Aleut languages. This linguistic connection shows that these people were in or near the areas that were also inhabited by Norse people.

There are other things that show that the Norse were very familiar with and accustomed to the Skræling people. It's very probable that the Norsemen coming into contact, either knew of or had dealt with Skræling people before. This is why they didn't concern themselves too much with meeting 'Native Americans' as did the latter explorers in the late 15th and early 16th centuries when they began coming to the New World and meeting the Native Americans.

The Norse were already very acquainted with a people they called Skræling. A more primitive people that Norse explorers and traders would occasionally come into contact with. The Norse also had contact with the Sami people that were located just North of them. These were a people the Norse had regular contact and interactions with due to proximity to each other. Contact between cultures which exists Today by modern Scandinavians.

This contact of Northern people was extended with the Thule people (Eskimos / Inuits) across the North where the Norse traveled all the way to the New World. A land which the Norse referred to as Vinland.

There were many commonalities of these people, such as how the Nordic Sami and the Skræling lived. Look below at the comparisons of Sami lavvo tents in North Scandinavia to that of the Native American (Skræling) teepees most commonly knows from the North American Great Plains.

A Sami indigenous northern European family in Norway around 1900.[34]

The above picture is of the Sami people in Norway and the picture taken below is of the Sami people in Lapland. Both in Northern parts of Scandinavia.

Nordic Sami (Saami) people in Sapmi (Lapland) in front of two Lavvo Tents.[35]

The following pictures are of teepees made by the Great Plains Natives (Indians) in North America. Note how they are almost identical to the tents made by the Sami.

A young Oglala girl sitting in front of a tipi, 1891.[36]

The above photograph and watercolor painting on the next page are both of Native American shelters in the North American Great Plains. The style of housing between the two cultures is astoundingly almost identical.

Sioux Teepees. 1832-1834.[37]

Not only did the Norse tell of the Skræling people that they encountered over the centuries, but the aboriginals also tell of making contact with the Norse. The Inuit (Eskimos) have a tale about a Kavdlunait (Inuit word for foreigner or European) that was speared by a Kayaker and how they feared revenge from the Kavdlunait because of the killing.

Violence was the usual interaction between the two people, inhibiting peaceful trade and any real successful settling of these areas by Viking explorers. Such stories are also mentioned in the Saga of Erik the Red and the Greenlander Saga written in the 13th century, about Thorvald and Thorfinn Karlsefni's attempt to settle in Vinland.

431

Thorvald's first contact with the native inhabitants, who would come to be known as the Skrælings. he'd captured and killed eight of the inhabitants when they were attacked at their beached ships. Thorvald is said to have been wounded by an arrow that flew between the edge of the ship and a shield, lodging into his armpit which had been the cause of his death.

Thorfinn, after barely surviving a rugged winter, had at first made peaceful interacts and trade with the Skræling they'd came into contact with. Only later did the peaceful interactions end when Thorfinn's men came under attack after a native had been frightened by a bull that had gotten loose. The settlement was forced to retreat to more defensible ground and fight back where it was reported that he had lost two men and the Skræling had lost several of theirs.

The Norse explorers pointed out that despite all that the land offered in these areas, they would be under constant attack by Skræling. At this point, the Norse and Skræling were already at war with one another and any further peaceful contact between the two people was simply not going to happen.

There have been recent findings in DNA research where they analyze a type of DNA that is passed only from mother to child. Using this research, scientists have found more than 80 living Icelanders with a genetic variation similar to one found mostly in Native Americans.

This signature DNA probably entered Icelandic bloodlines around the time period of 1000 AD when the first Viking-American Indian child was probably born. It is believed that a Native American female was transported from Vinland to Iceland on one of the Viking voyages, as the Norse were well known to capture inhabitants on their raids.

The North Americans and the North Europeans had known and had contact with each other for a very long time.

Additionally, new archaeological data and the latest DNA research have revealed that Europeans had indeed visited North American shores far earlier than the Vikings. These findings date arrivals to approximately 17,000 years before Columbus was even born. This was a time when the two regions were connected by land-ice bridges and from hunters following seals along the ice's edge.

This explains why the North American natives and the Norse Viking explorers were of no surprise to each other when the Norse explorers spoke of them. They had been in previous contact off and on with each other for not hundreds, but thousands of years.

Chapter 37 - The Jötnar (Giants or People)

The jötnar, pronounced "yoot-nar" *(singular: jotunn or jotun)* also known as the þursar *(singular þurs)*, are said to be a race of giants that live in Jötunheimr.

Jötunheimr literally translates from Old Norse as "Giant Home" or "Jötun Home", or more specifically:

"Home of the Jötun".

Jötunheimr was a place high in the mountains where men could not go. There is an actual reference to this location in Southern Norway called the Jotunheimen Mountains which is part of the Scandinavian Mountains. It was in these high mountains of Jotunheim where the Norse believed the majority of giants, or jötnar lived.

There is also referencing to Utgard *(Old Norse Útgarðr)* in Norse Mythology as being the home and stronghold of giants.

In poems and sagas, the Norse spoke quite frequently about the presence, or rather nuisance of giants. Within these tales, mostly there is mention of the frost giants, but there were many other types of giants and they came with a variety of names. Some of the descriptions went from trolls, to ogres, to many other large humanoid beings.

The Norse were very animate about the fact there were indeed giants, sharing the Earth with them. So much so that they mentioned some of the gods, kings, and a few heroes even marrying them and producing human/giant hybrids as offspring. Much like in the book of Genesis with the Nephilim from the breeding of angels and humans.

The Norse also mentioned that it was for the better of mankind to slay the giants and try to rid them from the world. From about every Norse account, there was always conflict and competition between giants and mankind.

From Jötunheimr, the giants menaced the humans in Midgard and the gods in Asgard. The river Ifing separates Asgard, the realm of the gods, from Jötunheimr, the land of giants.

In Norse mythology, Ifing (Old Norse, Ífingr) is the name of a river that separates Asgard, the realm of the gods, from Jotunheim, the land of giants, according to the poem Vafthrudnismal from the Poetic Edda:

> "Ifing the river is called, which divides the earth
> between the sons of giants and the gods;
> freely it will flow through all time,
> ice never forms on the river."

The Ifing is a river on which ice will never form because it runs swiftly and therefore is extremely difficult to ford,

436

thus forming an effective barrier between the worlds of gods and giants. Such a river is what traditionally separates Norway from Sweden as a border. The river that separated the Jotenheimen (home of the joten) from the land of the gods, or Gotland / Götaland or the Eastern Goths *(possibly Æsir Gots?)*.

Hjelmkollen and Ringdalsfjorden (Iddefjorden) seen from the Svinesund bridge. Norway on the left, Sweden on the right of the fjord. Overlooking Ringdalsfjorden (often mislabeled Iddefjorden) which is the fjord leading into Halden, Norway.

The Norwegian-Swedish border has changed many times because of wars over the centuries.

From the middle of Sweden in Dalarna and north of it,

the Norwegian-Swedish border usually follows the drainage divide in the Scandinavian Mountains between rivers that flow to the Skagerrak.

The Skagerrak is the strait running between the southeast coast of Norway, the southwest coast of Sweden, and the Jutland peninsula of Denmark, connecting the North Sea and the Kattegat sea area, which leads to the Baltic Sea.

But were they actually "giants", or was this simply a mistranslation?

438

The father of Icelandic scholarship, Arngrímur Jónsson 'the Learned' defined Goths as being Gotlanders who were the inhabitants of Gotland, which was home of the Gutes, who are the Jutes known as Jötnar.[235]

So who were the Jutes?

The Jutes were one of the three most powerful Germanic peoples of their time during the Nordic Iron Age. The other two being the Saxons and the Angles.

The Jutes are believed to have originated from the Jutland Peninsula and part of the north Frisian coast. In present times, the Jutlandic Peninsula consists of the mainland of Denmark and Southern Schleswig in Germany. North Frisia is also part of Germany.

The Jutes invaded and settled in southern Britain in the late 4th century during the Age of Migrations, as part of a larger wave of Nordic-Germanic settlements in the British Isles.

The venerable Bede, a very important chronicler of early Anglo-Saxon England, places the homeland of the Jutes on the other side of the Angles relative to the Saxons, which would mean the northern part of the Jutland Peninsula.

The Roman historian Tacitus portrays a people called the Eudoses living in the north of Jutland and these may have been the later Iutae.

The Jutes have also been identified with the Eotenas (ēotenas) involved in the Frisian conflict with the Danes as described in the Finnesburg episode in the poem Beowulf, lines 1068–1159.

Others have interpreted the ēotenas as jotuns ("ettins" in Old English), meaning giants, or as a kenning for "enemies".

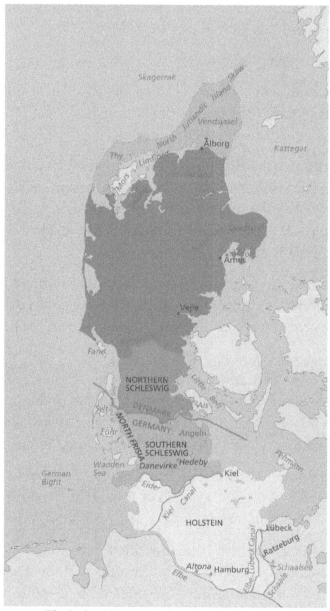

The Jutland Peninsula, homeland of the Jutes.

Disagreeing with Bede, some historians identify the Jutes with the people called Eucii or Saxones Eucii, who were associated with the Saxons and dependents of the Franks in 536 AD.

[536 AD nominated by a medieval scholar as being "the worst year to be alive" because of a volcanic eruption in Iceland blankets much of the Northern Hemisphere in clouds and ash, and dims the sun for 18 months, that caused average temperatures in Europe and China to decline and resulting in crop failures and famine for well over a year.]

The Eucii may have been identical to a little-documented tribe called the Euthiones and probably associated with the Saxons. The Euthiones are mentioned in a poem written 583 AD by Venantius Fortunatus as being vassal state under the rule of Chilperic I of the Kingdom of the Franks. This identification would agree well with the later location of the Jutes in Kent, since the area just opposite to Kent on the European mainland, present-day Flanders and was part of Francia.

Even if Jutes were present to the south of the Saxons in the Rhineland or near the Frisians, this does not contradict the possibility that they were migrants from Jutland.

The Jutish Hypothesis

A theory known as the "Jutish hypothesis" claims that the Jutes may be synonymous with the Geats of southern Sweden, or more probably their neighbors the Gutes.

The evidence for this theory includes that many primary sources refer to the Geats by alternative names such as

Iútan, Iótas, or Eotas as noted in the poem Beowulf.

In the *Life of Alfred*, written in 893 AD, Asser identifies the Jutes with the Goths in a passage explaining that Alfred the Great was descended, through his mother Osburga, from the ruling dynasty of the Jutish kingdom of Wihtwara, on the Isle of Wight.

The 13th Century Gutasaga states that some inhabitants of Gotland left for mainland Europe. This is confirmed by large burial sites attributable to either Goths or Gepids found near Wielbark, Poland.

However, it is possible that the tribal names were confused in the above sources. In both Beowulf and 10th century Old English poem Widsith, the Eotenas are clearly distinguished from the Geatas.

The Jutes, along with some Angles, Saxons and Frisians, sailed across the North Sea to raid and eventually invade Great Britain from the late 4th century onwards, either displacing, absorbing, or destroying the native peoples there.

According to Bede, the Jutes settled in Kent where they established the kingdom of Cantaware (Cantwarebyrig). On the Isle of Wight, they established the kingdom of Wihtwara where Alfred the Great's mother is said to be from.

They also settled in the area now known as Hampshire, where they established the kingdom of Meonwara in the Meon Valley area. Also the kingdom of Ytene, which the monk chronicler Florence of Worcester states was the name of the area that became the "New Forest".

There is also evidence that the Haestingas people who settled in the Hastings area of Sussex in the 6th century may also have been Jutish in origin.

The Jutes had settled and expanded into well established pagan kingdoms.

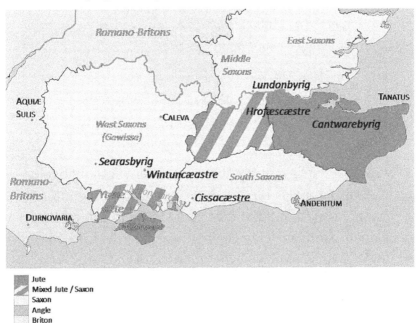

Map of Jutish settlements in Southern Britain around 575 AD.

While it is commonplace to detect their influences in Kent (for example, the practice of partible inheritance known as gavelkind), the Jutes in Hampshire and the Isle of Wight vanished, probably assimilated to the surrounding Saxons, leaving only the slightest of traces. However, the Jutes of Hampshire and the Isle of Wight were actually victims of a form of ethnic cleansing by the West Saxons.

Bede clearly records the Jutes as being victims of ethnic cleansing in 686 AD. From the Anglo-Saxon Chronicle:

"...Cædwalla, a young and vigorous prince of the Gewisse12.. came with an army and slew King Æthelwealh, wasting the kingdom with fierce slaughter and devastation... After Cædwalla had gained possession of the kingdom of the Gewisse he also captured the Isle of Wight, which until then had been entirely given up to idolatry, and endeavored to wipe out all the natives by merciless slaughter and to replace them..."

The Christian led West Saxons of Cædwalla King of Wessex slaughtered the heathen Jutes. Some were forcefully baptized and then executed, and replaced the population with his own Christian West Saxon people.

This was the last of the Jutes who were systematically pushed out of their homeland of Norway and the Jutland penisula. Pushed out of a region medieval chroniclers and saga poets claim as being the homeland of the Jutes or Jötun. Was this Nordic-Germanic tribe of the Jutes demonized in the sagas, most written a couple centuries after the fact, as being 'giants' to justify their tribe to be ethnically cleaned by the end of the 7th century?

Chapter 38 - Nisse

A nisse is a spiritual creature from ancient Scandinavian folklore that in modern times is usually associated with the Winter Solstice and Christmas season.

It is believed that nisse originated before the Asa belief, which also predates Christianity.

Nisse are one of the most familiar creatures in Scandinavian folklore and have appeared in many works of Scandinavian literature. They are both solitary and mischievous domestic sprites responsible for the protection and welfare of the farm and homestead.

It is generally described as being no taller than 90 cm (3 ft), having a long white beard, and wearing a conical or knit cap in red or some other bright color. They are often depicted as having the appearance somewhat similar to that of a garden gnome.

Most often nisse are imagined as being a small, elderly man (size varies from a few inches to about half the height of an adult man), often with a full beard; dressed in the traditional farmer garb, consisting of a pull-over woolen tunic belted at the waist and knee breeches with stockings.

This was common farmer clothing in rural Scandinavia.

Nisse/tomte (Norwegian farmers) harvesting oats at Fossum in Jølster during the 1880s

However, there are also folktales where nisse are believed to be shape-shifters able to take a shape far larger than an adult man. In The Hidden Hollow, a nisse is depicted as being about the size of a common house cat.

In modern Denmark, nisse are often seen as beardless, wearing grey and red woolens with a red cap.

Since nisse are thought to be skilled in illusions, they are also believed to sometimes be able to make themselves invisible.

Portrait of an invisible nisse.

One is unlikely to get more than a brief glimpse of a nisse, no matter hard they tried. Nisse are quick and work hard to stay hidden. This is the primary reason we don't really know what they look like to this day, except that of about how tall they are. Some Norwegian folklore claims that they have four fingers and sometimes have pointed ears and much like those of a cat, have eyes which reflect light in the dark.

They are called *nisse* in Denmark and Norway. *Tomte* in Sweden. 'Tomte' literally means "homestead man" and is derived from the word *tomt* which means homestead or building lot.

They are known as *tonttu* in Finland and also haugkall, haugebonde, tuftekall, and tomtegubbe.

The Lowland Scots refer to them as *brownie, brounie* or *urisk.*

The Scottish Gaels call them *brùnaidh, ùruisg,* or *gruagach.*

In England, they are simply known as *hobs* or *hobgoblins.*

A few other common names are: *household spirit, household diety, house elf, imp, Robin Goodfellow,* and *Puck.*

Most cultures consider them to be an ancestral spirit or wight with names such as: niðsi, dear little relative, and nixie.

The Slavic term for them is *domovoi* and the Germans call them *heinzelmännchen.*

Globally known, they're called *Koro-pok-guru* by the Japanese.

To say the least, nisse are very common in Scandinavia.

They are said to be good wights who take care of the house and barn when the farmer is asleep, but only if the farmer reciprocates by setting out food for the nisse and he himself also takes care of his family, farm and animals. This is with emphasis on treatment of the animals – they like them much more than they do humans.

They are also said to inhabit houses and aid in tasks around the house. However, they do not like to be seen and will only work at night, traditionally in exchange for small gifts of food. Among food, they especially enjoy porridge with butter and honey. They usually abandon the house if their gifts are called payments, or if the owners of the house misuse them.

If the nisse is ignored or maltreated or the farm is not cared for, he can sabotage a lot of the work on the farm to teach the farmer a lesson or two.

An illustration made by Gudmund Stenersen of an angry nisse stealing hay from a farmer.

An illustration made by Gudmund Stenersen of an angry nisse stealing hay from a farmer.

Although the nisse should be treated with respect and some degree of kindness, he should not be treated too kindly. In fact, there's a Swedish story in which a farmer and his wife enters their barn an early morning and finds the little grey old man brushing the floor. They see his clothing, which is nothing more than torn rags, so the wife decides to make him some new clothes but when the nisse finds them in the barn he now thinks he is too elegant to perform any more farm labor and thus disappears from the farm.

Incidentally, this is the Scottish-Anglo way to get rid of a nuisance nisse (brownie, house-elf, or hob). It is said to give them new clothes and they go away forever. (Dobby's a free elf now!)

In modern times, nisse are usually associated with Christmas and the yule time. It is normal that families may place bowls of porridge on the doorsteps in a similar manner that cookies and milk are put out for Santa Claus. In the morning the porridge would have been eaten and sometimes the nisse brings presents as well.

U.S. G.I.'s returning from WWII who' who saw nisse

decorations all over the place in Northern Europe during Christmas time and helped spread the concept in the U.S..

Coke Cola adopted the image of the Scandinavian nisse and made it into the Santa Claus you know today.

Nisse are a surviving echo of ancient ancestral spiritual beliefs.

Some scholars believe them to be wights which may have originated as general household gods or deities from before the Asa belief spread through Scandinavia.

In Old Norse, Asa (or ǫs, áss, ás, plural æsir; feminine ásynja, plural ásynjur) is a member of the principal pantheon in Norse religion. This pantheon includes Odin, Frigg, Thor, Baldr and Týr.

Many ancient Scandinavians believed them to be their ancestors and are often seen as being the farmer who originally cleared the forest to build the farm. A spirit that never leaves the farm or homestead they built in their day.

In pre-Christian times, this individual would have been buried on the farm in a mound. He was sometimes referred to as the haugkall or haugebonde, from the Old Norse haugr meaning mound. Mounds are common places in Scandinavian folklore as the lurking places for ancestors, even angry ones such as Draugr. Most often blóts are made in their tribute to keep them appeased.

Other names are tuftekall and tomtegubbe, which all connect the being to the origins of the farm (the building ground) or a burial mound. It was thought that the nisse was a more generalized spirits of previous generations at the homestead and there are references to them following the family/clan when they are moving.

The nisse is an echo of ancient spirit. Nisse may be derived from the Old Norse word "niðsi", meaning "dear little relative".

Most of the time these hidden folk are rather distant and do not meddle in human affairs. But do not meddle into theirs as they can be fearsome when enraged. They can make your life very very miserable or even dangerous – they do whatever it takes to drive you away, even arrange accidents that will harm or even kill you.

According to tradition, nisse live in the houses and barns of the homestead and secretly act as their guardian. If treated well, they will protect the family and animals from evil and misfortune and may aidwith the chores and farm work. However, they are known to be short tempered, especially when offended, and once insulted they will usually play tricks, steal items, and even maim or kill.

Traditionally, blóts are held every solstice and a gift (never payment) is left for the nisse, the ancestor protecting the home and family.

And you must ALWAYS remember to put out a bowl of porridge with butter and honey for him on Christmas Eve (Winter Solstice or Jul) to show your appreciation for his watchfulness!

Chapter 39 - The Helhest

The Danes have a creature in their folklore called a helhest (*"Hel horse" or "Hel's horse"*). It is a three-legged horse linked with the Norse goddess Hel and her cold underworld realm of the dead which bears the same name.

The Helhest is also associated death and illness and it is mentioned in folklore as having been spotted in various locations throughout Denmark. Usually in the frigid mist of dreary church cemeteries.

It is described as being pale and white-ish by those who've claimed to have witnessed it. Metaphors and mentionings of this horse has made their way into many Danish phrases and expressions, such as "han går som en helhest" ("he walks like a hel-horse") for a man who stumbles noisily.

Seeing a helhest is viewed as a very bad omen as they are sometimes described as 'going around the churchyard on his three legs fetching death'. A phrase is recorded that, in times of plague, it is said, "Hel riding about on a three-legged horse, destroying men".

An old Danish saying, "he gave death a pack of oats", refers to when someone survives a near-fatal disease, on the notion that they bribed the Helhest with an offering of a 'bag of oats' to escape death.

460

The cathedral yard of a church in Aarhus, Denmark, which was once an important town during early Viking times, at times features the Hel-horse.

The first church built in Aarhus' was a timber structure built during the reign of Frode King of Jutland around year 900 AD. It was built on top of a pagan burial site in what was then the town center. Some believe the spotting of the Helhest are because of the church being built over the site and disturbing pagan ancestors.

A tale recorded in the 19th century details that, looking through his window at the cathedral one evening, a man yelled "What horse is outside?" A man sitting beside him said "It is perhaps the Hel-horse."

"Then I will see it!" exclaimed the man, and upon looking out the window he grew deathly pale, but would not detail afterward what he had seen. Soon thereafter he grew sick and died.

At the Roskilde Cathedral, people used to spit on a narrow stone called the helhesten where a Helhest was said to be buried underneath.

Roskilde Cathedral helhesten

Legend dictates that "in every churchyard in former days, before any human body was buried in it, a living horse was interred. This horse re-appears and is known by the name of 'Hel-horse.'"

Prior to the Christianization of the Norse, Jacob Grimm in *Teutonic Mythology* says that the helhest was originally the steed of the goddess Hel. No mention as to why the Helhest only had three legs.

Chapter 40 - The Valravn

In Danish folklore, a valravn ("raven of the slain") is a raven that tranformed into a 'terrible creature with supernatural powers' from eating the flesh and blood of the dead left on the battlefield.

These horrifically transformed 'Ravens of the Slain'

appear in many traditional Danish folksongs which describe them as originating from ravens who ate the bodies of the dead on the battlefield.

Danish legend also says that when a king or jarl was killed in battle and if his fallen body not found and buried, that ravens would come and eat his corpse.

These ravens then became some very terrible valravn.

Jacob Grimm in his *Deutsche Mythologie* tells us that the valravn who ate the king's heart would gain human knowledge and would do great malicious acts. This special valravn also gained superhuman powers and would lead people astray, leading them to their dooms. These creatures were said to have become terrible corrupted beings associated with death and disaster.

There is no description of what any of these valravn forms looked like.

Even more horrific, valravn are said to gain the ability to turn into the form of a knight after eating the entire heart of a child. In this version, a valravn is described as a peaceless soul in search of redemption that flies by night, avoiding the day *(avoiding the sun like a vampire)*. This version claims that the valravn can only free itself from its terrible form by consuming the blood of a child.

This is story is reflected in a Danish traditional song that describes how after refusing offers of riches, a valravn made an agreement with a maiden to take her to her betrothed after she promised it her first-born son.

After making the agreement, the valravn flies away.

466

Time gently passes and eventually the couple have a child and guess what, the Valravn returns, and reminds the maiden of her forgotten promise to him. The valravn takes the child away and tears into the chest of his won wager and consumes the blood contained within the child's heart.

As a result, the valravn transforms into a knight.

In some storys, it is said that a valravn that eats the heart of a child will turn into half-wolf and half-raven creatures. These are much like 'were' creatures in other folklore, such as the werewolf being that is half-wolf / half-man *(were)*.

This being, however, was in the form of raven-wolf.

Chapter 41 - The Night Mare

A Mare is an evil spirit or huldrefolk (hidden folk) in folklore which rides on people's chests while they sleep, often bringing on bad dreams or "nightmares".

The mare (Old Norse: mara) is mentioned in the Eyrbyggja saga, Ynglinga saga, and Vatnsdæla sagas. In English, the name appears in the word for "nightmare". The Swedish word "mardröm" literally means mara-dream, the Norwegian word "mareritt" and the Danish "Mareridt", both mean 'Mare-ride' or the Icelandic word 'martröð' means mara-dreaming repeatedly. The Mara is also a demon in Buddhism and some Buddhists have amulets blessed by monks to ward off these evil spirits called ผีอำ ((pee ahm), pee meaning "ghost") in Thailand.

The mare is thought to sometimes appear as a skinny young woman dressed in a night gown with pale skin and long black hair and nails.

It is believed to be a dark spirit that takes a form of a beautiful woman and then visits men in their dreams, torturing them with desire while dragging the life out of them – much like a Judeo-Christian Succubus (Lilith).

Wait,.. torturing men with desire while dragging the life out of them… Does marriage come from mara? *(Okay bad joke *snicker*)*

Folklore claims that mares can slip through the slightest cracks in walls or floors like sand or smoke and re-emerge to terrorize their sleeping victim by "riding" on their chest. By sitting on their chests the mare cause their victim to have nightmares (and sleep paralysis if they awaken) as they are slowly being smothered to death.

There is controversy as to how they came into being and in some tales the Maras are simply restless children or adolescents whose souls leave their body at night to haunt the living. Much like how poltergeist (German for "noisy ghost") activity is believed to be the subconscious psychokinesis of an unaware preteen. The general belief is that these mare manifestations are the disembodied spirits of the living.

In folklore, zmora or mara are believed to be the souls (Old Norse: hugr) of living people that leave their bodies (Old Norse: likami) during the night. Odin was well known to travel out of his body. He did it so much that he even feared that one day he may not be able to return to his body. In the The Poetic Edda: Grímnismál, a disguised Odin expresses that he fears that they may not return from their daily flights.

His wife was very concerned about this as well. "Freyja's (probably Frigg) husband, the god Óðr (Probably Odin), is frequently absent. She cries tears of red gold for him."

These 'out-of-body' mara are seen as being wisps, orbs, or as being moths.

Incidentally the words, mara (in Polish) and můra (in Czech), denote both a kind of elf or spirit as well as being the word for a "sphinx moth" or "night butterfly". Other Slavic languages with cognates that have the double meaning of moth are: Kashubian "mòra" and Slovak "mora".

They would sometimes ride cattle that, when touched by the Mara, would have their hair or fur tangled and energy drained, while trees would curl up and wilt.

The night mare was believed to entangle the hair of the sleeping individual or beast, which resulted in "marelocks", called marflätor ("mare-braids") or martovor ("mare-tangles") in Swedish or marefletter and marefloker in Norwegian.

The belief probably originated as an explanation to the Polish plait phenomenon, a hair disease.

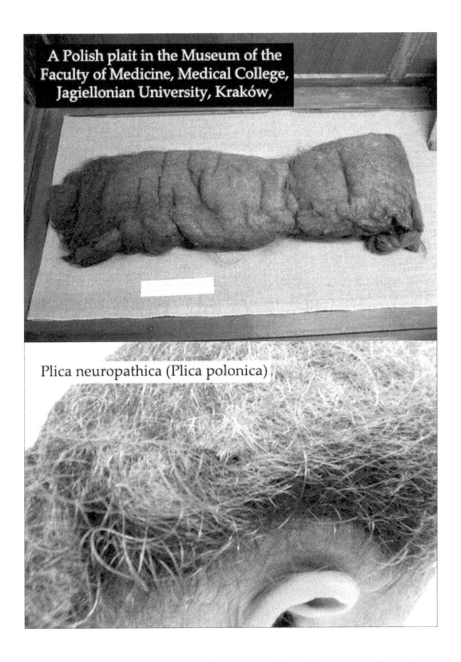

A Polish plait in the Museum of the Faculty of Medicine, Medical College, Jagiellonian University, Kraków,

Plica neuropathica (Plica polonica)

Polish Plait believed to be caused by Mares tangling the victim's hair at night.

Even trees thought to be ridden or even touched by the mare would cause their branches to become entangled. The undersized, twisted pine-trees growing on coastal rocks and on wet grounds are known in Sweden as martallar ("mare-pines") or in German as Alptraum-Kiefer ("nightmare pine").

Similar to an angry nisse/tomte, the mare was also believed to "ride" horses, which left them exhausted and covered in sweat by the morning.

Mares were also believed to be witches (or völva /seiðr) who took on the form of animals when their spirits went out and about while they were in trance.

In folklore, these included animals such as frogs, cats, horses, hares, dogs, oxen, birds and often bees and wasps.

In the modern Norse fiction The Hidden Hollow, an apparition shape-shifted as a cat and sat on the chest of its victim as it grew bigger and heavier, trying to crush and smother them to death.

In the Eyrbyggja saga, the sorceress Geirrid is accused of assuming the shape of a "night-rider" or "ride-by-night" (marlíðendr or kveldriða) and causing serious trampling bruises on Gunnlaug Thorbjornsson. The marlíðendr mentioned in the saga is believed to be the same as a mara.

King Vanlandi Sveigðisson of Uppsala lost his life to a nightmare (mara) conjured by the Finnish sorceress Huld or Hulda, hired by the king's abandoned wife Drífa.

In the saga, the king had broken his promise to return within three years and after ten years had elapsed the wife engaged the sorceress to either lure the king back to her, or failing that, to assassinate him. Vanlandi had scarcely gone to sleep when he complained that the nightmare "rode him;" when the men held the king's head the it "trod on his legs" on the point of breaking, and when the retinue then "seized his feet" the creature fatally "pressed down on his head."

The Nightmare by Henry Fuseli, 31 December 1780.

According to the Vatnsdæla saga, Thorkel Silver (Þorkell Silfri) has a dream about riding a red horse that barely touched ground, which he interpreted as a positive omen, but his wife disagreed, explaining that a mare signified a man's fetch (fylgja), and that the red color boded bloodiness. This association of the nightmare with fetch (fylgja) is thought to be of late origin, an interpolation in the text dating to circa 1300, with the text exhibiting a "confounding of the words marr and mara."

A female Mare riding on a sleeping man's chest. (Andy Renard Artwork)

To ward off a mare people took many precautions. These went from possessing blessed amulets to leaving a broom upside down behind the door or putting their belt on top of their sheets. After the Norse became Christianized, the elaborate prayer poem was recited before going to sleep.

Westphalia Germany, people were taught a prayer to ward off mares:

Hier leg' ich mich schlafen,
Keine Nachtmahr soll mich plagen,
Bis sie schwemmen alle Wasser,
Die auf Erden fließen,
Und tellet alle Sterne,
Die am Firmament erscheinen!
[Dazu helfe mir Gott Vater, Sohn und heiliger Geist. Amen!]

Here I am lying down to sleep;
No night-mare shall plague me until they have swum through all the waters that flow upon the earth,
and counted all stars that appear in the skies.
[Thus help me God Father, Son, and Holy Ghost. Amen!]

Chapter 42 - The Selkie

Selkies are said to live as seals in the sea but shed their skin to become human on land.

These mythological creatures from the sea are found in Irish, Scottish, Faroese, and Icelandic folklore.

The stories frequently revolve around female selkies being coerced into relationships with humans by someone stealing and hiding their sealskin, often not regaining the skin until years later upon which they commonly return to the sea, forsaking their human family.

Male selkies are described as being very handsome in their human form, and having great seductive powers over human women. They typically seek those who are dissatisfied with their lives, such as married women waiting for their fishermen husbands.

If a woman wishes to make contact with a selkie male, she must shed seven tears into the sea.

If a man steals a female selkie's skin she is in his power and is forced to become his wife.

"The Selkie Wife" by Michelle Bradshaw

Female selkies are said to make excellent wives, but because their true home is the sea, they will often be seen gazing longingly at the ocean. If she finds her skin she will immediately return to her true home, and sometimes to her selkie husband, in the sea.

Sometimes, a selkie maiden is taken as a wife by a human man and she has several children by him. In these stories, it is one of her children who discovers her sealskin (often unwitting of its significance) and she soon returns to the sea. The selkie woman usually avoids seeing her human husband again but is sometimes shown visiting her children and playing with them in the waves.

Chapter 43 - The Huldra

A huldra is a dangerous seductive forest creature found in Scandinavian folklore.

She is a member of a family of a very ancient beings that inhabit the forest, but remain hidden from humankind.

In Scandinavian folklore, the huldra (Norwegian, derived from a root meaning "covered," "hidden," or "secret") is a very elusive and seductive creature of the forest. The huld-rå being is a rå, which is a keeper or warden of a particular location or landform.

The different species of rå are sometimes distinguished according to the different spheres of nature with which they were connected, such as skogsrå or huldra (forest), sjörå (freshwater) or havsrå (saltwater), and bergsrå (mountains).

Other names include: huldra, huldrå, hylda, skogsrå or skogsfru/skogfru (meaning 'lady (ruler) of the forest' or 'forest wife/woman/spirit') and tallemaja ('Pine Tree Mary'). They are often referred to as Ulda by the Sámi.

As a whole, they are known as huldrefolk or huldufólk. They are hidden folk of the forest.

Her name suggests that she is originally the same being as the Völva Huld and the German Holda.

"In Scandinavian mythology, Huld is only referenced by völva or seiðkona, which is a woman who practiced the seiðr. She is mentioned in Icelandic tales and sagas, such as the Ynglinga saga, Sturlunga saga and a late medieval Icelandic tale. One source states that she is Odin's mistress and the mother of the demi-goddesses Thorgerdr Holgabrudr and Irpa. As her name suggests, Huld may be in origin the same being as the Huldra and the German Holda." *(Nordisk familjebok (1909))*

The males are called Huldrekall (hulder man), huldu, or huldrekarl are often said to be hideous in appearance and have grotesquely long noses.

Both the male huldrekarl and female huldra are forest and mountain dwelling creatures that take the form of tall and very beautiful humans with long flowing hair.

488

The female huldra is almost invariably described as being incredibly, seductively beautiful.

Huldra are said to hallow bark backs, similar to a rotting tree trunk.

The huldra is a stunningly beautiful, sometimes naked woman with long hair; though from behind she is hollow like an old tree trunk and has an animal's tail. In Norway, she has a cow's tail and in Sweden she may have that of a cow or a fox. Further in the north of Sweden, the tail can be entirely omitted in favor of her hollow or bark-covered back.

Most Tales tell of a tail. *(ba dum tss)*

In Norway, the huldra has often been described as a typical dairymaid wearing the clothes of a regular farm girl, although somewhat more dazzling than most girls.

One of her methods is to appear suddenly out of the rain and mist, friendly and enticing to the point that no man can resist her charm.

They lure them into the forest in order to secure her freedom or sometimes to suck the life out of a man.

She has a long cow's tail that she ties under her skirt in order to hide it from men. Hulder collab by am markussen

They may appear nude in their most basic form, or disguise themselves and hide among humans, masquerading as farm maidens. If a human manages to somehow see their back or tail, the spell is broken and the human is no longer susceptible to the huldra or huldrekarl's seductive advances.

Lore of huldra and huldrekarl tell of them using their beautiful appearance and seductive charm to lure young men and women back to their caves or subterranean homes where they may be kept a slaves, lovers, or worse – depending on the tale.

Sometimes the humans are released, but are cursed with the constant temptation to return to their captor. Other tales describe them getting married to humans, losing their tails, and becoming human themselves – but retaining their magic.

Some huldra or huldrekarl are inherently deceptive and evil, but many respond to the treatment they receive. If treated kindly, they have been known to use their magic to help humans and solve their problems. If treated unkindly, they can be hateful and vengeful. Much like any other being in the world.

Christian Norse say that if a huldra can manage to get married in a church, her tail falls off and she becomes human.

However, it is also said that she can become very ugly. It is often said, that the young and beautiful Huldra is moody and dangerous, but when she becomes old and ugly that she also becomes gentle and caring to the man who made her Christian.

Den lille Havfrue (The Little Mermaid) bronze statue by Edvard Eriksen in Copenhagen, Denmark.

The huldra has an aquatic counterpart called the 'havsfrun', 'sjörå', or 'Havsrå' (sea wife/woman) who is very similar to the Sirens Odysseus meets in the Odyssey. Or possibly that of mermaids luring men to their deaths at sea.

There is also the bergsrå, which are in caves and mines. They make life tough for the poor miners, but this is perhaps because the miners are encroaching in their dwellings.

The mountain huldra (bergsrå) are said to lure men down into endless cave systems that they wouldn't be able to find their way out from. The bergsrå (Mountain Rå), Bergatrollet (Mountain Troll), or Bergakungen (Mountain King) are a mythical creature of the mountain, or Rå, in Norse mythology.

Like the forest huldra, the mountain bergrå can be either male or female. It lives in the mountain with a court of relatives and sometimes surrounded by trolls. It was a common phenomena in the mythology about the bergsrå for humans to be bergtagen (literary: "taken into the mountain") and spend time with the bergså in the mountain.

A typical description of such a claimed occurrence was given by Sven Andersson in 1691, when he was on trial for having sexual intercourse with a female bergrå.

The forest huldras were held to be kind to colliers (wood burners that make charcoal) and watched their charcoal kilns while they rested. The colliers knew that she would wake them if there were any problems. This allowed the to sleep and be rested. In exchange for her help they left provisions for her in a special place.

Huldra by MrMyte

One day, a boy in Tiveden went fishing, but he had no luck.

Then he met a beautiful lady and she was so stunning that he felt he had to catch his breath. But, then he realized who she was because he could see a fox's tail sticking out below the skirt. He knew that it was forbidden to comment on the tail to the lady of the forest, so if it must be done, it must be done in the most polite manner. He bowed deeply and said with his softest voice, "Mi'lady, I see that your petticoat shows below your skirt".

The lady thanked him gracefully and hid her tail under her skirt, telling the boy to fish on the other side of the lake. That day, the boy had great luck with his fishing and he caught a fish every time he threw out the line.

This was the huldra's recognition of his politeness.

However, there are tales of kind huldra and there are tales of huldra that are not so kind.

In some traditions, the huldra lures men into the forest to have sexual intercourse with her, rewarding those who satisfy her and often killing those who do not. The Norwegian huldra is a lot less bloodthirsty and may simply kidnap a man or lure him into the underworld. She sometimes steals human infants and replaces them with her own ugly huldrebarn (huldre children, a changeling).

Sometimes she marries a local farm boy, but when this happens the glamour leaves her when the priest lays his hand on her or when she enters the church. Some legends tell of husbands who subsequently treat her badly. Some fairy tales leave out this feature and only relate how a marriage to a Christian man will cause her to lose her tail, but not her looks and let the couple live happily ever after.

However it is said that if she is treated badly by her husband, she will remind him that she is far from weak by straightening out a horseshoe with her bare hands, sometimes while it is still glowing hot from the forge.

If betrayed, the huldra can punish a man severely. In one case from Sigdal, a huldra avenged her pride on a young braggart she had sworn to marry on the promise that he would not tell anybody of her. The boy instead bragged about his bride for a year and when they met again she beat him around the ears with her cow's tail. He lost his hearing and his wits for the rest of his life.

There is legend of the 'hunder's blessing'. Legend states the hulder has long been associated with hunting and that she might blow down the barrel of a huntsman's rifle, causing it to never miss a shot thereafter.

Some men are not so lucky, or perhaps skilled enough, and escape her only after surrendering their sanity.

A man returning from the forest without wits has indubitably met with the hidden folk of the forest.

In modern day Iceland, stories still abound of the huldufólk. It is said that work crews building new roads will sometimes divert the road around particular boulders which are known to be the homes of the huldufólk.

Chapter 44 - The Draugr

The will of the Norse appears to be very strong. Strong enough for them to draw their hugr back to their own body.

Reanimating it so they can walk amongst the living again.

These are the Walking Dead in Norse folklore.

Draug are undead figures from Norse and Icelandic mythology/folklore that appear to retain some semblance of intelligence. They exist either to guard their treasure, wreak havoc on living beings, or torment those who had wronged them in life. Thorolf Halt-Foot was known to have reincarnated as a draugr and become a frightening marauder who left his tomb to cause devastation around Þórsnes (Stykkisholmur, Iceland). *(Eyrbyggja Saga (ch 31))*

A draug can be created by a curse or by the will of the deceased by simply refusing to die.

Hard to imagine going against a Viking Warrior that had to be re-killed. Slain warriors ignoring the beckoning of a valkyrie and going back into their dead bodies, reanimating the corpse and picking their shield and ax back up.

The Norse described the undead as being either hel-blár ("black as death" or "blue as death") or ná-folr ("corpse-pale).

In the Eyrbyggja Saga, a shepherd who is killed by a draug and who was destined himself to become undead as well was said to be "coal-black." The draugr that killed him was described as hel-blár when its corpse was disinterred (dug up). Glamr, the undead shepherd of Grettirs Saga (ch 32) was reported to being dark blue in color.

You always know when you are near a draug or its grave or howe. The air will be foul with the unmistakable stench of decay. Powerful enough to bring even those with the strongest constitutions to their knees retching.

Draug possess superhuman strength and can increase their size at will.

And with the increase with its size also to increase was its weight.

The body of the draugr was described as being extremely heavy in the Eyrbyggja saga, It was said that the draug of Thorolf had swollen to the size of an ox and his body was so heavy that it could not be raised without the use of levers.

Draug were deadly to any living being they came around or got too close to their howe.

They were known to decimated livestock by running the animals to death while either riding them or pursuing them in some hideous, half-flayed form to frighten them.

He (Thorolf Halt-Foot) was buried near Þórólfr. Of all the sheep in the valley, some were found dead, and the rest that had strayed into the mountains were never found. Whenever birds landed on Þórólfr's grave, they fell down dead.

The oxen which had been used to haul Thorolf's body were ridden to death by demons, and every single beast that came near his grave went raving mad and howled itself to death.

Draugr are also known for having numerous magical abilities (trollskap) that resemble those of living witches and wizards. They're able to shape-shift into various creatures. Some of the creatures that draugr are said to turn into are: a seal, a great flayed bull, a grey horse with a broken back but no ears or tail. Draug have shapeshifted into the form of a cat that would sit upon a sleeper's chest and grow steadily heavier until the victim suffocated.

The draugr Þráinn (Thrain) shape-shifted into a "cat-like creature" (kattakyn) and a troll.

Then Thrain turned himself into a troll, and the barrow was filled with a horrible stench; and he stuck his claws into the back of Hromund's neck, tearing the flesh from his bones..

Draugr are also said to have the ability to rise from the grave as wisps of smoke. They form into a mist so they can swim through the rock and exit their graves.

The presence of a draug was not without end. Even though the draug's body was reanimated, it was still simply just a reanimated corpse and continued to rot and decay.

A draug didn't walk for long before the corpse eventually would rot away, and the undead deceased would eventually experience a second and permanent death. The corpse of a draug could no longer rise again once their body became too decayed, dismembered, or was destroyed in any manner such as burning.

This might explain why Christians were so eager to burn witches, heathens, and pagans. They knew a pissed off Norseman was sure to rise back from the grave and kick some ass.

Once a draug's body was destroyed, the corpse could no longer be reanimated and their hugr would be released.

The Hugr is part of the Norse concept of the self. The Nordic and Germanic folk had a deep concept of the self that expanded as a differentiation from the body (líkami), the mind or will (munr) and their very being (hugr). The mind being apart of the very being which would be best described as a soul or spirit. The Hugr was the very essence of an individual's being that could be separated from the body at will and returned. It left the body upon death.

There were careful steps taken to prevent the dead from returning.

The Nørre Nærå Runestone is interpreted as having a "grave binding inscription" used to keep the deceased in its grave.

The Icelanders' Sagas, in the Eyrbyggja Saga (ch 33), instructs that upon someone's death, a hole was to be cut in the wall closest to where the corpse was and the body was to be removed from the house through the hole. It was believed that, if a dead person was carried through the front door, their ghost would remember how to enter and exit the house and come back to haunt the house.

The most effective means of preventing the return of the dead was believed to be the corpse door.

A special door would be built for which the corpse would be carried feet-first with people surrounding it so the corpse couldn't see where it was going. The door was then bricked up to prevent a return.

It's also said that the coffin should be lifted and lowered in three different directions while it's being carried from the house. This practice was meant to confuse a possible draug's sense of direction, in case it tried to return.

The practice of placing a pair of open iron scissors or some other iron item on the chest of the recently deceased.

Iron was to be placed on the deceased body because draug, like other undead, vættir, and fea folk, hate iron. Iron was often used as a means of keeping the undead away by placing iron somewhere at the threshold. Most often something of iron would hung by iron nails above the doorway of a longhouse.

Often the feet of the departed would be bound to prevent them from rising and walking. Sometimes just the big toes would be tied together. An extra measure was also taken by driving needles through the soles of the feet in order to keep the dead from being able to walk.

Gravesites, mounds, and howes weren't the only place to encounter a draug. Even the sea and coast held the dangers of the undead.

Draug were also said to rise from their graves in the sea and described as the spirits of those drowned at sea. The North Seas were already danger. The cold unforgiving nordic sea became downright hazardous with the dead coming out of the deep gloom and crawling into your longship or knarr.

Chapter 45 - Ratatoskr

Ratatoskr is a squirrel who runs up and down the world tree Yggdrasil to carry messages between Veðrfölnir, perched atop Yggdrasil, and the wyrm Níðhöggr, who dwells beneath one of the three roots of the tree.

Ratatoskr is attested in the Poetic Edda, compiled in the 13th century from earlier traditional sources, and the Prose Edda, written in the 13th century by Snorri Sturluson.

Veðrfölnir is a hawk sitting between the eyes of an

unnamed eagle that is perched on top of the world tree Yggdrasil.

An illustration from a 17th-century Icelandic manuscript shows a hawk, Veðrfölnir, on top of an eagle on top of a tree, Yggdrasil.

Níðhöggr is a dragon/serpent/wyrm who gnaws at a root of the world tree, Yggdrasil.

Níðhǫggr gnaws the roots of Yggdrasill in this illustration from a 17th-century Icelandic manuscript.

In the Poetic Edda poem Grímnismál, the god Odin

508

(disguised as Grímnir) says that Ratatoskr runs up and down Yggdrasil bringing messages between the eagle perched atop it and Níðhöggr below it:

Benjamin Thorpe translation:

Ratatösk is the squirrel named, who has run
in Yggdrasil's ash;
he from above the eagle's words must carry,
and beneath the Nidhögg repeat.

Henry Adams Bellows translation:

Ratatosk is the squirrel who there shall run
On the ash-tree Yggdrasil;
From above the words of the eagle he bears,
And tells them to Nithhogg beneath.

Ratatoskr is described in the Prose Edda's Gylfaginning's chapter 16, in which "High" states:

An eagle sits at the top of the ash, and it has knowledge of many things. Between its eyes sits the hawk called Vedrfolnir [...]. The squirrel called Ratatosk [...] runs up and down the ash. He tells slanderous gossip, provoking the eagle and Nidhogg.

Ratatoskr is described as a red squirrel.

European Red Squirrel

In ancient artwork, he is depicted with extremely long ears, but this could be an artifact of the art style of the time, rather than a meaningful statement about Ratatoskr's physique. Texts that describe Ratatoskr don't mention him having any features that set him apart from your typical bright-eyed and bushy-tailed red squirrel.

Ratatoskr is regarded as a troublemaker.

He enjoys fueling spiteful relationships, and he may sometimes add his own embellishments to the messages sent between Veðrfölnir the hawk and Níðhöggr the dragon.

Some scholars believe that Ratatoskr may have higher ambitions than just inflaming the fraught relationship between Veðrfölnir and Níðhöggr. In some interpretations, Ratatoskr is intent on destroying the tree of life. Because he lacks the strength to do much damage to the tree by himself, Ratatoskr manipulates Veðrfölnir and Níðhöggr into attacking the tree, which stands between them and the opportunity to fight each other.

Ratatoskr tells Níðhöggr of a particularly vicious comment Veðrfölnir made about him, and Níðhöggr gnaws at the roots of the tree, hoping to cause it to fall and crush Veðrfölnir. Then, Ratatoskr returns to Veðrfölnir with the news that Níðhöggr is gnawing at the tree, in an attempt to do him harm. Veðrfölnir begins to pluck branches from the tree and rain them down on Níðhöggr. With his well-placed accusations, Ratatoskr succeeds at doing great damage to the tree of life.

Occasionally, the squirrel might even chip into the effort with his reputed "gnawing teeth."

Ratatoskr, the Gossip Squirrel. European Red Squirrel (Sciurus vulgaris)

Chapter 46 – The Dragon, the Gold and the Magical Ring

The Völsunga saga tells of the legendary hero Sigurd and of his slaying of the dragon Fafnir.

Fafnir was a dwarven prince that was cursed into becoming a dragon from Andvari's stolen gold and magical ring.

Andvari, meaning "careful one" in Old Norse, is a dwarf who lives underneath a waterfall and has the power to change himself into a fish at will. Andvari had a treasure of gold and a magical ring named Andvaranaut. It is said, his magic ring helped him become wealthy.

The Völsunga saga tells us: Loki used a net provided by the Norse goddess Rán, to catch Andvari while he was shape-shifted as a pike. Loki then forced Andvari to give up his gold and his magic ring, Andvaranaut.

Furious at Loki and at losing his precious, Andvari cursed the stolen gold and magical ring which would destroy anyone who possessed it.

One day, the Æsir gods Odin, Loki, and Hœnir, were

traveling and came across Ótr (otter), who was shape-shifted as an otter. Ótr was the son of Hreidmar, King of the Dwarves. Loki killed the otter (which was Ótr shape-shifted as an otter) with a stone and the three Æsir, Odin, Loki, and Hœnir, skinned the otter.

Note: Loki is referred to as an Æsir in the Völsunga saga.

Later that day, the gods came to King Hreidmar's dwelling and showed off the otter's skin. Hreidmar, King of the Dwarves recognized the otter skin as being the hide of his son Ótr and demanded justice

King Hreidmar and his remaining two sons, Fafnir and Regin, seized the gods and held them captive while Loki was sent to gather a ransom (weregild). Loki was to have the otter skin of Ótr stuffed with gold and have the outside of it covered with red gold. This was the weregild demand as reparations for slaying Ótr.

Loki fulfilled the task by gathering the cursed gold of Andvari as well as the magical ring, Andvaranaut. Loki knew because of Andvari's curse that the items would bring about the death and destruction of whoever possessed them.

The dwarven king Hreidmar accepted the Ótr filled bag with Andvari's magical ring and gold as weregild and released the three Æsir.

The curse causes Fáfnir to kill his father Hreidmar and take all the ring and all the gold for himself. He became very ill-natured and greedy, so he went out into the wilderness to keep his fortune, eventually turning into a serpent dragon (wyrm) to guard his treasure. Fafnir had denied his brother Regin any share of the gold.

Some versions are more specific about Fáfnir's treasure hoard, mentioning, not only the vast hoard of gold and the magic ring Andvaranaut, but also the swords Ridill and Hrotti, the helm of terror, and a golden coat of chainmail. ..and perhaps, an Arkenstone?

Being denied his share of the gold, his brother Regin seeks out the aid of the legendary hero Sigurd.

Sigurd agrees to kill the now dragon Fafnir to avenge him and his father Hreidmar.

Regin instructed Sigurd to dig a pit in which he could lie in wait under the trail Fáfnir used to get to a stream for a drink of water and plunge his sword, Gram, into Fafnir's heart as the dragon crawled over the pit to get to the water. Regin then ran away and hid in fear, leaving Sigurd alone to the task.

As Sigurd dug, Odin appeared in the form of an old man with a long beard, advising the warrior to dig more trenches for the blood of Fafnir to run into, presumably so that Sigurd does not drown in the blood.

The earth quaked and the ground nearby shook as Fafnir appeared, blowing poison into his path as he made his way to the stream. Sigurd, undaunted, stabbed Fafnir in the left shoulder as he crawled over the ditch he was lying in and succeeded in mortally wounding the dragon.

As the creature laid there dying, he spoke to Sigurd and asked for his name, his parentage and who sent him on such a dangerous mission. Fafnir figured out that his own brother, Regin, plotted this, and predicts that Regin will also cause Sigurd's death. Sigurd tells Fafnir that he will go back to the dragon's lair and take all his treasure. Fafnir warns Sigurd that all who possess the gold will be fated to die.

Sigurd replies that all men must one day die anyway, and it is the dream of many men to be wealthy until that dying day, so he will take the gold without fear.

Alternatively; Sigurd kills Fafnir and drinks some of Fafnir's blood, gaining the ability to understand birds. The birds advise Sigurd to kill Regin, because he'd been corrupted by the ring and was plotting Sigurd's death. Sigurd beheads Regin and keeps the ring and treasure for himself.

Sigurd then meets the shieldmaiden Brynhildr, who pledges herself to him but also prophesies his doom and marriage to another. The ring's curse affects Gudrun. a beautiful but evil woman rumored to be a sorceress. Sigurd given the magical ring of Andvaranaut and gave it to Gudrun as his *morning gift* to marry her daughter.

Morning Gift, or "Dower" (German: Mitgift), is a provision accorded by law, but traditionally by a husband or his family, to a wife for her support in the event that she should survive her husband (i.e., become a widow). It was settled on the bride by agreement at the time of the wedding, or provided by law. ("Settled" here refers to a gift into trust.)

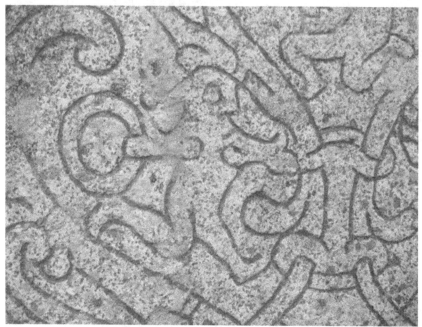

This part of the Drävle Runestone is held to depict Andvari.

Corrupted by the Andvari's cursed ring (Andvaranaut), Gudrun plots against Sigurd and Brynhildr to get the gold for herself and her family. Tragedy follows and after the deaths of Brynhild and Sigurd, Grimhild's brother Gunnar acquires Andvari's gold and hides it in a cave.

Years later, Andvari discovers the cave and finds his hidden lost gold.

However, his ring, Andvaranaut was lost forever.

Legend claims he spent the remainder of his days in search of his lost ring, his Andvaranaut, …his precious.

Chapter 47 - Naglfar, the Ship of Nails

It was foretold that during the events of Ragnarök, a massive ship called Naglfar will carry an army of jötnar to a large field called Vígríðr to host a battle between the forces of the gods and the forces of Surtr (a jötunn).

Naglfar (also Óskópnir or Naglfari), means "nail ship" in Old Norse. It is a massive ship which was foretold that will ferry hordes to do battle with the gods – and it is not held together by timber and iron nails, but by finger and toe nails!

Yo-ho-yuck is right!

It's a ship made entirely from the fingernails and toenails of the dead.

(We don't recommend eating anything from the ship's galley.)

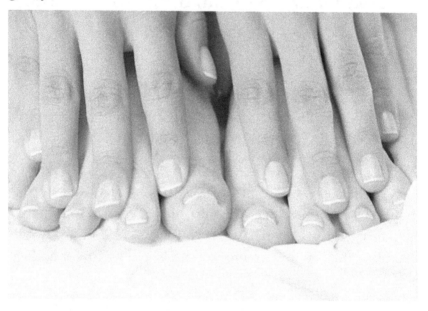

In order to deny the jötnar their much-needed building material, Nordic people trimmed or even removed the fingernails and toenails of the dead.

Snorri Sturluson in the Prose Edda references a funeral rite involving the cutting of nails, "lest unpared nails from the dead be available for the completion of the construction of Naglfar, the ship used to transport the army of jötnar at Ragnarök."

– No fingernails left on the dead means no nails for the

jötnar.

– No nails, no ship, and no Ragnarök.

High describes the composition of Naglfar as that of the untrimmed nails of the dead, and warns about burying the dead with untrimmed nails, stating that "the ship is made of dead people's nails, and it is worth taking care lest anyone die with untrimmed nails, since such a person contributes much material to the ship Naglfar which gods and men wish would take a long time to finish".

High, Just-As-High, and Third (Old Norse Hár, Jafnhár, and Þriði, respectively) are three men that respond to questions posed by Gangleri (described as king Gylfi in disguise) in the Prose Edda book Gylfaginning. The three figures sit upon thrones; High upon the lowest, Just-As-High on the mid-highest, and Third on the highest of the thrones.

It is stated in Chapter 20 of Gylfaginning (translation by Anthony Faulkes) that these names are pseudonyms employed by Odin:

[Odin] called himself various other names on his visit to King Geirrod:

"I call myself [...] Third, [...] High, [... and] Just-as-high"
— Snorri Sturlusson, Prose Edda

The gods did whatever it took to prevent or delay the coming of Ragnarök, even binding Fenrir.

One version of foretold events of Ragnarök, states:

"After the stars disappear from the sky, the landscape will shake so severely that mountains fall apart, trees uproot, and all binds will snap, causing the wolf Fenrir to break free. After, the Midgardr Serpent Jörmungandr will fly into a rage and swim to the shore, causing the ocean to swell unto land. Naglfar, too, will be break free from its moorings."

High adds that the ship will be captained by the jötunn Hrym and that Naglfar will be carried along with the surging waters of the flood that were caused by the Midgard Serpent.

The poem continues: "The Midgard serpent
Jörmungandr furiously writhes, causing waves to crash.
"The eagle shrieks, pale-beaked he tears the corpse," and
the ship Naglfar breaks free thanks to the waves made by
Jormungandr and sets sail from the east. The fire jötnar
inhabitants of Muspelheim come forth."

A variation: In chapter 51 of Gylfaginning when High describes the events of Ragnarök:

"Amid this turmoil the sky will open and from it will ride the sons of Muspell. Surtr will ride in front, and both before and behind him, there will be burning fire. His sword will be very fine. Light will shine from it more brightly than from the sun." High continues that when the sons of Múspell ride over the bridge Bifröst it will break, and that they will continue to the field of Vígríðr. The wolf Fenrir and the Midgard Serpent will also arrive there. By then, Loki will have arrived with "all of Hel's people", Hrym, and all of the frost jötnar; "but Muspell's sons will have their own battle array; it will be very bright".

Hrym (Old Norse "decrepit") is a jötunn (plural: jötnar) and the captain of the ship Naglfar according to the Gylfaginning (chapter 51). During the end time conflict of Ragnarök, he will set sail from Jotunheimr (Home of the Jötnar) , transporting the legions of jötnar toward the battlefield of Vígríðr to confront the gods in the final battle.

Yet in the eddaic poem Völuspá, it is said that it is the god Loki who is the captain of Naglfar, but Hrym is still described arriving for Ragnarök in stanza 50 as follows :

"From the east comes Hrym with shield held high"

This changes the ship's captain, but still includes both Hrym and Loki as arriving at the battle.

There are other references to this massive ship Naglfar.

The ship is also on the Tullstorp Runestone.

Tullstorp Runestone in Scania, Sweden.

If the images on the Tullstorp Runestone are correctly identified as being from Ragnarök, then Naglfar is the ship depicted below the monstrous wolf Fenrir. (see sketch image below)

Sketch highlight from the Tullstorp Runestone in Scania, Sweden.

It is also noted that the ship image on the Tullstorp Runestone has beakheads, both fore and aft unlike any known Viking ship, and is thus likely to be a symbolic ship.

A beakhead is the protruding part of the foremost section of a sailing ship. It was fitted on sailing vessels from the 16th to the 18th century and served as a working platform by sailors working the sails of the bowsprit, the forward-pointing mast that carries the spritsails. The beakhead would be one of the most ornate sections of a ship, particularly in the extravagantBaroque-style ships of the 17th century. The sides were often decorated with carved statues and located directly underneath was the figurehead, usually in the form of animals, shields or mythological creatures.

The bow and beakhead of the 17th century warship Vasa seen from above.

There is no mention or hint as to what these beakheads were used for or what they represented on this massive ship. There has also been argument that they are not beakhead, but rather rams such as those on Greek and Roman Triremes, for example.

The only other references to Naglfari are when the ship is first mentioned in chapter 43 of Gylfaginning, where the enthroned figure of High notes that while Skíðblaðnir is best the ship—constructed with the finest skill—"the biggest ship is Naglfari, it belongs to Muspell".

Naglfar receives a final mention in the Prose Edda in Skáldskaparmál, where it is included among a list of ships.

Chapter 48 - The Viking Board Game
Hnefatafl

How did Vikings fight boredom? Well that answer's easy!

They raided, burned villages, half naked women, lots of explosions in the background, ham and bacon sandwiches, and a never ending flow of mead.

Okay, maybe not. That's the Hollywood version of Viking life. Not to mention Hollywood's obsession for horned helmets and warriors that never took off their armor. In truth, the Vikings were simply like anyone else and occasionally got bored and played games.

The Norse played a variety of tafl or hnefatafl *(try pronouncing it: "neffa-taffle")* type board games. Tafl games are ancient Germanic and Celtic strategy board games that were played on a checkered or latticed gameboard with two opposing armies of uneven numbers.

These board games have been found in several Viking grave sites and have even been found depicted on Runestones.

Illustration from the Ockelbo Runestone, Sweden.

The board game Hnefatafl has also been mentioned in several medieval sagas, including the Orkneyinga saga, Friðþjófs saga, Hervarar saga, and others. The Sagas

536

simply mention them and don't tell us the exact rules of how to play the game. They do, however, tell us how popular and widespread the use of these board games were in the Viking era.

In the Orkneyinga saga, the notability of Hnefatafl is evident in the nine boasts of Jarl Rögnvald Kali Kolsson, who tops his list with skill at playing Tafl, a variation of Hnefatafl.

We do get a hint of the rules in some sagas by some mentions of game play.

In the Friðþjófs saga, a conversation over a game of Hnefatafl reveals that the king's men are red and the attackers game pieces are white. We also learn that the word hnefi does indeed refer to the king-piece. Making the game's name to be a version of tafl called 'king's tafl"

The most revealing – and yet most ambiguous – clues to Hnefatafl lie in a series of riddles posed by a character identified as Odin in disguise (*Gestumblindi*) in Hervarar saga. One riddle, as stated in Hauksbók (*'Book of Haukr'*), refers to "the weaponless maids who fight around their lord, the [brown/red] ever sheltering and the [fair/white] ever attacking him," although there is controversy over whether the word weaponless refers to the maids or, as in other versions, to the king himself, which may support the argument that a "weaponless king" cannot take part in captures.

One may also note that the assignment of the colors of brown or red to the defenders and fair or white to the attackers is consistent with Friðþjófs saga.

Another of Gestumblindi's riddles asks, "What is that beast all girded with iron, which kills the flocks? He has eight horns but no head, and runs as he pleases." Here, it is the answer that is controversial, as the response has been variously translated as: "It is the húnn in hnefatafl. He has the name of a bear and runs when he is thrown;" or, "It is the húnn in hnefatafl. He has the name of a bear and escapes when he is attacked." The first problem is in translating the word húnn, which may refer to a die (as suggested by the former translation), the "eight horns" referring to the eight corners of a six-sided die and "the flocks" that he kills referring to the stakes the players lose.

Alternatively, húnn may refer to the king, his "eight horns" referring to the eight defenders, which is more consistent with the latter translation, "He has the name of a bear and escapes when he is attacked."

Ultimately, the literary references are inconclusive on the use of dice in Hnefatafl. There have been many dice finds in graves that also contained the board game, but the Norse also played and gambled with dice games.

It is not known if dice were used in the game play of Hnefatafl.

Although a widely spread board game in the Viking world; game boards, play, and game rules varied from region to region.

There are different variants of Tafl, such as

Brandub

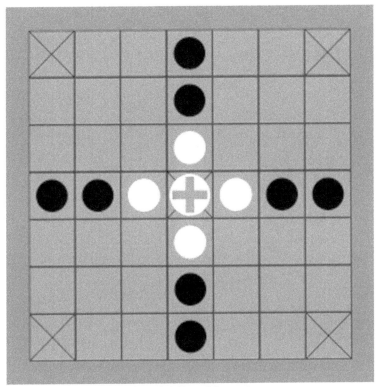

Brandub Board Layout

Brandub *(bran dubh)* was the Irish version of tafl. We know from two poems that it was played with five men against eight and that one of the five was a called "Branán", or chief. A number of 7×7 boards have been found, the most famous being the elaborate wooden board found at Ballinderry in 1932, featuring holes for pegged pieces, possibly to allow for portability of the game.

The Ballinderry gaming board – National Museum of Ireland

The name brandub *(bran dubh)* means "black raven".

Ard Rí

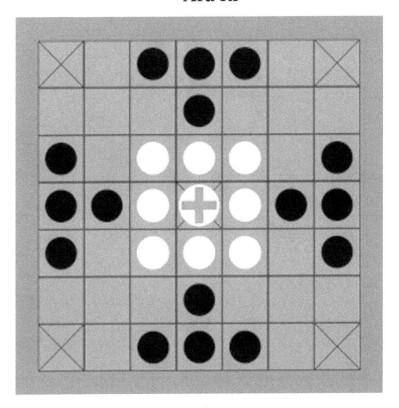

Ard Rí *(Gaelic meaning: High King)* was a Scottish tafl variant played on a 7×7 board with a king and eight defenders against sixteen attackers. Sadly, this is the least documented version of the known tafl variants.

Tablut

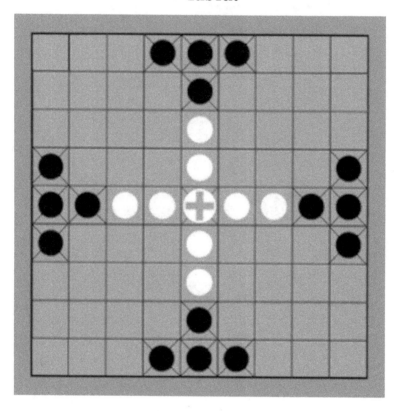

This variant from Sápmi, is the best documented version of the Tafl games. Carl Linnaeus recorded the rules and a drawing of the board in his journal during his 1732 expedition to Lapland. His description, in Latin, was incomplete, as he did not speak the Sami language of his hosts and described the game only from observing the players. The game was played on a 9×9 mat of embroidered reindeer hide. In his diary, Lachesis Lapponica, Linnaeus referred to the light (defending) pieces as "Swedes" and the dark (attacking) pieces as "Muscovites".

This may have been the same game was still being played in the late 19th century, as described in P.A. Lindholm's Hos Lappbönder (1884).

Tawlbwrdd

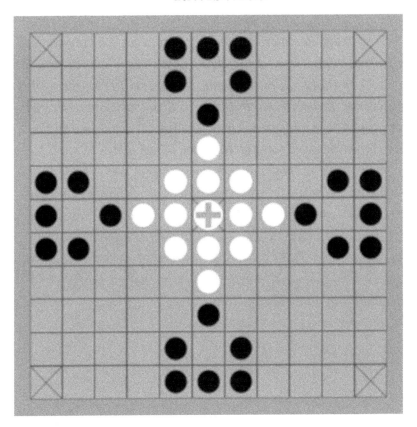

This variant was played in Wales. It is described as being played with 8 pieces on the king's side and 16 on the attacker's side. Robert ap Ifan documented it with a drawing in a manuscript dated 1587. His version was played on an 11×11 board with 12 pieces on the king's side and 24 pieces on the opponent's side.

His passage states:

"The above tawlbwrdd should be played with a king in the centre and twelve men in the places next to him, and twenty-four men seek to capture him. These are placed, six in the centre of each side of the board and in the six central positions. And two move the men in the game, and if one [piece] belonging to the king comes between the attackers, he is dead and is thrown out of the game, and the same if one of the attackers comes between two of the king's men in the same manner. And if the king himself comes between two of the attackers, and if you say 'Watch your king' before he moves to that space, and he is unable to escape, you capture him. If the other says 'I am your liegeman' and goes between two, there is no harm. If the king can go along the [illegible] line, that side wins the game."

Alea evangelii

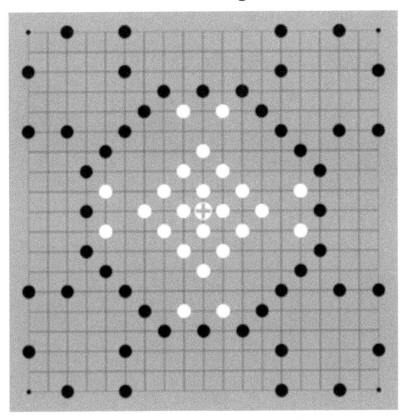

Alea evangelii, which means "game of the gospels", was described with a drawing in the 12th-century Corpus Christi College, Oxford manuscript 122, from Anglo-Saxon England. It was played on the intersections of a board of 18×18 cells. The manuscript describes the layout of the board as a religious allegory, but it is clear that this was a game based on Hnefatafl. This is where we assume the rules for game play for Hnefatafl.

Hnefatafl

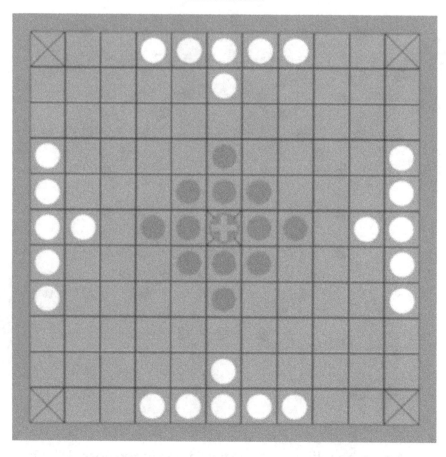

Hnefatafl was a popular game in medieval Scandinavia and was mentioned in several of the Norse Sagas. Some of these saga references have contributed to controversy over the possible use of dice in playing hnefatafl. The rules of the game were never explicitly recorded and only playing pieces and fragmentary boards have been discovered, so it's not known for sure how the game was played. If dice were in fact used, nothing has been recorded about how they were employed. Archaeological and literary sources indicate Hnefatafl may have been played on a 13×13 or an 11×11 board. It is known that it became a popular game in Northern Europe during the Viking era.

When chess became a popular game during the Middle Ages, the rules of Hnefatafl were forgotten over time. Hnefatafl was particularly popular in Nordic countries and followed the Viking civilization to other parts of Europe, primarily to the British Isles and the Viking country of "Gardarike". The game developed differently at different locations.

Archaeologists have found editions in places such as Ireland and Ukraine.

Hnefatafl literally translates to "fist table," from the Old Icelandic (equivalently in modern Icelandic) hnef, 'fist', and tafl, 'table'. The study of medieval manuscripts and examination of pieces and boards has allowed researchers to figure out how the game was probably played. It was last recorded to have been played in Wales during 1587 and Lapland in 1723.

How to play Hnefatafl

The board game is much like Chess in which it is based on pure strategy. It is played on a 13×13 or 11×11 square board, with the latter being the most common size played.

One player's side consists of a king and a small force of defenders which occupy the center of the board – they are the defenders. The other player has a much larger force which is twice as numerous as the defenders – they are the attackers. The attacker player occupies positions around the edge of the board.

The defending player *(usually the lighter pieces)* places their pieces with the king piece occupying the center, surrounded by his defending army pieces.

The attacking player *(usually the darker pieces)* will divide their pieces equally on all four outer sides.

The objective of the defending king is to escape to one of the outer edges or side of the board. The objective of the attacking player is to capture the defending king and prevent his escape.

All pieces move one square orthogonally *(forwards and backwards or side to side)* like rooks in the game of chess.

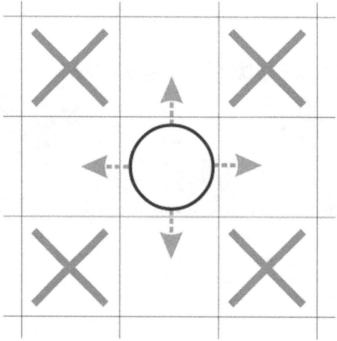

You may move a face-up piece of your color to any empty orthogonally adjoining square. Diagonal moves are not allowed.

The defending player with the centered king moves first. Players take turns moving and try to capture each other's pieces and remove them from the board.

A capture is achieved by surrounding a piece on two opposite sides.

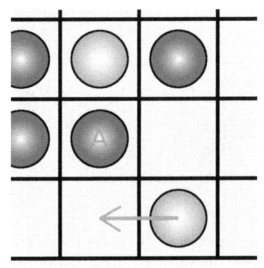

Example of a capture: the white player is moving into the square under the red player (marked A). With a white piece already on the opposite side of the red piece (A), the red piece is captured and thus removed from the board.

The game is won by the attacker if they are able to capture the defender's king, regardless if the defending player has other pieces on the board or not. However, the defender wins if their king is able to make it to the side or edge of the game board.

Some variations of the rules state that the defender's king must make it to one of the corners of the board.

Much like any other game, there were many minor variations to the rules, as the game was popular and widespread across Northern Europe. Most developed their own set of "house rules", depending on where you were and who you played with.

Chapter 49 - The Viking Ball Game Knattleikr

Knattleikr *('ball-game')* was an ancient ball game played by the Norse of Iceland during, and perhaps before, the Viking Age. It is a Nordic sports game which dates to antiquity that no one today knows the exact rules. We only have 'hints' and some information which survived from around the 9th century in Iceland.

We know that players were divided into teams, each with a captain. The game demanded so much time that it was played from morning to night. It was a spectator game, with tournaments drawing huge crowds from all over Iceland.

There are some descriptions of the game in a few Icelandic sagas, such as Egils saga chapter 40, *"Of Egil's and Skallagrim's games"*.

Putting together what information we can for various sagas, we know that game-play involved using a hard ball and that was hit by a stick, even though players could also use their hands if they chose. Body contact was allowed in the fight for the ball where the strongest had the best chance to win. Much like other full contact sports, raw aggression and intimidation went hand in hand.

Several hostile exchanges of words beyond friendly 'flyting' have been recorded in the old sagas. There were penalties and much like the modern sport of hockey, there was a penalty box.

Many sources state that the playing field was lined and usually played on a flat ice covered surface, such as a frozen pond or a land-based ice svell. The players may have used tar and sand under the soles of their boots for traction. However, ice cleats or spikes strapped to the bottoms of their feet could have been used as well.

There were two iron spikes found in a woman's grave in Birka, Sweden that date from 800 to 1099 AD. The iron spikes would be strapped to the bottom of the wearer's shoes or boots to prevent them from slipping on ice, according to the Swedish History Museum who hold them in their collection.

In Grettis saga chapter 15, "Of the ball-play on Midfirth Water", it speaks of men settled to have ball-play together on Midfirth Water (Iceland). The saga says men from the Midfirthers, Willowdale, Westhope, Waterness, and Ramfirth came from afar to play in a match.

It is said that those most even in strength were paired together and the game play often became heated enough whereas other players and spectators had to jump in and physically pull them apart.

The Knattleikr ball game was very popular amongst the Vikings. It was one of the roughest games invented and often deaths were reported from the games.

One Norse writer reports that at the time of a game between Sands and Botn, that before dusk, six of the Strand players lay dead, though none on the Botn side. In this story, one person by the name of Tord Blig was the worst and was barred from playing completely due to his 'bad temper'.

It appears that even in those days the worst berserkers where understandably thrown out of the game.

The Story of the Ere-Dwellers (*Eyrbyggja Saga*) chapter 43, *"Of Egil The Strong"* speaks of great 'play-halls' or 'play-meads' that were built specifically for the games. There were men who traveled to play who made their abodes there for half a month or so.

Records from Iceland report that at Lekskalvollane (*Ballgame Shelters*) there were annual tournaments that usually lasted fourteen days. Shelters and tents were erected where people lived during the tournaments.

Perhaps maybe Norse explorers brought the game of knattleikr to North America which formed into hockey when they built their first settlements in Greenland and Vinland over a 1000 years ago.

References

1 Kouwenhoven, Arlette P. "World's Oldest Spears." Archaeological Institute of America. Volume 50 Number 3, May/June 1997.

2 A drawing of a point from the paleolithic Hamburg culture arrow head. Drawing by Micke. 2007.

3 Drawing of a Ahrensburg point, Germany. José-Manuel Benito. August 2006.

4 Linear Band Pottery, Collection University of Jena, Bereich für Ur- und Frühgeschichte an der Friedrich-Schiller-Universität Jena. Photo by Roman Grabolle. January 2005.

5 Map of European Middle Neolithic Period. Created by Joostik. December 2012.

6 Tunnackigyxa (thin-neck axe), from Skåne. 1st (1876–1899), 2nd (1904–1926) or 3rd (1923–1937) edition of Nordisk familjebok.

7 Boat-shaped battle axes typical of the Battle Axe Culture. Pottery vessels and axes, chisels and arrows made of flint were also common. The National Museum of Denmark. 2013.

8 Corded ware pottery from around 2500 BC in the Museum für Vor- und Frühgeschichte (Museum of prehistory and early history), Berlin. Photo by Einsamer Schütze. June 2011.

9 Two of the viking stone ships (burial grounds) at Badelunda near Västerås, Sweden. Photo by: "Berig." 1 May 2005.

10 A modern version of England 878 AD made using Inkscape by Hel-hama. 13 June 2012.

11 The approximate extent of Old Norse and related languages in the early 10th century. Created by Wiglaf, based on Europe plain rivers by Dbachmann. 20 April 2005.

12 Gwyn Jones. A History of the Vikings. Oxford: Oxford University Press. 1968. p. 177.

13 Ian Riddler. Two Late Saxon Combs from the Longmarket Excavations. Canterbury's Archaeology 1989/1990, The 14th Annual Report of Canterbury Archaeological Trust Ltd.

14 Reconstruction of the Køstrup apron-dress at the National Museum of Denmark. Photo by Hilde Thunem

15 Wikinger Museum Foteviken auf Skanör. Wikinger (Guide in Wikingerkleidung) Wolfgang Sauber. 17 August 2007.

16 Germanic thing, drawn after the depiction in a relief of the Column of Marcus Aurelius (AD 193)

17 Egill Skallagrímsson engaging in holmgang with Berg-Önundr, painting by Johannes Flintoe (1787–1870)

18 Fig. 885. Drawing of a Shield from Gokstad ship. CH 6, pg 98. "The Viking Age" vol. 1 by Paul B Du Chaillu. 1889.

19 Modern reconstructions of Viking shield. Danish National Museum. Photo: Jacob Nyborg Andreassen. Accessed online 2013.

20 Viking "bearded axe" blade 1000 AD (top), and a German horseman's axe blade 1100 AD (bottom). Incitatus. 4 December 2006.

21 Replica Danish ax head. Forged by Bronze Lion. 14 August 2008.

22 Infantry armed with spears, swords and battle axes that fought the huscarls Harold Hastings. Bayeux Tapestry, Bayeux. Picture by Urban, February 2005.

23 Viking Spearheads. The Vikings (Pelican Books ISBN 10: 0140204598 / ISBN 13: 9780140204599) by Brondsted, Johannes. 1960.

24 From Njáls saga: Gunnar fights his ambushers at Rangá. Illustration from "Vore fædres liv" : karakterer og skildringer fra sagatiden / samlet og udggivet af Nordahl Rolfsen ; oversættelsen ved Gerhard Gran., Kristiania: Stenersen, 1898.

25 Ulfberth sword found in Finland at the National Museum in Copenhagen, Denmark (Historisk Viden, Danmark). 2013 online.

26 Example of pattern forged sword at the National Museum in Copenhagen, Denmark (Historisk Viden, Danmark). 2013 online.

27 Thorsberg moor, Germany find. Fig. 412. Brynja or coat of chain mail, 3 feet long. CH 12. pg 215. "The Viking Age" vol 2 by Paul B Du Chaillu. 1889.

28 Chainmail sample from the mail shirt found in Gjermundbu, Norway. Universitets Oldsaksamling in Oslo, Norway. Accessed 2013.

29 Viking warrior with leather lamellar armour. Via Elettra Gardini www.pinterest.com 2013. Note: the original source of this picture is of yet to be found. It was used in 'fair use' as the best example of replicated lamellar armor in use to educate the reader in their research on Viking armor.

30 Viking helmet from the Gjermundbu gravesite now in the Museum of Cultural History, University of Oslo. Photo: NTNU Museum February 10, 2010.

31 Replica Conical Spangenhelm with nasal made from 16 gauge steel by Royal Oak Armoury Artisan Crafts / Metal Work. Photo taken by Royal Oak Armoury on June 15, 2012.

32 Gokstadskipet, Vikingskipmuseet, Oslo. Photo by Karamell 2005.

33 Iceland spar, perhaps the medieval sunstone. Decemeber 2010 by ArniEin.

34 A Sami indigenous northern European family in Norway around 1900. The picture was probably taken in 1896 by an unknown author.

35 Nordic Sami (Saami) people in Sapmi (Lapland) in front of two Lavvo Tents. Photo taken 1900-1920 by Granbergs Nya Aktiebolag.

36 A young Oglala girl sitting in front of a tipi, with a puppy beside her,

probably on or near Pine Ridge Reservation. Photo taken 1891 by John C. H. Grabill.

37 Sioux Teepees. Watercolor on paper by Karl Bodmer from his travel to the U.S. 1832-1834.

Cover art made from original painting: The Ravager (1909) by artist John Charles Dollman (1851-1934).

38. Christian Krohg: Illustration for Olav Tryggvasons saga, Heimskringla 1899.

39. Hamilton, Hugo. 1830. Sketches of Scandinavia's ancient history. Stockholm: Gjöthström & Magnusson.

40. "The destruction of Irminsul by Charlemagne" (1882) by Heinrich Leutemann. - Wägner, William. 1882. Nordic-Germanic gods and heroes. Otto Spamer, Leipzig and Berlin. Page 159.

41. Lindisfarne Priory Viking stone, a 9th Century grave marker with seven warriors carved into the surface. Holy Island, Northumberland.

42. Statue of a Viking in Gimli, Manitoba (Canada). Photo by Magickallwiz, 2008.

43. Lindisfarne shown within Northumberland. Northumberland UK location map by Nilfanion, 2010.

44. One of three wooden spears found at Schöningen, Germany. Photo by: Chip Clark, Smithsonian Institution. 1995.

45. John Cassell. 19th century depiction of a Pict. *John Cassell's Illustrated History of England: volume 1 From the earliest period to the reign of Edward the Fourth.* Cassell, Petter & Galpin. 1865.

46. The Danish Ship called the Raven, Viking Ship, Pre-800 AD. Historical archives of LIFE Magazine.

47. "King Rorik" by Hermanus Willem Koekkoek (1867–1929) *Teutonic Myth and Legend* by Donald A. MacKenzie, London, Gresham Publications. 1912.

48. *King Ælla of Northumbria's execution of Ragnar Lodbrok.* Hamilton, Hugo. 1830. Teckningar ur Skandinaviens Äldre Historia. Stockholm: Gjöthström & Magnusson.

49. Peter Nicolai Arbo. *Battle of Stamford Bridge.* December 31, 1869.

50. A battle between 'Anglo-Saxons' and 'Vikings'. Staged by 're-enactors.' Source: bbc.co.uk.

51. King of Mercia Athelred seen on the exterior of Lichfield Cathedral.

52. Reenactors depicting King Alfred with the West Saxon (Wessox) forces battling the Danish Norsemen of the Great Summer Army.

53. Statue of King Alfred at Wantage created by DJ Clayworth. 2004.

54. Statue of the first King of Norway, Harald Hårfagre (Fairhair). Made by Einar Jónsson in 1924 and located on Arnarhóll, Reykjavík.

55. *Viking Ships besieging Paris.* Der Spiegel Geschichte (6/2010): The Vikings - Warriors culture: The life of the Northmen. Spiegel-Verlag Rudolf Augstein GmbH & Co. KG, Hamburg 2010, p.33

56. Portrait of Charles the Bald (823-877) at Palace of Versailles, France.

57. A map of the routes taken by the Great Heathen Army from 865 to 878 based on Stenton 'Anglo-Saxon England' chapter 8 and Hill ' An Atlas of Anglo-Saxon England' p40-1. by Hel-hama. June 26, 2012.

58. Map of the Duchy of Normandy.

59. Portrait of Robert I of Western Francia, King of the Franks.

60. British Isles in 10th century represented with the coastline at the time. Created by Ikonact. August 31, 2013.

61. Rollo statue depicted among the 6 dukes of Normandy in the town square of Falaise.

62. Silver penny of Eric Bloodaxe. A coin of the last Viking King of York, Northumbria. It circulated during the Viking Age at 947 to 954 AD. British Museum.

63. Raven's Banner (hrafnsmerki) as used by Jarl Sigurd.

64. Erik the Red statue at Qagssiarssuk, Greenland.

65. Leif Erikson statue in front of Hallgrimskirkja.Iceland.

66. A depiction of the death of Thorvald Eriksson which took place somewhere in North America in 1004 AD. *Did the Vikings Beat the Pilgrims to Plymouth?* By Patrick Browne. July 24, 2014

67. Death of Ymir. Lorenz Frølich (25 October 1820 – 25 October 1908).

68. Illustration of Auðumbla licking Búri out of a salty ice-block, from an Icelandic 18th century manuscript by Jakob Sigurðsson.(1765-1766).

69. Two dwarfs as depicted in the Poetic Edda poem Völuspá by Lorenz Frølich. 1895.

70. "The Wolves Pursuing Sol and Mani." J.C. Dollman. 1909.

71. Scultpure of the first living people, Ask and Embla, at the main square in Sölvesborg, Sweden.

72. Artist's depiction of Yggdrasil and the nine realms.

73. Odin the Wanderer by George von Rosen. 1896.

74. Odin sits atop his steed Sleipnir, his ravens Huginn and Muninn and wolves Geri and Freki nearby by Lorenz Frølich. 1895.

75. Odin Hanging on the World Tree. Illustration for Die Edda: Germanische Götter und Heldensagen by Hans von Wolzogen. 1920.

76. "Frigg and Odin in Grímnismál by Frølich" by Lorenz Frølich. Published in Gjellerup, Karl.1895.

77. Statute of Balder. Sculpted by Bengt Erland Fogelberg. 1842.

78. Artist depiction of Thor Odinsson with Toothgrinder and Toothgnasher. mytholipedia.com. 2014.

79. Drawing of silver amulet representing Mjöllnir, the hammer of Thor. Discovered in Skåne, Sweden.1877.

80. Artist's depiction of the Tyr, God of War.

81. The Battle of Thor with the serpent of Midgard. Painted by Henry Fuseli. Royal Academy of Arts, London. 1788.

82. Artist's depiction of the Symbol of Jörmungandr, The Midgard Serpent.

83. "The Punishment of Loki", by Louis Huard. *The Heroes of Asgard: Tales from Scandinavian Mythology* by A & E Keary. MacMillan & Co, London. 1891.

84. The Norse god Heimdallr blowing the horn Gjallarhorn by Lorenz Frølich (1820-1908).

85. "The goddess Sif" by John Charles Dollman. *Myths of the Norsemen from the Eddas and Sagas* by Guerber, H. A.. London. 1909.

86. "Hermod before Hela" by John Charles Dollman. *Myths of the Norsemen from the Eddas and Sagas* by Guerber, H. A.. London. 1909.

87. The god Freyr by Johannes Gehrts. 1901.

88. "Kampf der untergehenden Götter" by Friedrich Wilhelm Heine.1882.

89. Njord's desire of the Sea by W. G. Collingwood. 1908.

90. Skadi's longing for the Mountains by W. G. Collingwood. 1908.

91. Týr and Fenrir by John Bauer. 1911.

92. Hel by Johannes Gehrts. 1889.

93. An illustration of Lífþrasir and Líf by Lorenz Frølich.Published in Den ældre Eddas Gudesange by Gjellerup, Karl. 1895.

94. The battle between Surtr and Freyr at Ragnarök, illustration by Lorenz Frølich. Published in Den ældre Eddas Gudesange by Gjellerup, Karl. 1895.

95. The Sutton Hoo helmet located at the British Museum. 2011.

96. Replica of Viking Era Merchant Knarr. Publishied in *Mobility, the Viking Way*. By Alan Robert Lancaster. March 28, 2015.

97. Grimm, Jacob (James Steven Stallybrass Trans.) (1883). Teutonic Mythology: Translated from the Fourth Edition with Notes and Appendix by James Stallybrass. Volume II. London: George Bell and Sons.

98. Thorpe, Benjamin (1851). Northern Mythology, Compromising the Principal Traditions and Superstitions of Scandinavia, North Germany, and the Netherlands: Compiled from Original and Other Sources. In three Volumes. Scandinavian Popular Traditions and Superstitions, Volume 2. Lumley.

99. Vicary, J. F. (1884). A Danish Parsonage. London: Kegan Paul, Trench & Co.

100. Kelchner, Georgia Dunham (2013) [orig. 1935]. Dreams in Old Norse Literature and their Affinities in Folklore. Cambridge University Press. ISBN 1107620228.

101. Ashliman, D. L. "Origin of the Hidden People: Two Legends from Iceland by Jón Arnason". D. L. Ashliman's folktexts.
102. Devereux, Paul (2003). Haunted Land: Investigations into Ancient Mysteries and Modern Day Phenomena, Piatkus Publishers. ISBN: 0749923571
103. Hall, Alaric Timothy Peter (2004). The Meanings of Elf and Elves in Medieval England (PDF). Glasgow, Scotland, UK: Department of English Language, University of Glasgow.
104. Eyrbyggja saga
105. Ynglinga saga
106. Vatnsdæla saga
107. Sturlunga saga
108. Grimberg, Carl; Åberg, Alf (1960). Svenska folkets underbara öden. Stockholm.
109. Grimberg, Gunnar (1935). Skogsrået i yngre nordisk folktradition. Skrifter / utg. av Kungl. Gustav Adolfs akademien för folklivsforskning, 99-0440828-9 ; 3 (in Swedish). Uppsala: Lundequistska bokh.
110. Hultkrantz, Åke, ed. (1961). The supernatural owners of nature: Nordic symposion on the religious conceptions of ruling spirits (genii loci, genii speciei) and allied concepts. Stockholm studies in comparative religion, 0562-1070 ; 1. Stockholm: Almqvist & Wiksell.
111. Thomson, David. The People of the Sea: A Journey in Search of the Seal Legend. Counterpoint. (2002) ISBN: 9781582431840.
112. Briggs, Katharine. An Encyclopedia of Fairies, Hobgoblins, Brownies, Boogies, and Other Supernatural Creatures. ISBN 0-394-73467-X.
113. Williamson, Duncan. Tales of the seal people: Scottish folk tales. New York: Interlink Books. (1992) ISBN 0-940793-99-7.
114. Ashliman, D. L. "Origin of the Hidden People: Two Legends from Iceland by Jón Arnason". D. L. Ashliman's folktexts.
115. Hall, Alaric Timothy Peter (2004). The Meanings of Elf and Elves in Medieval England (PDF). Glasgow, Scotland, UK: Department of English Language, University of Glasgow.
116. Nordisk familjebok (1909)
117. Ynglinga saga
118. Sturlunga saga
119. Grimberg, Carl; Åberg, Alf (1960). Svenska folkets underbara öden. 4, 1660–1707. Stockholm.
120. Grimberg, Gunnar (1935). Skogsrået i yngre nordisk folktradition. Skrifter / utg. av Kungl. Gustav Adolfs akademien för folklivsforskning, 99-0440828-9 ; 3 (in Swedish). Uppsala: Lundequistska bokh.
121. Hultkrantz, Åke, ed. (1961). The supernatural owners of nature: Nordic

symposion on the religious conceptions of ruling spirits (genii loci, genii speciei) and allied concepts. Stockholm studies in comparative religion, 0562-1070 ; 1. Stockholm: Almqvist & Wiksell.

122. Häll, Mikael (2013). Skogsrået, näcken och djävulen: erotiska naturväsen och demonisk sexualitet i 1600- och 1700-talens Sverige (in Swedish). Stockholm: Malört. ISBN 978-91-978751-2-7

123. Hrómundar saga Gripssonar

124. Eyrbyggja Saga

125. Grettirs Saga

126. Grímnismál

127. Gylfaginning

128. Bellows, Henry Adams (Trans.) (1936). The Poetic Edda. Princeton University Press. New York: The American-Scandinavian Foundation.

129. Thorpe, Benjamin (Trans.) (1907). The Elder Edda of Saemund Sigfusson. Norrœna Society.

130. Krappe, Alexander Haggerty. Science of Folklore. Kessinger Publishing, 2003. ISBN 0-7661-5813-6.

131. Anderson, Rasmus Björn (1891). Norse Mythology Or The Religion Of Our Forefathers: Containing All The Myths Of The Eddas. Kessinger Publishing, LLC, 2006. ISBN 978-1428641846

132. Jackson Crawford, The Poetic Edda: Stories of the Norse Gods and Heroes. Hackett Classics, 2015. 978-1624663567

133. Jesse L. Byock. The Prose Edda. Penguin Classics, 2006. 978-0140447552

134. Bellows, H. A. (trans). The Poetic Edda: The Mythological Poems. Dover Publications, 2004. 978-0486437101

135. Crumlin-Pedersen, Ole & Thye, Birgitte Munch (eds.) (1995). The Ship as Symbol in Prehistoric and Medieval Scandinavia: Papers from an International Research Seminar at the Danish National Museum, Copenhagen, 5th-7th May 1994. Nationalmuseet. ISBN 87-89384-01-6

136. Snorri Sturluson (Author), Faulkes, Anthony (Trans.) (1995). Edda. Everyman. ISBN 978-0460876162.

137. The Poetic Edda. Gylfaginning.

138. The Prose Edda. Skáldskaparmál

139. The Poetic Edda. Völuspá

140. Steinsland, Gro (2005); Norrøn religion. ISBN 82-530-2607-2 (access via interlibrary loan)

141. Clunies Ross, Margaret (1994); Prolonged echoes, vol 1. ISBN 978-87-7838-008-1

142. Lee M. Hollander (tlr)(1986); The Poetic Edda. ISBN 978-0292764996

143. Vern L. Bullough and James Brundage (1982). Sexual Practices and the

Medieval Church. ISBN-13: 978-0879752682

144. The Poetic Edda: Þrymskviða

145. De Vries, Jan (2008) [First published 1938]. Boon-de Vries, Aleid; Huisman, J.A., eds. Edda - Goden- en heldenliederen uit de Germaanse oudheid. Deventer, Netherlands: Ankh-Hermes. ISBN 978-90-202-4878-4.

146. Iona and Peter Opie, The Classic Fairy Tales. ISBN 0-19-211559-6.

147. Acker, Paul; Larrington, Carolyne. The Poetic Edda: Essays on Old Norse Mythology. London: Routledge. ISBN 978-0415653855.

148. Byock, Jesse. Feud in the Icelandic Saga. Berkeley: University of California Press, 1982. ISBN: 0520045645

149. Jochens, Jenny. "Women in Old Norse Society". Ithaca: Cornell UP, 1998. Print.

150. Rapp, Linda. "Iceland." GLBTQ Archive. 2004, 2015.

151. Dumézil, Georges. "From Myth to Fiction: the Saga of Hadingus." Chicago: University of Chicago Press. 1973.

152. Cherici, Peter. Celtic sexuality: power, paradigms, and passion. Tyrone Press. 1995. Print.

153. Boswell, John. Same-Sex Unions in Premodern Europe New York: Villard Books, 1995.

154. Conner, Randy P, Sparks, David, & Sparks, Mariya. "Cassell's Encyclopedia of Queer Myth, Symbol and Spirit: Gay, Lesbian, Bisexual and Transgender Lore (Cassell Sexual Politics Series)." Cassell. 1998. Print.

155. Saxo Grammaticus, Mark Ludwig Stinson (Editor). "The Nine Books of the Danish History: Gesta Danorum." 2012. Print.

156. David F. Greenberg. "The Construction of Homosexuality". University Of Chicago Press, 1990. 978-0226306285

157. Publius Cornelius Tacitus. "De Origine et situ Germanorum (On the Origin and Situation of the Germanic Peoples)". 98AD.

158. "Bog Bodies of the Iron Age" Nova: PBS.

159. Brøndsted, Johannes. The Vikings. (transl. by Kalle Skov). Penguin Books; 2 Sub edition (January 1, 1999).

160. The Gesta Danorum (Danish History), Books I-IX, by Saxo Grammaticus ("Saxo the Learned")

161. Kane, Njord. "The Viking Age." The Vikings : The Story of a People. 2nd ed. Yukon: Spangenhelm, 2015. Print. 978-1943066018

162. Ibn Rustah, Encyclopaedia Iranica, C.E. Boswort, New York 2003

163. Ibn Rustah, Kitāb al-A'lāk an-Nafîsa, ed. M. J. De Goeje, Bibliotheca Geographorum Arabicorum [BGA], Leiden, E. J. Brill, 1892

164. Islamic ring in Viking grave sheds new light on ancient ties. by Jim Stenman and Susannah Cullinane, CNN, Thu March 19, 2015.

165. A Tale of Two Civilisations: The Viking and the Muslim World.
166. Analysis and interpretation of a unique Arabic finger ring from the Viking Age town of Birka, Sweden. Authors: Sebastian K.T.S. Wärmländer, Linda Wåhlander, Ragnar Saage, Khodadad Rezakhani, Saied A. Hamid Hassan, Michael Neiß. published: 23 February 2015.
167. Eaters of the Dead by Michael Crichton
168. The film, The 13th Warrior
169. Viking raids on the spanish peninsula by Rolf Scheen
170. "Digging up the 'Spanish Vikings." University of Aberdeen. 2014.
171. "Vikings and Pilgrims in Galicia" by Birgitta Olsen, 2005.
172. Georg Heinrich Pertz, Georg Heinrich Saint-Bertin. Annales Bertiniani (Latin Edition), 2010
173. Andrew Marr. A History of the World. 2014.
174. S.B. Samadi (Ed.)., Haft Iqlim: the Geographical and Biographical Encyclopaedia of Amin Ahmad Razi, 1972.
175. Reconstructing Hnefatafl by Damian Walker
176. TAFL: Ancient Board Games of the Norse and Celtic Peoples of Scandinavia and the British Isles (Ancient Games Book 1) by Jesse Robinson
177. An Introduction to Hnefatafl by Damian Gareth Walker
178. Orkneyinga Saga: The History of the Earls of Orkney (Penguin Classics) by Anonymous (Author), Hermann Palsson (Translator), Paul Edwards (Translator)
179. Fridthjof's Saga; a Norse romance by Esaias Tegnér (Author), Thomas Addis Emmett Holcomb (Translator), Martha A. Lyon Holcomb (Translator)
180. Hervarar Saga Ok Heidreks Konungs (Norwegian Edition) by N. M. Petersen
181. Jómsvíkingadrápa
182. Styrbjarnar þáttr Svíakappa
183. Eyrbyggja saga
184. Gesta Danorum
185. Olaf Tryggvasson's Saga
186. Hollander, Lee M. (1989). The Saga of the Jómsvíkings. University of Texas Press. ISBN 978-0292776234.
187. Jones, Gwyn (2001). A History of the Vikings (2d ed.). Oxford Univ. Press. ISBN 978-0192801340.
188. Palsson, Hermann (1989). Eyrbyggja Saga. Penguin Classics. ISBN 978-0140445305.
189. Sturlason, Snorre (1990). Erling Monsen, ed. Heimskringla: Or the Lives of the Norse Kings. Dover Publications. ISBN 978-0486263663.

190. N. F. Blake. "The Sagas of the Jómsvíkings". Thomas Nelson and Sons, 1962.

191. Reimund Kvideland and Henning Sehmsdorf. Scandinavian Folk Belief and Legend (The Nordic Series). Univ Of Minnesota Press. 1991. ISBN 978-0816619672

192. Marie Ericsson, Jörgen I Eriksson, Mikael W Gejel, Mikael Hedlund. Sejd:En vägledning I nordlig shamamism. Gimle, 1985. ISBN 978-9178102754

193. Snorri Sturluson, Jesse L. Byock (trans). The Prose Edda: Norse Mythology. Penguin Classics, 2006. ISBN 978-0140447552

194. Paul S. MacDonald. History of the Concept of Mind: Speculations About Soul, Mind, and Spirit from Homer to Hume. Ashgate Pub Ltd, 2003. ISBN 978-0754613657

195. Thomas Oswald Cockayne, Saint Augustine. "The shrine: a collection of occasional papers on dry subjects" British Library, 2011. ISBN 978-1241159030

196. Chapter XV, De mensibus Anglorum. "Blot-monath mensis immolationum, quia in ea pecora quae occisuri erant diis suis voverent."

197. Gwyn Jones, tr., "Thidrandi who the Goddesses Slew," Eirik the Red and Other Icelandic Sagas, Oxford, 1961. ISBN 978-0199539154

198. John Porter (tr), Viðar Hreinsson (ed)."The Tale of Thidrandi and Thorhall," The Complete Sagas of Icelanders: Including 49 Tales (5 vols). ISBN 978-9979929307

199. Kane, Njord. "Norse Religion." The Vikings : The Story of a People. 2nd ed. Yukon: Spangenhelm, 2015. Print. 978-1943066018

200. Turville-Petre, E. O. G.. Myth and Religion of the North: The Religion of Ancient Scandinavia. Holt, Rinehart and Winston. 1964. ISBN 978-0837174204

201. Snorri Sturluson, Arthur Gilchrist Brodeur (Trans.).The Prose Edda. 2014. ISBN 978-1497424180.

202. Snorri Sturluson, Faulkes, Anthony (Trans.) (1995). Edda. Everyman. ISBN 978-0460876162.

203. Snorri Sturluson, Jesse L. Byock (Trans.). The Prose Edda: Norse Mythology. Penguin Classics, 2006.

204. Carolyne Larrington (Translator). The Poetic Edda. Oxford University Press, 2014. ISBN 978-0199675340

205. N. M. Petersen. Hervarar Saga Ok Heidreks Konungs. Kessinger Publishing, LLC, 2009. ISBN 978-1104175641

206. Robert Kellogg, Jane Smiley, Various Authors. The Sagas of Icelanders. Penguin Classics, 2001. ISBN 978-0141000039

207. Snorre Sturlason. Heimskringla: or, The Lives of the Norse Kings. Dover

Publications, 1990. ISBN 978-0486263663

208. Geir T. Zoëga. A Concise Dictionary of Old Icelandic. Dover Publications, 2011. ISBN 978-0486434315

209. Welch, Martin (2011). "Pre-Christian Practices in the Anglo-Saxon World". In Timothy Insoll (ed.).The Oxford Handbook of the Archaeology of Ritual and Religion. Oxford: Oxford University Press. pp. 863–876. ISBN 978-0-19-923244-4.

210. Jesch, Judith (2004). "Scandinavians and 'Cultural Paganism' in Late Anglo-Saxon England". In Paul Cavill (ed.). The Christian Tradition in Anglo-Saxon England: Approaches to Current Scholarship and Teaching. Cambridge: D. S. Brewer. pp. 55–68. ISBN 978-0859918411.

211. Reynolds, Andrew (1996). "Anglo-Saxon human sacrifice at Cuddesdon and Sutton Hoo?". Papers from the Institute of Archaeology. 7. pp. 23–30.

212. Reynolds, Andrew (2002). "Burials, Boundaries and Charters in Anglo-Saxon England: A Reassessment". In Sam Lucy and Andrew Reynolds (eds.). Burial in Early Medieval England and Wales. The Society for Medieval Archaeology Monograph Series 17. London: The Society for Medieval Archaeology. pp. 171–194. ISBN 978-1902653655.

213. Shaw, Philip A. (2002). Uses of Wodan: The Development of his Cult and of Medieval Literary Responses to It (PDF) (Doctoral thesis). University of Leeds.

214. Shaw, Philip A. (2011). Pagan Goddesses in the Early Germanic World: Eostre, Hreda and the Cult of Matrons. London: Bristol Classical Press. ISBN 9780715637975.

215. Doyle White, Ethan (2014). "The Goddess Frig: Reassessing an Anglo-Saxon Deity". Preternature: Critical and Historical Studies on the Preternatural. 3 (2): 284–310.

216. Price, Neil (2010). "Heathen Songs and Devil's Games". In Martin Carver, Alex Sanmark, and Sarah Semple (eds.). Signals of Belief in Early England: Anglo-Saxon Paganism Revisited. Oxford and Oakville: Oxbow Books. pp. xiii–xvi. ISBN 978-1-84217-395-4.

217. Pluskowski, Aleks (2011). "The Archaeology of Paganism". In Helena Hamerow, David A. Hinton, and Sally Crawford (eds.). The Oxford Handbook of Anglo-Saxon Archaeology. Oxford: Oxford University Press. pp. 764–778. ISBN 978-0199212149.

218. Dunn, Marilyn (2009). The Christianization of the Anglo-Saxons c.597–c.700: Discourses of Life, Death and Afterlife. London and New York: Continuum.

219. Wood, Ian N. (1995). "Pagan Religions and Superstitions East of the Rhine from the Fifth to the Ninth Century". In G. Ausenda (ed.). After Empire: Towards an Ethnology of Europe's Barbarians. Woodbridge:

Boydell. pp. 253–279. ISBN 978-0-85115-853-2.

220. Jesch, Judith (2004). "Scandinavians and 'Cultural Paganism' in Late Anglo-Saxon England". In Paul Cavill (ed.). The Christian Tradition in Anglo-Saxon England: Approaches to Current Scholarship and Teaching. Cambridge: D. S. Brewer. pp. 55–68. ISBN 978-0859918411.

221. Worm, Olao. Fasti Danici. (Latin) Apud Salomonem Sartorium Regium et Academie Typographii, 1633 (ed. II, 1643).

222. Arild Hauge. Runekalender (Rune Calendar). Denmark, 2002.

223. Gylfaginning

224. Prose Edda (complete)

225. Jana K Schulman, The Laws of Later Iceland: Jónsbók: The Icelandic Text According to MS AM 351 fol. Skálholtsbók eldri. With an English Translation, Introduction and Notes (2010).

226. Grágás (Gray Goose Laws)

227. Map of the Kievan Rus' realm, 1015-1113 CE, of the medieval Rus' culture in Eastern Europe created by Koryakov Yuri 30 July 2009, translation by Hellerick.

228. Forte, Angelo; Oram, Richard; and Pedersen, Frederik. Viking Empires. Cambridge University Press, 2005 ISBN 0-521-82992-5

229. A.D. Stokes, "Kievan Russia," in Robert Auty, and Dimitri Obolensky, eds. Companion to Russian Studies: vol 1: An Introduction to Russian History (1981)

230. Klejn, Leo S. (2013). "From Goths to Varangians: Communication and cultural exchange between the Baltic and the Black Sea". In Lind, John; Bjerg, Line Maj-Britt Hojberg; Sindbaek, Soren M. The Russian Controversy over the Varangians. Aarhus: Aarhus University Press.

231. Andrushchuk, Fjodor (2008). "The Vikings in the East". In Price, Neil S.; Brink, Stefan. The Viking World. London: Routledge.

232. Stephen Turnbull, The Walls of Constantinople, AD 324–1453, Osprey Publishing, ISBN 1-84176-759-X.

233. Viktor Vasnetsov, The Invitation of the Varangians: Rurik and his brothers arrive in Staraya Ladoga. (1913)

234. John Skylitzes, John Wortley. John Skylitzes: A Synopsis of Byzantine History, 811-1057: Translation and Notes. Cambridge University Press,, 2010. ISBN 978-0521767057

235. Gustav Freytag. Our Forefathers. Arkose Press, 2015. ISBN: 978-1345050028

236. Stenton, Frank M. (1971). Anglo-Saxon England, 3rd ed. Oxford: Oxford University Press. ISBN 0-19-821716-1.

237. Venerable Saint Bede (1723). The Ecclesiastical History of the English Nation. John Smith, trans.

238. Smith, L. (2009). G.E.Jeans, ed. Memorials of Old Hampshire: The Jutish Settlements of the Meon Valley

239. R. Coates. On the alleged Frankish origin of the Hastings tribe in Sussex Archaeological Collections Vol 117.

240. Chadwick, Hector Munro (1911). "Jutes". Encyclopædia Britannica (11th ed.).

241. Jordanes, Giles Lauren (Ed), and Charles Christopher Mierow (Cm).The Gothic History of Jordanes. Kessinger Publishing, LLC, 2010. ISBN 978-1167082405

242. H.R. Ellis Davidson. Gods and Myths of Northern Europe. Penguin Books, 1965. ISBN 978-0140136272.

243. Edwin W. Teale. The Golden Throng: A Book about Bees. Universe Publishing, NY, 1982. ISBN 978-0876634073.

244. Peter Godfrey Foote, David M. Wilson. The Viking Achievement: The Society and Culture of Early Medieval Scandinavia. Sidgwick & Jackson, 1983. ISBN 978-0283979262.

245. Gsbriel Turville-Petre. Dreams in Icelandic Tradition (pp. 30-51). Nine Norse Studies. Viking Society, University College London, 1972. ISBN-13: 978-0903521055